# PHILOSOPHY

## AN INTRODUCTION

*JOHN HERMAN RANDALL, JR.*
*Columbia University*

*JUSTUS BUCHLER*
*State University of New York at Stony Brook*

Revised Edition

BARNES & NOBLE, INC., NEW YORK

PUBLISHERS • BOOKSELLERS • FOUNDED 1873

L. C. Catalogue Card Number: 74-149835

SBN 389 00089 2

**Distributed**

*In Canada*
by McGraw-Hill Company of Canada Ltd., Toronto

*In Australia and New Zealand*
by Hicks, Smith & Sons Pty. Ltd., Sydney and Wellington

*In the United Kingdom, Europe, and South Africa*
by Chapman & Hall Ltd., London

Manufactured in the United States of America

# Preface

The first edition of this book, published in 1942, stated in its Preface:

> This book has been written to serve different possible uses: (1) as a textbook, to be used either alone or with readings in the philosophic classics; (2) as a guide to independent study by the general reader; (3) as a background reading for lectures or discussions; (4) as a rapid survey and review of outstanding philosophic issues discussed in introductory courses. . . .
>
> We wish to thank Professor Ernest Nagel of Columbia University for reading the manuscript and giving without stint of his time to make many useful, constructive suggestions; Dr. Milton K. Munitz of the College of the City of New York, and Professors James Gutmann and Horace L. Friess of Columbia University for the same generous contribution of labor and helpful criticism; and Professor Irwin Edman of Columbia University for the benefit of his long experience in making philosophic ideas lucid and clear.

The first edition met the needs of students and teachers with gratifying success. In making revisions, therefore, we have tried to preserve the original framework and organization. And in taking account of major philosophic interests and developments over the past thirty years, our emphasis has been on the long-term theoretical underpinning of these developments rather than on this or that trend of the moment.

We should like to call attention to the volume *Readings in Philosophy* published in the present series. That book and this one, in our view, can be used together with advantage.

The preparation of this revised edition has profited from critical comments made on the first edition by Evelyn Shirk and Hugh Van Rensselaer Wilson.

J.H.R., Jr.
J.B.

## ABOUT THE AUTHORS

John Herman Randall, Jr., author of the classic *The Making of the Modern Mind*, is Frederick J. E. Woodbridge Professor Emeritus of Philosophy at Columbia University. Among his books are *Aristotle, Nature and Historical Experience, The Career of Philosophy*, and *Plato: Dramatist of the Life of Reason*.

Justus Buchler, formerly Johnsonian Professor of Philosophy at Columbia University and now Distinguished Professor of Philosophy at the State University of New York at Stony Brook, is the author of, among other books, *Toward a General Theory of Human Judgment, Nature and Judgment, The Concept of Method*, and *Metaphysics of Natural Complexes*.

Dr. Randall and Dr. Buchler with Evelyn Shirk are the authors of another book in the College Outline Series: *Readings in Philosophy*.

# Table of Contents

## Part One

### THE RÔLE OF PHILOSOPHICAL THINKING IN HUMAN LIFE

# PART TWO

## THE ANALYTICAL FUNCTION OF
## PHILOSOPHY

Accumulated. Experience as the Quality of Sensation
or Emotion. Experience as Consciousness. Experience as Deliberate Observation. Experience as the
World of Fact. Experience as a Relation or Interaction. The Logic of a Philosophy.

When Have We Assurance that We "Know"? Dogmatism and Scepticism. Descartes' Problem. Methodological Scepticism. Scepticism as an Attitude:
Kant's Critical Philosophy. Scepticism concerning
Extra-empirical Knowledge. The Kantian Contrast
of Knowledge and Faith. Historical Illustrations of
the Contrast. Extreme Scepticism: a Fourth Type.
The Argument from Historical Changes in Science.
The Argument against Any Method. Critical Re-
marks on the Latter Argument. Critical Remarks on
Anti-scientific Scepticism. Further on Methodologi-
cal Scepticism. Outgrowths of Modern Empiricism:
Positivism. The Positivist Limitation of Inquiry.
The Positivist Interpretation of Scientific Method.
Critical Remarks. The Phenomenology of Husserl.
Phenomenological Reduction. Two Standpoints and
Two Kinds of Experience. Pure Seeing: the Abso-
lute Knowledge of Essences.

How Important Is Language in Knowing? Bergson's View. Points of Difference between Symbolical and Intuitive Knowledge. Intuition, Symbols,
and Empirical Science. The Meaning of Non-symbolical Intuition. Critical Remarks. Scepticism and
Non-symbolical Intuitionism. Insight and Analysis
in Science. Knowledge and Communication. General Methodological Implications. Other Conceptions
of Intuition: the Romantic Craving for Immediate
Insight. Mysticism. Critical Remarks on Intuitionism
in General. Art and Intuition. Does the Artist Communicate? Philosophy and Language. The Linguistic
Movement in Recent Philosophic Thought.

Pragmatism as Experimentalism; Genuine and
Pseudo-Problems. Literal Meaning and Psychological Meaning. The Experimental Standard of Definition. The Requirement of Scientific Verifiability.
The Broad Conception of Experience and Verification. Kantianism, Positivism, and Experimentalist
Pragmatism. Pragmatism as Practicalism: the View

# PART THREE

## THE SPECULATIVE FUNCTION OF
## PHILOSOPHY

___

# PART ONE

# The Rôle of Philosophical Thinking in Human Life

## CHAPTER ONE

❖    ❖    ❖

# What Is Philosophy?

It is very difficult to give a satisfactory formal definition of philosophy. For philosophy is like those other great human enterprises of ideal society—art, science, and religion: every definition turns out to be the expression of an individual and limited conception, reflecting the practice of that enterprise in the definer's own culture, and shutting out as much as it includes. And no definition conveys much illumination apart from a knowledge of the concrete philosophies men have formulated, the philosophical problems out of which those formulations have grown, and the rôle which philosophical thinking has played in their own lives and in that of their culture. Philosophy, in other words, is a human and cultural enterprise to be inquired into, rather than a mere term to be defined. Any definition must emerge from a careful analysis of what men have been doing when they philosophized, and how that is to be distinguished from what they do when they engage in their other cultural enterprises. The boundaries between these different pursuits are notoriously vague; and different definitions reflect a more or less arbitrary drawing of the lines.

**Philosophy and Religion, Science, and Art.** Philosophical thinking, indeed, has very close relations with religion, with science, and with art. It has normally culminated in the attempt to do intellectually what religion has always done practically and emotionally: to establish human life in some satisfying and meaningful relation to the universe in which man finds himself, and to afford some wisdom in the conduct of human affairs. Historically, philosophy arose as the reflective

I

criticism of religious and moral beliefs, and it has never ceased
to have that critical concern. But in its methods it has been
allied rather with science, even when it has been most critical
of the scientific assumptions and conclusions prevailing at a
given time. Philosophic and scientific thinking, in fact, were
born together; and again and again philosophic reflection has
been revitalized by fresh contact with the concepts, methods,
and standards of scientific inquiry. And finally, those comprehensive visions of the world and of human destiny which we
cherish as the great philosophic systems of speculative thought
are surely among the most imposing artistic achievements of
the spirit of man. The outstanding philosophers, indeed, have
been endowed with something of poetic imagination, critical
acumen, natural piety, and spiritual insight.

So closely allied has philosophic thinking been with all the
other basic cultural institutions of human society that we often
call the general intellectual temper of an age—its pervasive
world-outlook, its distinctive methods of thinking, its unquestioned assumptions and climate of opinion— "the philosophy"
of that period. But this usage hardly suffices to define the function of philosophic thinking itself; that is both more self-
conscious and more critically analytic than this would suggest.
In every age there are men who, aware of this distinctive intellectual temper, either give it systematic expression or seek to
modify certain of its aspects. It is they who carry on actual
philosophic thinking and merit the title of "philosophers," because they are concerned with the *conscious* analysis of methods of thinking, and with the *conscious* formulation of a world
outlook.

**Is Philosophy Critical and Reflective Thinking?**  There
is a sense in which we speak of "the philosophy" of an age,
or "the philosophy" of a man, meaning thereby the sum total
of beliefs entertained. But for philosophic thinking much more
is required than merely to have beliefs. It may be said that
every man absorbs from his society a certain philosophy; but
that does not mean that every man is himself therefore a phi-

losopher. For only a small minority possess the *critical* or *reflective attitude* that is necessary in thinking properly called philosophical. So essential is this temper and method that philosophy has sometimes been defined in its terms, as "critical and reflective thinking." But this definition is likewise unsatisfactory; for it does not indicate the distinctive character of the problems with which philosophic thinking is concerned, nor the distinctive cultural and historical function which has determined them in detail. For those whom we call "scientists" certainly think reflectively, and yet we make a distinction between philosophy and the special sciences. Moreover, the craftsman, the industrialist, the housewife, the lawyer also think reflectively on occasion — in fact, all men do — and yet they are not necessarily either philosophers or scientists.

**Abstract Concepts and Theory.** Philosophic thinking differs from ordinary reflective thinking in one characteristic which it shares with the thought of the scientist. It employs *concepts* or *abstractions,* and in terms of these formulates *principles* or *laws.* This is what is ordinarily meant when philosophy and science are called "theoretical" pursuits: they are interested in formulating "theories" of a wide range of applicability. This does not mean that their theories may not have grown out of practical problems, or that they have no bearing on practice. The relation between theory and practice is itself a philosophical problem on which there has been wide difference of opinion. In any event, history has proved again and again that nothing is so practically valuable as "pure theory." But the ordinary man does not often especially concern himself with such abstractions. The industrialist is not necessarily an economist, the lawyer not necessarily a legal philosopher. They are interested primarily in specific objectives, and in concepts and principles only in so far as these may apply to a given situation. The philosopher and scientist, on the other hand, are interested primarily in concepts and principles, and only secondarily in their application — though what particular concepts and principles they are interested in may be very intimately bound up with the activities and problems of their society. In ordinary reflective thinking, men think in terms of achieving this or that sale, winning this or that case, driving to the country, participating in games, writing, fighting, loving. The scientist and philosopher, however, are interested not in particular situations but in the general concepts by means of which such situations can be understood and dealt with. Thus the scientist is interested in "utility," "price," "labor," and "demand"; in "property," "equity," "contract," and "tort"; in "energy," "density," "acceleration," and "specific gravity"; and so on. The philosopher is concerned with "experience" and "knowledge," "meaning" and "truth"; with "purpose" and "God," "nature" and "mind."

This abstractness and generality of its concepts and principles, which philosophic thinking shares with that of the scientist, may serve also to distinguish the two types of thought. The concepts of each of the sciences relate to different specific fields of inquiry. Those of astronomy are concerned with stellar phenomena, those of biology with the phenomena of life, those of sociology with the phenomena of social groups. The concepts of philosophy are not limited in this way. They are broader and more general than those of the special sciences; they apply to a wider range of phenomena. Indeed, one branch of philosophy, metaphysics, has been traditionally defined as "the science of existence as existence," that is, as the examination of those pervasive traits that appear in every field of inquiry, and the analysis of the concepts in which they are expressed, like "matter" and "form," "contingency" and "law," "cause" and "effect," "structure," "activity," and "process."

**The Central Problems of the Meaning of Human Experience.** But philosophic thinking is not merely critical and reflective, operating, like science, with abstract notions and principles. The problems with which it is concerned have a distinctive character which sets them off from the problems of specialized scientific inquiry. And this characteristic trait consists not merely in the fact that they cut across the lines of the particular sciences, and arise in connection with the basic ideas and assumptions in many different fields. The many specific problems of philosophic thinking, which often become very technical and abstract, are ultimately connected with a central set of problems from which they radiate and to which they return if pushed far enough.

The term "philosophy" means literally "the love of wisdom." Now what "wisdom" consists in is something on which different men and different cultures have varied widely. What kind of knowledge is it, and how is it related to other kinds, especially to the kind we call scientific? The Greeks thought the relation was very close. Their "wise" men were much concerned with the sun, the moon, and the stars, with living things and how they came into existence. That group of Greeks who first proclaimed their devotion to "the love of wisdom," or philosophy, the Pythagoreans, felt that it was intimately bound up with mathematical knowledge, which they hence cultivated with enthusiasm. Philosophy has been well called "the mother of the sciences"; for philosophic thinking has again and again directed attention to certain problems and fields like astronomy and mathematics which have then been made the subject of independent inquiry. Other Greeks, like Heraclitus, held that "the learning of many things teacheth not understanding," and even that "wisdom is apart from all." But this attitude has been more characteristic of other cultures; much more typical of Greek thought is the statement of Aristotle: "All men by nature desire to know."

But whatever its precise relation to other kinds of knowledge, there is general agreement on the type of problems with which "wisdom," and hence philosophy, is centrally concerned. They are those which raise the question of the *meaning* of human life, and the *significance* of the world in which man finds himself. What is the general nature of the universe in which human life has its setting, in so far as that character has a bearing on human destiny? And what is that destiny itself? How far can man affect it by his own actions; and, within the limits of his choosing, what activities and pursuits should he follow? What kind of life is most worth while leading, individually and collectively?

**Philosophy Presupposes Existent Knowledge.** In identifying philosophic thinking with a concern with what is significant and meaningful in human experience, it is clear that we are assuming familiarity with what is thought to have been already found out about the world. Men must have some acquaintance with and some understanding of their experience if they are to estimate what in it is of significance. There is indeed no type of knowledge, or alleged knowledge, which philosophic thinking cannot take as the starting-point of its critical reflection; no field or phase of human experience which cannot provide it with material. Historically, of course, philosophers have always commenced with what passed for knowledge in their own society, with the beliefs current in their own day or their own tradition; and they have clearly done so even when, like Descartes, Locke, or Kant, they have imagined they were starting "at the very beginning." Beliefs specifically about human destiny and man's relations to the controlling powers in the universe, which every society possesses in connection with its religious institutions long before critical philosophic thought begins to reflect upon them, have naturally furnished a large part of its materials. Ever since the attempt to understand the world "scientifically" made its appearance in Greece, and especially since the revival of scientific inquiry in the later Middle Ages, scientific conclusions, as the best attested beliefs, within whatever limits they might be found to possess, have been taken as the point of departure for further philosophic reflection. Today it would be bold indeed to disregard "scientific knowledge" completely in the search for the meaning of human experience. But every social institution has its theoretical side, its beliefs about its ends and goals, its norms and standards of excellent functioning; and all this funded knowledge has a bearing on the meaning of life. Indeed, ever since science has come to dominate our intellectual life, many philosophies have been primarily protests against the undue neglect of these other fields of reflective human interest.

Ideally, every phase of human experience and all the institutionalized activities of men should be examined for what they reveal, by the philosopher seeking a really comprehensive view of the world and the destiny of man. The great architectonic visions of the speculative system-builders, those which stand out as the intellectual expressions of what we have called "the philosophy" of an entire age, have managed to be fairly inclusive. And at least one philosopher, Hegel, made his central task this examination of all phases of human experience in their historical development. But in practice few have considered them all with equal thoroughness; and many of the analytic thinkers who have contributed the most solid and enduring conclusions to the funded body of philosophic method, have actually based their critical achievements on a very limited body of beliefs.

**The Interpretation and Evaluation of Knowledge.**  Philosophic concern with the central problems of the meaning and significance of human experience presupposes an acquaintance with the widest range of facts and the possession of the conclusions of all types of knowledge, as materials on which to reflect. But "meaning and significance" is an affair of more than mere knowledge: it raises the fundamental questions of importance, of relevance, and of relative value. In this sense, philosophy is often called an interpretation of knowledge, or of human experience in the light of available knowledge. This means that philosophic thinking tries to *organize* the materials of human experience into some reasonably coherent arrangement. It fits opposing or irrelevant beliefs together into some not too chaotic scheme, and it adjusts warring ideals to give some direction to life without excluding too much. It involves a reflective appraisal of what we know piecemeal in various particular fields. It estimates how this bears upon the central problems of man's status in the great scheme of things

and the importance and worth-whileness of his various enterprises. Hence we reach the important conclusion that the philosophic search for what is significant in experience is fundamentally a process of *reflective evaluation.*

Now it is often held that philosophy is to be distinguished
from science in that it is concerned with "values," whereas
science is not. This distinction, however, is difficult to maintain. For whereas philosophy has always been very consciously
interested in the relative value of different ideas and aims, it
is by no means clear that science is not also. In a sense, as
we shall see, the "truth" which science seeks can be considered as one very specific kind of value, and its methods can be
taken as a process of determining which ideas "best" satisfy
its tests of validity. Those methods can clearly be applied also
to the evaluation of ethical and aesthetic beliefs, the goods or
"values" of conduct and of art. The traditional distinction is
responsible for the usage which still considers as branches of
philosophy the three "normative" sciences of logic, ethics, and
aesthetics, concerned with the standards, methods, and tests of
thinking, conduct, and art respectively. But even if the distinction be only relative, it remains true that philosophic thinking
is basically a process of critical evaluation. And it operates
at a more fundamental level than evaluation in the particular
sciences, for it is concerned with the relative value of their
respective goods and standards, and with the critical appraisal
of their procedures and of scientific inquiry itself.

The process of philosophic evaluation and interpretation is
thus an intimate combination of two co-operating processes.
On the one hand, it is the *organization* and adjustment of ideas
and beliefs in terms of their relevance and importance for a
world-view and a scheme of living. On the other, this problem of organization involves a careful *analysis* of ideas to
determine just what they are and what they imply. Philosophic thinking thus performs a double function, one *analytic,*
and one *synthetic* or *speculative.* In practice the two are usually carried on together, though the emphasis may be on one

or the other. But since each function has historically involved and raised a distinctive set of problems, we shall consider them separately in the body of this volume.

**The Analysis and Clarification of Ideas and Methods.** The philosophical interpretation of the meaning of human experience and of different types of knowledge and aim involves the analysis of just what the concepts and principles and beliefs mean, and what their bearing is on other ideas. This is often called the "clarification" of ideas. But it leads also to an examination of the basis for maintaining them and the evidence for their validity, in the light of other and seemingly conflicting ideas drawn from different areas of experience. Thus philosophic thinking, in performing this analytical function, is confronted with the task of clarifying and criticising the fundamental methods, rules, procedures, and standards or norms of all theoretical enterprises, including those of scientific inquiry itself. This type of analysis and criticism has always played a very large part in the body of philosophic writing, especially in modern times, when the interpretation of human experience has involved so many problems of adjusting scientific ideas to traditional beliefs. The examination of methods and procedures has recently assumed still greater importance. For we now realize that the very meaning of ideas and their range of applicability, especially of the novel and unfamiliar ideas of contemporary science, are closely dependent on the way in which they are arrived at. We see that to attempt to appraise their broader bearing apart from these procedures leads only to confusion — as in popular interpretations of "relativity," for example. So important and illuminating has such analysis proved that it has often been carried on for its own sake, quite apart from the bearing of such clarified ideas on the broader interpretation of human experience. Many philosophers today wish to confine their reflection to such problems of analysis, and to abandon the organizing or speculative function of philosophy to the scientists and poets.

But the clarification and criticism of intellectual methods and procedures have from the beginnings of Greek philosophy been closely associated with the central problems of the meaning of human experience. Parmenides, early proclaiming, "It is the same thing that is and can be thought," initiated an eager examination of what it is "that can be thought." And Socrates, intensely preoccupied with the problems of those human excellences that make up the good life for men and cities, taught generations that if one could only find the right way of getting the right kind of knowledge, the problem of living well would be solved. The most practical of men, like the hard-headed Englishman John Locke, have been led by philosophic reflection starting from pressing political problems to impressive and influential analyses of the "original, extent, and certainty of human knowledge." The methods and tests of knowing have always occupied a central place in philosophical thinking. For unless a man can know when he is justified in being confident that he knows, how can he be sure that he knows what is best?

❖  ❖  ❖

# The Organization
# and Interpretation
# of Experience

This business of analyzing and criticising ideas and intellectual methods is all very well, the average man is likely to exclaim, but after all it is mere preliminary spade-work. We are not really interested in these technical details. What we want to know is what it all means. What is this world we are living in really like? And what is it worth while to try to do? When we go to church, we find the preacher is as much at sea as the rest of us. Our children won't listen to him anyway. And what he has to say about love and goodwill and serving others certainly doesn't seem to have much to do with the way the world is going. Is there nothing to do but to blame it all on original sin? And the politicians are no better. They clutter up the air about the American way, and then they go on and do things that would make my father turn over in his grave. Talk about the new society! It's here now! What has philosophy got to say about all this? For God's sake, why doesn't it stop hair-splitting and tell us the answer?

**The Average Man Demands a Faith.** Today it is not merely the restless stirring of adolescence that drives men to reflect upon the meaning of human life in the world that confronts us. And the first impulse of that reflection is to demand "the answer." Those who have read a little of the story of philosophy have learned that there were times in the past when philosophy did proclaim the answer. They forget that men lived it before philosophers put it into winged words: "Those answers, you say, were well enough in their day; but we have got beyond them now. You would hardly call them true; we have learned so much since then. But if we really know so much, why don't you tell us what it is all about? What is the Truth about the world, and the way the world is going? Can't you give us something we can all join in believing? Look at those fellows in the 'people's democracies.' They've really got something! Of course, it's all dead wrong, but—"

To the average man, philosophy has always seemed a seductive deceiver: she has promised all things, but has delivered not even truth — only a quarrel about its definition. It is little wonder that he prefers the loud and clear-cut summons of faith, especially in times when he so desperately needs something reassuring to cling to, something to sustain him in a world where everything familiar and dear seems to be going by the board, that he would gladly welcome any kind of faith that would give him a sense of direction and purpose, anything that would with sufficient assurance promise him a way out of hopelessness and meaninglessness. Our average man, in demanding "the answer," is clearly asking for a faith; he is not really interested in philosophic thinking, he is not concerned with understanding *why* the answer is an answer.

**But Philosophy Cannot Create a Faith.** Now a faith, all ready-made, is something philosophy cannot provide men with. Only experience can do that, and it is a slow and painful process. But philosophy can help our inquirer in that hardest of human tasks, learning from experience. And it can clarify the faith that is already in him, and help him enlarge that faith by experience: it can make it more humane and less fanatical and dogmatic. And it can ask him whether he really wants in America the kind of unifying social faith whose fruits are so clear in Communist lands.

We have consulted the average man in his demand for what he conceives to be the important thing philosophy has to offer him; and we have tried to explain that it is something philosophic thinking does not and cannot give at all. And yet the questions that trouble him are precisely those upon which philosophic thinking ultimately focuses — what is the answer? What is it all about? And philosophy does organize and adjust men's beliefs and ideals in terms of their relevance to a world-view and a scheme of living; it is vitally concerned with a sense of direction and purpose. Its interpretation and evaluation of human experience does culminate in a world-view and a "philosophy of life." But philosophic thinking does not perform its organizing or synthetic work in quite the way the average man supposes.

**How Philosophy Proceeds in Interpreting Experience.** "With all our immense store of knowledge at your disposal," the philosopher is asked, "why don't you examine and sift it and arrive at the Truth?" Now we have already recognized that philosophy presupposes an acquaintance with the widest range of facts and the possession of the conclusions of all types of knowledge, as materials upon which to reflect. But this does not mean that the philosopher first gathers all facts and all knowledge together, and then proceeds to interpret them by picking out what is important and significant. Herbert Spencer, indeed, tried some such organization of the conclusions of all the sciences in his "synthetic philosophy"; the first volumes were antiquated long before he arrived at the final pages. His effort stands as the classic warning against the danger of attempting to build a philosophy on the temporary "results" of a rapidly growing scientific enterprise. For human thought never operates by first assembling all the facts or data, and then asking them to deliver their meaning. Philosophic inquiry resembles all other human inquiry in seizing upon some organizing hypothesis as the tool with which to search for further data; the interpretation goes on simultaneously with the discovery of fresh facts which are relevant to it. Philosophic inquiry should indeed consult all phases of human experience in formulating a comprehensive interpretation; the neglect of any is bound to render its conclusions one-sided and in obvious need of supplementation. But this inclusiveness of its materials is something at which, if it be carried far enough, philosophy eventually arrives, not something with which it sets out; it comes at the end, after a long process of clarification and criticism, not at the beginning with its initial insights.

**Organizing Principles Have Been Varied and Manifold.** These insights which philosophic reflection employs when it tries to interpret man's experience, these hypotheses in terms of which it performs its organizing function, arise like those in all inquiry in connection with some particular area of experience, normally in considering some particular problem or set of problems that has there assumed importance. Now these problems can be either theoretical or practical; they can occur anywhere. What makes them "philosophical" is that they generate a *philosophical response*: they introduce some modification in the broad interpretation of experience. The philosophical temper of mind or intellectual attitude consists in just this ability to see the further ramifications of ideas arising from particular problems, to trace their various bearings and implications, and to realize their generalized significance, their meaning in a wide variety of other fields. The fundamental concepts with which philosophy operates are just those major ideas which because they have been able to illuminate so many fields of experience have served to order and organize men's other beliefs. They are "philosophical ideas" because of what philosophical reflection has been able to do with them.

It often takes several generations or several centuries of use as instruments of interpretation to bring out the full implications of such ideas. The ancient notions of a providence, of atomism, and of a mathematical order of nature have not yet been exhausted; they are still finding new applications and revealing new possibilities. The idea of man's organic relation to his environment, introduced by evolution over a century ago, is at the center of philosophic attention today. The organizing possibilities of the basic ideas of recent biological theory, like modern views of genetics and DNB, have so far been barely scratched. It is in the course of this long-continued and co-operative use by a succession of thinkers that the limitations of principles of interpretation in their original form are gradually removed; they are modified to take account of the facts of other phases of experience, and adjusted to the ideas that seem of most immediate significance there. Thus the idea of mechanism, which emerged as a central principle of interpretation in the seventeenth century, seemed then, to Spinoza, for example, in fundamental conflict with any notion of purpose. But the renewed interest in biological concepts in the late nineteenth century led to a revision of both ideas. And today, formulated more precisely in the light of facts from all areas of human experience, they are seen as both involved in all natural processes, and as both contributing to the interpretation of our world. This is an excellent illustration of the way in which the organization and adjustment of ideas is bound up with their careful analysis and clarification (See pp. 253-4.)

The insights which serve as principles of interpretation can thus spring from problems related to any type of belief; any reflective human interest can generate a philosophical response, and lead, if pushed far enough, to a broad formulation of the meaning of human life in the world. This fact is of fundamental importance. It is made clear by the examination of how philosophical thinking has actually and concretely operated, of how philosophers have gone about their distinctive task and what problems and ideas have seemed of central importance to them. And it in turn explains a great many of the problems about the actual character and history of philosophic thinking which puzzle the average man.

**Philosophy Has Given Many Different Interpretations.** Our average man wants the answers; he wants to learn what his experience is all about. He is eager to know what the wisest men have thought about life, confident that somewhere he will find the answer to all his own doubts and perplexities. He hopes to find somewhere, in some philosophic insight, something that will do for him what religious or social certainty used to do for men. He is looking for something solid and indisputable, something he can use immediately and apply to his personal problems. Or more often today, he is seeking something that will take him out of himself by charting the exact course the world should take from here. He is too anxious to be saved, or to save the world, to waste time trying to understand, even to understand the ways in which other men and other ages have been saved, if they don't have in evidence at first glance all the gadgets of the latest model. For other men and other ages, after all, have been saved, as fully as we can ever hope to be. The world has been saved again and again, and it will always need to be saved; and what we do to save it today will necessitate saving it another way tomorrow. This at least philosophy can teach; and it teaches also why thoughtful men will always feel the need of philosophy.

The average man discovers, to his surprise, that most of the great philosophers have been worried about quite different problems from those that bother him, problems that are not issues in getting rid of the atomic bomb, and that seem to have no immediate bearing on how to end international anarchy or organize industrial society; that the visions of human life they have beheld seem often quite irrelevant to fighting against totalitarianism or for it. He finds that the Greeks were far more interested in understanding their world than in changing it, that they believed the only salvation worth while lay in seeing how the world is intelligible, that to them tracing the pattern of its intelligible structure was far more important than getting a substitute for religious faith. He learns that Plato early pointed out the sad but inescapable fact that while you can teach even an ignorant slave-boy the beautiful but apparently useless science of geometry, Pericles himself could not teach his own sons how to live the good life — in our more familiar jargon, to display good-citizenship and social-mindedness. He notes that the Greeks, in fact, managed to lay the foundations for the intellectual life of all who have come since without ever solving the problem of social organization for themselves or for us; that modern scientists likewise have devoted their energy to the intellectual and technical problems they could solve, rather than to the moral and social problems they could not; and that for many of the greatest thinkers, like Aristotle, Spinoza, and Hegel, a rational vision of an intelligible universe was in itself a sufficient salvation, a satisfactory meaning of life.

To his dismay, our average man finds, instead of the One Answer he has hoped for, a pageantry of variegated answers, some irrelevant to each other, some actually contradictory; and he finds many of them vigorously maintained by intelligent men today in our own society. He finds that wise philosophers have discerned, and discern today, quite different meanings in life, and that they have often vigorously combatted all who disagreed with their own. Even on the way of getting there, on the question of intellectual methods, he finds nearly all the roads to Truth and the ways of knowing men have used in the past earnestly advocated today; and if some do not in our society enjoy the same prestige they used to, they have able spokesmen, and they have managed to enlist whole nations in their service.

**Philosophy Has Reached No Final Truth.** Confronting this situation, our inquirer is naturally confused, bewildered, and disheartened. He had hoped to find the One Truth; instead he is led to ask, What is Truth? He had hoped to have his doubts set at rest; instead, he finds that philosophizing raises far more doubts and perplexities than it settles, and asks far more questions than it can answer. The outcome is often disillusionment, scepticism, cynicism. What's the use? Philosophy can't prove anything, for it proves too many different things; and philosophers never agree. It's all moonshine anyway! And so our sceptic is a ready prey for some dogmatically preached faith. It is an old story, and the Greeks knew the ending. Lucian has told it in classic form in his dialogue *Hermotimus*.

Now this ancient complaint against philosophy, that it never arrives at any definitive and accepted answers to its central problems of the meaning of life, is hardly justified. Indeed, it is not even true. For, as we shall see, the philosophic enterprise has slowly but surely built up a cumulative body of well-grounded knowledge, much like science itself; and if this body of funded knowledge is concerned more with concepts and methods, with intellectual tools for use in inquiry, than with results that stand in no need of further investigation, that character it likewise shares with the scientific enterprise. It is sometimes objected that this leaves philosophy with "no greater certainty than that of science." But one who can seriously count this as an objection is obviously not looking for any kind of thinking, philosophic or otherwise; he is in search of a faith, and will not be satisfied until he has found one.

But the facts on which the familiar complaint against philosophy's pretensions is founded have enough truth in them to demand an answer. And philosophy can be justified against the charge in two ways. The first is directed more particularly to our average man, for it denies his basic assumption that philosophy has failed because it has not discovered the One Answer. The second justification goes on to try to understand what philosophic thinking has actually been doing, what its distinctive historical and cultural function has been and is in human life.

**The Many Answers Are All Answers.**   It is true that different men and different ages have given different answers to the central problems of philosophy, and that most of them are still living answers today, capable for some at least of making life meaningful and significant. Hence the individual cannot conscientiously accept a philosophy on the authority of experts, as he usually accepts his science. On the fundamental issues he must make his own decisions, if he is to participate in philosophic thinking at all. But if there is no such thing as "the Meaning of Life" on which all men will some day agree, it is quite possible for different men, and for different ages and cultures, to find quite different meanings in life, and for all to be equally right and valid — all equally able, under the

circumstances for which they are significant, to make life meaningful. Even the fact that philosophy has not yet discovered
the One Truth about the world, and never will discover it,
does not mean that it has found no truths. For it is possible
that there are many truths about the world in its relation to
man — it is possible that man may understand the world in
many different ways, in terms of many different principles of
interpretation growing out of different kinds of experience. It
is even possible that there may be many forms of social organization under which men can live a richly satisfying life.
To all these possibilities the facts of history seem to point.
And to realize how many meanings of life, how many visions
of the world men have found, sets tolerance in the place of
intolerance, and sympathy and understanding in the place of im-
patience and contempt.

A tolerance based on an enriched understanding is indeed
one of the priceless fruits brought by an acquaintance with
man's philosophic thinking, even if its critics' severest com-
plaints be accepted. If a man looks for The Truth in the historical record of philosophy, he will find only a bewildering
succession of rash assumptions, and may be tempted to reflect
on the futility of human thought. If he looks for vision and
insight, he will not be puzzled by the variety of visions. He
will welcome every insight as enlarging his own experience
and giving him richer materials to work into the organization
of his own life and thought.

**Principles of Interpretation Must Be Relevant to Living
Experience.** For the philosophic insights that serve men
as principles for interpreting their knowledge and activities
spring out of their own experience, and in the last analysis it
is *that experience* which they render meaningful. The vision
of life a man proclaims is significant *for* the experience it expresses, and for all those who in some measure share that
experience — perhaps an entire society or age. This is of
course true for any principle in terms of which men understand anything — for any idea which causes a confused situa-

tion or field to "fall into line" and "make sense." The principles which organize any field of scientific inquiry have been
formulated on the basis of the experience of the investigators
in that field, and they are relevant to or apply to that co-
operative experience. When further observation and discovery enlarge that scientific experience, those principles need to
be modified to apply to the wider range of facts they must
now embrace. Critical analysis of scientific concepts and principles has revealed how closely their basic meaning is determined by the actual scientific procedures in which they are
used and tested.

Now scientific experience is open and public, subject to the
scrutiny of exact methods of observation and measurement,
and available to anyone who has learned to employ its methods. The experience out of which come the insights in terms
of which men try to organize their lives and their total world-
views is much more complex and subtle if less precise and
less capable of exact formulation. It embraces not just one set
of institutionalized activities, but a host of others as well —
there are none, we have pointed out, which may not give rise
to a philosophic response. This "philosophic experience," like
that of science, is of course shared and co-operative — only a
lunatic would find satisfaction in an interpretation significant
to himself alone. But like the religious and the social experience with which it has often been so closely allied, it is a shar-
ing of feeling and attitude and habitual co-operative activity
as well as of belief and observed fact. By common consent,
it is the poet who has most successfully caught and expressed
this complex, living human experience, not the analytic thinker
or scientist. And it is in its choice of principles of interpretation, its grasp of those insights that can then be imaginatively
extended to embrace all man's ideas and activities, that the
organizing or speculative function of philosophic thinking most
closely approaches the function of the poet or artist. "Speculation" is a synonym for "vision," for the intellectual and
imaginative "seeing" of things whole and clear. After all the

labor of analysis and criticism, there comes the moment when the philosopher "sees," and makes us see; and his intellectual vision is so akin to the imaginative vision of the poet that this culmination of philosophic thinking is often called the "poetry of ideas."

**Philosophic Experience Has Varied.** It should now be clear why the visions or "world-views" of philosophers have varied, why philosophers have found different meanings in life. Their experience has been different; even when they have looked at the same world, it has been from different vantage-points. Different aspects or characters of it have seemed important; in terms of those aspects, they have surveyed the other phases of experience, and found them somehow to make sense. The major interpretations have not completely left out important areas of human activity in sheer neglect; they have, as we say, "taken account" of most of them. But it is one thing to "take account" of art, shall we say, and another to have that sense of intimate participation in artistic activities which makes them central in the interpretation of life, or at least accords them their proper place in the scheme of things. Plato and Aristotle made "art" a basic organizing concept for understanding the universe; Kant left it hanging as a kind of bridge between science and moral activity. Now we can understand a great deal of this difference in terms of the Greek institutions in which Plato and Aristotle participated and of the eighteenth century world in which Kant lived. But which was right? For some men, art will always be the central key to the meaning of things; for others it will always be in the appendix.

**Distinctive Types of Philosophic Experience.** This example suggests two major ways in which men's experience, and consequently men's principles of interpretation, have varied. No man can actually participate in the entire range of human experience as it has appeared in the countless societies and cultures of history, and in those yet unborn; till our institutions have reached a fixed unchanging uniformity there will be new visions of the world. Philosophies change with men's changing social experience; as we shall see, they play a central role in that change itself. But likewise no man can participate equally in all the activities and experiences of a single complex culture. The scientist, the artist, the religious man, the moral prophet, the social revolutionary — each has his own insights, his own way of understanding *his* world. These characteristic types of experience and reflective human interest have each received philosophic expression again and again, in various cultures and ages, and within the limits of various intellectual traditions. Presumably, so long as these institutionalized activities have a place in our society, and philosophic thinking is allowed free play, some such differences in focus and vision will persist. Even the scientific philosophies of today are split in their interpretation of science itself between those which make central the concepts and methods of mathematics and physics, and those which have sprung rather from the experience of the biological and social sciences. Nay, within the first group the philosophy of a mathematical physicist is characteristically different from that of the experimental physicist.

**Major World-Views Persist because of Distinctive Types of Experience.** This does not mean, of course, that each of these phases of experience is bound up with a single world-view, a single vision of life. The accumulating common stock of philosophical ideas is at the disposal of each; the concepts and methods of thinking of any age, or any intellectual tradition, can be organized to express the distinctive concern of each. A strong religious interest, for example, can orient any world-view or comprehensive philosophy about itself — even one anti-clerical and atheistic, we are tempted to say, thinking of Epicurus and Marx. Conversely, most of the basic philosophical issues in the interpretation of present-day science were clearly expressed and fought over in the philosophical theology of the Middle Ages. But the continued vitality of the major intellectual methods examined in Part Two of this volume, and of the major world-views set forth in Part Three, is impressive. For the individual philosophical thinker, they all represent possibilities that have to be examined seriously in any considered choice. They have clearly persisted because each is bound up in countless subtle ways with some phase or combination of phases of experience which finds that method or world-view especially congenial. But this affiliation is very complex in detail; to unravel its strands requires a careful examination of the actual concrete social functioning of these philosophical methods and interpretations.

**The Limits of a Common Interpretation.** Does this mean that philosophical differences due to what we have called differences in reflective human interest will always persist? At any given time, will the scientist, the artist, the religious man, and the rest find their experience expressed in different philosophies? This depends on just what we mean by "philosophical differences." Any major interpretation of knowledge, if it becomes embodied in an intellectual tradition, and is worked on co-operatively by a group of men — if it becomes institutionalized in a given culture — tends through a process of clarification, criticism, and assimilation of neglected facts to become more comprehensive and more adequate to the entire range of experience in that culture. Thus the different philosophical traditions present in a culture tend, in the absence of some strong new impulse, to approach each other, as has been often illustrated historically. Sometimes the outcome is the formulation of a philosophy broad enough to interpret all the major intellectual interests of an entire age. More often the new impulse—some new experience or new set of ideas— interferes, and creates new differences. Such an approach of the different philosophical traditions in our culture was clearly in evidence during the late nineteenth and early twentieth centuries, with the gradual assimilation by them all of the expanding scientific experience of our society. In that sense, these philosophical differences within our culture might quite possibly tend to disappear with the adoption of common methods and concepts, and a common view of man's status in nature. Philosophical differences in the sense of distinctive vision and scales of values, however, even if only as differences of emphasis, would still not be wholly eradicated. At present, however, it seems more likely that the "new impulse" has come with our pressing social problems, and that the major varieties of method and interpretation will be focused on schemes of social organization rather than on attitudes toward science, which still determine the world-views of Part Three. It is even possible that the need for a unifying social faith will submerge all other differences in the conflicts of the near future. But even then, it is hard not to foresee different philosophical interpretations of that faith in terms of the different areas of reflective human interest.

❖   ❖   ❖

# The Cultural
# and Historical Function
# of Philosophy

We have still to consider the second way in which men's experience has varied, and with it their principles of interpretation and organization. Philosophies change as men's cultural and social experience changes *historically:* there is no final interpretation of the meaning of life. The average man, accepting the bare conclusion without further question, often finds it a reason for discounting all philosophic thinking. We have pointed out that the fact that different ages and different cultures have organized their experience in different ways does not mean they have not organized it, and that though the meaning and significance they have found has been primarily a significance for them and for their experience, it has not been the less meaningful. The lesson is clear: we have to attempt the task once more for our day and generation. We cannot rest on the achievements of the past, but must engage in philosophical thinking ourselves. And we have in fact found our average man insistently asking for just such thinking, demanding "the answer" and "what it is all about" — posing, that is, the questions of the bearing of all our knowledge on human destiny, which we have recognized to be central in philosophy. We have found him asking them in connection with specific problems — the breakdown of the traditional religious answers, the transformation of our accustomed social institutions, the probable nature of an automated and computerized society. And he makes it clear that the answer he expects must satisfy him on these very particular doubts.

Our average man, in fact, is illustrating in his own questions something to which we have been led again and again, but have not yet examined carefully. We have said that the distinctive character of philosophical problems lies in their bearing on the meaning of man's experience in his world. But we have also pointed out that any problem whatever can generate a philosophical response, and lead ultimately to a new organization of experience, a new vision of human destiny. We have touched on a number of problems that may well seem to us to be fairly remote from this central concern of philosophy, but which in past philosophical thinking have been intimately connected with it. And we have noted the many different world-views and schemes of life that philosophers have found meaningful, and the number still vigorously defended today which the thoughtful man must consider in making his own choice.

**Philosophical Thinking as a Social and Cultural Enterprise.** We have, in fact, been considering what philosophical thinking is in the life of the individual led for any reason to reflect on his experience and knowledge until he comes to ask finally, What after all is the world really like? What kind of life is really worth living? We have recognized that such an individual is limited by the intellectual materials and the experience of his culture; but we have not really considered philosophical thinking as itself a cultural enterprise. We have not examined the rôle of philosophical thinking among the other intellectual activities of human societies, its distinctive cultural and historical function. When we do, we find that many of the questions we have raised about philosophy are answered. We see why particular problems generate a philosophical response, and under what conditions they assume a central importance. We understand more clearly the great concern of philosophic thinking with questions of analysis and critical evaluation, with intellectual methods and standards of validity, with the procedures and tests of knowing. It becomes plainer why this analytic function of philosophy, this concern with the precise formulation of method, is no mere spade-work but rather its most cumulative and enduring achievement. And we realize that the objection that philosophy reaches no final and accepted conclusions, that it never definitively answers its central questions, but is forever asking them in new forms, that its task, in a word, is never-ending, far from invalidating the philosophic enterprise, is really its chief glory, and of the essence of its function in human life.

**Philosophy Reorganizes and Reinterprets Social Experience.** Now we have spoken as though in performing its organizing or speculative function philosophic thinking surveys the range of human experience and beliefs in search of some insight or principle of interpretation and evaluation. We have indeed noted that the survey does not come first, but is in fact carried on in the light of some initial promising insight or hypothesis. But we have assumed that the different types of experience and knowledge are spread out awaiting interpretation, that the idea that will significantly interpret them is hit upon more or less accidentally because of the special reflective interests of the interpreter, and that in the end the individual will find one world-view and scheme of living better validated than the others offered him because it is more successful in making his own experience meaningful. We have assumed an individual setting forth in search of the meaning of life, without preconceptions, and relatively free to choose among the different possible philosophic interpretations displayed for his consideration.

Now this of course is hardly the way in which philosophic thinking actually operates. There is a sense in which it may describe the situation of the student first beginning his formal acquaintance with philosophy, and anxious to make a systematic survey of what the "field" contains. It is perhaps appropriate enough as a scheme for an introductory study like the present one to follow. But it is doubtful whether any original philosophic thinking ever arose in this fashion. Even our average man, with no academic interest in philosophy as

a "field," makes it clear that there are certain definite doubts
and perplexities that have driven him to reflection, and that
he is not so much trying to understand his experience for the
first time as to *regain* a sense of meaning and direction he
once had but has lost. And it is certain that when we consider philosophic thinking as a cultural enterprise with a definite social function, we find that function historically and concretely has been not so much to organize and interpret the
social experience and institutionalized beliefs and aims of men
in a given society, as to *reorganize* and *reinterpret* them.

**Social Experience as Given Embodies a Meaningful Pat-
tern.** For every society is in fact a going concern with a
complexly organized "culture" or scheme of acting, feeling,
and thinking. It provides its members with a set of habitual
or customary ways of performing these activities; its social
and cultural habits or "institutions" regulate and direct all the
basic practical, emotional, and intellectual relations in which
its members stand to each other and to their world. The ends
or goods they seek are already organized in their institutionalized activities; the beliefs in terms of which they interpret and
express their social experience are likewise matters of social
and cultural habit. Thus activities and goals or values do not
come isolated and piecemeal, but as integral parts of this complex habitual way of doing things. Beliefs and ideas all have
their familiar place and function: they interpret an experience
that is meaningful in its own terms because it embodies a
functioning pattern of living. Philosophic reflection thus does
not have to create an organization of experience; experience
always comes organized in the institutions of a culture. Philosophy does not have to provide all "meaning" for life; life
normally follows some meaningful pattern. When that pattern
has broken down, philosophy may help an alienated individual
to *find* such organization and meaning; but socially speaking,
philosophic thought could never invent them if their elements at
least were not still present in the living experience and functioning institutions of even a disintegrating culture, and it is futile

to ask it to make the attempt. This is merely another way of repeating that philosophy cannot of itself generate a faith, individual or social, or create values and ideals that will impel men to seek them. Its function is not to generate faiths but to clarify and modify them, to give not driving force and impulse to life but guidance and direction.

**"Expression" and "Criticism" Are Both Reorganizations of This Pattern.** Even when we speak of "the philosophy" of an age or a culture, it is clear that it is not philosophic thinking that gives the age its intellectual temper, its assumptions, its controlling beliefs, and its scale of values and general direction. These things must all be implicit in its institutions before they can be consciously formulated and expressed in a philosophy. This does not mean that the expression makes no difference: a society conscious of its assumptions and methods and aims is certainly not the same as one in which they are only implicit. And imagine the difference in subsequent intellectual life if Greek philosophers had not given expression to the life of Greek society! It does mean that every such philosophic organization and interpretation of a culture is really a *re*organization and a *re*interpretation of materials already organized and meaningful in their own right. Even the most "conservative" of philosophies, those which are most obviously "rationalizations" of the pattern of the establishment and its institutional arrangements, in being rationalized formulations at all are reorganizations of beliefs and values in terms of some critical standards, and involve analysis, modification, and adjustment. Conversely, even the most "radical" philosophies, introducing revolutionary ideas and drastically criticising some part of existing beliefs, accept without question the vast majority of the ideas and activities of their society. They modify the interpretation of the meaning of experience, but they embody most of the ideas and aims that have actually been giving it meaning.

**Philosophy Presupposes the Values of an Organized Culture.** Now if philosophical thought is the critical reorganization and reconstruction of the beliefs of a culture, it

of necessity presupposes an organized culture, with a functioning set of aims and objectives and values and standards, as
the material on which to work. This is so fundamental to the
understanding of the function of philosophy as a social enterprise, that we shall be still more explicit as to how men live
their lives without philosophy, how they understand their world
and pursue their ends without consciously raising its central
problems. We shall then see how this pre-reflective "answer"
to what it is all about generates the need for philosophical reinterpretation.

### Social Institutions Generate Meanings, Aims, and Values.
Our Western society, like most others, used to provide the
young with the accepted answer to the question, "What is the
chief end of man?" through its institutions of organized religion. More recently, the answer has been given by the pattern of suburbia and the establishment it represents. Most men
were content to go through life satisfied with what they were
there taught about the controlling power in the universe and its
relation to their destiny. The pattern of their daily living was
provided by the various activities in which they normally took
part without much question — their family obligations, their
way of making a living, their intercourse with their neighbors,
their recreations and diversions. Each of these activities carried
with it its own set of social expectations — it was what men in
that position would naturally engage in. Such is the power of
habit, especially of socially accepted or institutionalized habit,
that the great majority wanted to do these things, and found
satisfaction in doing them well and successfully. The bitter
hardships involved — and it is well, even today, not to senti-
mentalize over "primitive society" or "the good old days" —
were accepted as inevitable. It was at this point that the "chief
end of man," the conscious "meaning of life" provided in
that society, impinged upon the many ends of daily living, to
bring endurance and peace.

   In such a relatively stable society, in which the various institutions are functioning fairly well, it is these institutions

themselves — the various activities which men customarily perform and are expected to perform — which prescribe the aims or ends men set themselves and the acts and qualities they find good. To hunt, to fight, to be wise in counsel, to have strong sons — these make up the life of a man. To possess skill in the chase, to be brave in battle, to be loyal and just to one's fellows, to be able to make cunning weapons — these things are good. It is all so clear as to require no debate. The things to be done are meaningful and significant, they all fit together into a familiar and well-rounded pattern; they need no reason why. The things that are good are to be sought after; their value needs no questioning. The beliefs of such a society normally include a good many glorifying these ways and these values by telling how powers more mighty than man respect and perhaps even practice them. It seems but natural for any being to act and feel that way.

Such a state of affairs is found in most stable societies. It is well exemplified in those simpler communities we call "primitive" still lingering in our world, like the Latin-American Indian groups relatively untouched by the white man's ways. It prevailed, with a more complex institutional development, in the Oriental civilizations and in medieval Europe. And it is well to remember that, compared with our present situation, even our own Western society has nearly always been "relatively stable," and the vast majority of men have usually been able to find life meaningful on this pre-reflective level.

**The Major Intellectual Tension in Western Society.** But certain features of Western civilization have generated in it, more than in most others, the conscious need for philosophical reinterpretation. Now in most civilizations the "meaning of life" and the "chief end of man" explicitly formulated in their religious beliefs has been the expression and consecration, and usually the clarification, of the significant activities and the cherished ends associated with their secular social institutions. Beliefs about the destiny of man and the powers that control it have been intimately connected with man's social experience, both growing out of it and modifying it in turn. But in the

civilization of the Western peoples the relation between these
two ways of interpreting and giving significance to human life
— the meaning expressed in its professed religious and ethical
beliefs, and the meaning implicitly embodied in the activities
and aims it actually pursued — has been much more complex.
For the Western peoples invented neither their own religion
nor their own ethical wisdom; they borrowed them from other
societies in the ancient world, the Hebrew, the Greek, and that
Hellenistic culture of the Roman Empire that fused so many
different strains. Western Europe was converted to Christianity, and for centuries it went to school to ancient wisdom.
At the same time it was creating a civilization of its own quite
different in character from those from which it was borrow-
ing. Its social experience and institutional arrangements, very
unlike to begin with, grew more and more divergent from those
that had originally generated the beliefs and ideals it was trying to profess. This divergence grew still more extreme when
it developed its novel scientific enterprise and its quite unprecedented institutions of industrialism, and with the spread of
a mature technology, there ensued a break with the entire past.

**The Persisting Demand for Reinterpretation and Adjust-
ment.** As a result, Western society has from the beginning found a gulf between its professed interpretation of life
and scale of values, and the interpretation and set of goals it
was consecrating in practice. This tension has operated to keep
alive, for its intellectual class at least, the question of the meaning and end of human life as a conscious problem, always demanding reflection and critical analysis. Our culture has rarely
been able to find a satisfying meaning, as have most other societies, in what it was actually doing: those activities have stood
condemned by its inherited ideals. Nor has it on the other
hand been able to rest in its traditional beliefs: those have been
either irrelevant to or at variance with what it was really pursuing. Hence prophets have had to condemn a degenerate generation in the light of the chief end of man. Thinkers have
had to formulate new beliefs and new ideals based on and in
defense of the new ways. Other thinkers have had to build

imposing systems to show that there is no real incompatibility: the new ideas and new experience can be adjusted to the old beliefs and values in a new synthesis. And both have had to work out and clarify methods of analysis, criticism, and proof.

Now this persisting tension might have been overcome by the analysis, clarification, criticism, and adjustment of philosophical thinking; the different elements inherited from the ancient world, themselves incompatible enough, like Aristotelian science and the Neoplatonic philosophy, might eventually have been brought into harmony with European social experience. The great Schoolmen of the thirteenth century, of whom St. Thomas Aquinas is the best known, did in fact measurably accomplish the task for that time. They stamped the name "Scholasticism" on the philosophical enterprise of systematically reformulating a body of ideas and giving it a vital meaning in reorganizing social experience.

**Social and Intellectual Expansion Has Demanded Constant Reinterpretation.** But European society was in a state of constant expansion, forever outgrowing the institutional forms in which its activities were organized. Its developing economy, and later its mushrooming industrialism, and now the sharp leap into an electronic technology, again and again confronted it with novel types of social experience, together with the ever repeated problems of liberation from older institutional organizations and their reconstruction into new ones. Its beliefs and forms of knowledge were likewise kept in a constant turmoil by the recurrent impact of new ideas that had to be assimilated — first the discovery of one intellectual element after another of ancient culture, which came in successive waves, each one upsetting the adjustment already tentatively made; and then the still more disturbing ideas which its own enterprise of science began to produce in ever-increasing profusion.

Now each of these novel forms of experience, each of these unfamiliar ideas, produced far-reaching reverberations throughout Western culture. Each proved a shock to the accustomed ways of acting and thinking in terms of which men found their life meaningful and their world intelligible. Each not only had somehow to be assimilated to those accustomed ways; each posed anew the broader problems of the meaning of human life and the significance of the new world in which it now found itself. Each problem of conflict and adjustment, in other words, generated a philosophical response. It not only provoked the process of analysis and clarification of ideas, both new and old, to harmonize the conflict and effect the adjustment; it forced fundamental reinterpretations of the meaning of human experience, and gave rise to new world-views and new speculative visions of human destiny.

**The Cultural and Historical Genesis of Philosophical Problems.** We can now see what was lacking in our definition of philosophic problems, and why we insisted that the function of philosophic thought is to *re*organize and *re*interpret ideas and experience. Viewed concretely in the light of its actual historical operation, philosophy never sets out from scratch to survey the world and organize men's beliefs into a significant world-view. It always starts with some existing interpretation and some functioning set of values that has been challenged by fresh experience or novel ideas, and it reconstructs that interpretation and that scheme of values to take account of the challenging element. Often the idea or method by which the intellectual conflict is resolved is itself so significant that it leads to a further drastic reconstruction and to a new intellectual vision of the world. Often the challenging idea, when analyzed and clarified, serves as a new focus from which to reinterpret all phases of experience. But the problems which generate such a philosophical response, though they can arise in any field, do actually arise at those points where the strife of ideas and experience forces men back to fundamental assumptions. It is the impingement of novel experience upon traditional beliefs and values which impels men to philosophical thinking, the emergence of new ideas irrelevant to or, in their initial form, logically incompatible with the old, but which yet have somehow to be adjusted to them and worked into the accustomed pattern of living and thinking.

**Philosophy as the Intellectual Phase of Cultural Change**. The problems of philosophy in this sense have varied from age to age, and are historically unique. They are to be understood only as the expressions of those basic conflicts within a culture which drive men to the searching thinking that is philosophy, and force them to thoroughgoing analysis and criticism, to intellectual reinterpretation and reorganization, and perhaps to new insight and vision. In the light of these historical facts, we can venture a definition of philosophy as a social and cultural enterprise. Philosophical thinking is the intellectual expression of the process of cultural change; it is the intellectual phase of the process by which conflicts within a culture are analysed and clarified, resolved and composed. This distinctive social and historical function explains why Western civilization, with its never-ending succession of tensions and conflicts, exhibits so rich a record of philosophical thought. A civilization that has become stable and static may have inherited "a philosophy," but it produces no philosophical thought; that comes only with problems of fresh assimilation and adjustment.

If the social function of philosophy be to serve as the method of criticising and reorganizing beliefs, the philosophic problems of adjusting different ideas to each other are obviously analogous to the political problems of adjusting different ways of acting. At his proudest the philosopher is the statesman of ideas, organizing some new synthesis of intellectual materials within whose constitutional framework men can thenceforth carry on their intellectual pursuits. At his humblest he is the politician of ideas, effecting through analysis compromises and working-agreements to live and let live. It is because the starting-point of his enterprise is the adjustment of intellectual tensions and conflicts that the *history* of philosophy is best understood in terms of its analytic function, of problems of method, rather than in terms of its speculative function, of their culmination and fruit in imaginative vision. And that is why also the method of philosophic criticism and reconstruction, though always very intimately bound up with the prevalent "scientific method," is never wholly exhausted in it, but always retains something of the art of the politician of the mind.

❖   ❖   ❖

# The Cumulative Achievements
# of Philosophy

We have been at some pains to point out why the task of philosophic thinking is never-ending, since the function it performs will always be needed in any culture that has not crystallized into complete immobility. In the light of what it does do, it is not surprising that it does not do some of the things often expected of it — provide final answers, for example, to its central questions concerning the nature of the world and the meaning of life, or impose a unifying faith on a society that has not achieved one in its experience. We have dwelt on how both the analytic and the speculative functions of philosophy are historically related to man's growing knowledge and changing social experience.

But by the side of this relevance to particular historical situations we must set also those aspects of philosophical thinking that represent a genuine cumulative achievement, in much the same sense that the scientific enterprise is a genuine growth in knowledge, though its theories also are subject to constant reconstruction in the light of fresh evidence. Since this funded body of intellectual materials and instruments and assured results is at once something that every philosophical student ought to have in his possession and something that can be taught and learned, it is naturally emphasized in Parts Two and Three of this volume. To acquire it forms a large part of philosophical training; not to possess it is a mark of philosophical naïveté and incompetence.

**The Clarification and Evaluation of Methods and Standards.**   This cumulative achievement is most clearly in evidence in connection with the analytic function of philosophy, its examination of methods and intellectual procedures and standards of validity. The recurrent and still persisting ways in which men support and try to establish their beliefs have been scrutinized in detail. We have found out a great deal about the way those methods operate in practice, the consequences to which each leads and the limitations and difficulties to which it is subject. We know the intellectual dangers lurking in the appeal to intuition and self-evidence, to which intelligent men have fallen prey. We have examined the assumptions involved in such historic methods as rationalism, empiricism, and positivism, and seen the intellectual impasses to which they have led. We have searchingly analyzed the methods of the sciences, themselves built up so painstakingly over a long period through the patient practice of inquiry, with all their elaborate techniques and procedures and safeguards. We know something of the reasons for their success, and we know the kind of questions with which they cannot deal. We know the consequences of thinking in terms of confused and ambiguous concepts, and of using ideas which have no ascertainable meaning; we have formulated methods for attaining precision in the clarification of ideas. In Part Two we shall see concretely how, out of various differing viewpoints, definite clarifications and conclusions emerge which command universal assent.

**The Analysis of Assumptions.**    Secondly, there are classic pieces of philosophical analysis that have stood the test of time. Historic and familiar arguments which men still employ today have been punctured once and for all, so far as any claim to validity goes. Above all, it has been made clear what consequences and what assumptions a man commits himself to in adopting certain positions, what further difficulties certain lines of reasoning entail. The assumptions involved in various intellectual traditions have been brought to light as men have used them in confronting a variety of intellectual problems. Some of them have been revealed to have great explanatory and interpretative value; others have been shown to lead again and again to insoluble and purely verbal problems. Philosophical experience in this sense of the use of ideas has taught lessons which deserve careful study. Thus, for example, no one today who asserts belief in miracles can reckon without Hume's critique of the concept of miracle; no one who has anything to say on the so-called free will problem can neglect the contribution of Spinoza. These and other classical pieces of philosophizing will be discussed in Parts Two and Three.

**The Refinement of Philosophical Concepts.** Thirdly, there has been built up a large common store of carefully formulated philosophical concepts which have been subjected again and again to thoroughgoing analysis in the light of their intellectual values in formulating and dealing with a wide variety of problems. The crudities of their initial vagueness of meaning have been gradually refined away, until they have become much more adequate intellectual instruments. With each further extension of their use to new problems and new ranges of experience or ideas, they undergo further reformulation; but no competent thinker will handicap himself by disregarding the clarifying elaboration and refinement to which they have already been subjected. Among these philosophical concepts are certain recurrent types of antithesis, certain persistent distinctions — the one and the many, permanence and change, the real and the ideal, reason and experience, form and matter, structure and process, and the like. These fundamental antitheses or distinctions, often called "metaphysical," first formulated by the Greeks, and slowly elaborated by subsequent generations, have often been regarded as problems to be settled once and for all. But they seem rather a set of concepts to be employed in rendering man's changing experience intelligible, an intellectual instrument of criticism in meeting cultural conflicts. They are not so much problems to be solved, as distinctions to be used, used in the good fight and the enduring quest. The enemy, the fight, the quest are ever new; but fighting is not, nor are the weapons by which the thinker can conquer. In Parts Two and Three we shall discover how concepts like "truth," "meaning," "value," "cause," "idea," and "happiness" are the more readily manipulatable by us, the more subject to our conscious control, as a result of having passed through the ever-finer filter of philosophic history.

**The Store of Insights and Visions.** And finally there are the enduring insights and visions of the great philosophies of the past. The philosopher is not merely the statesman of ideas, he is also the poet of the mind; and his great imaginative achievements, the dialectic of a Plotinus or a Hegel, the architecture of a Thomas, the symbolic logician's world of pure form, possess an eternal appeal quite apart from any use they may find in the problems of intellectual adjustment. It is no accident that the major philosophers, though they start as statesmen or even politicians of ideas, have ended as poets. They have risen above their particular problems of adjustment and partisan loyalty to behold the same world; and though they speak in differing languages, each in his own dialect seems, to an attentive ear, to be speaking of the same permanences of man's experience of that world. For one seeking, like them, the universal structure of that experience and that world, for one likewise endeavoring to formulate what is and how it is to be understood, it is well to look through as many eyes as he may, and to ponder as many reports as he can.

**Introduction to Succeeding Parts.** We have remarked that the two fundamental concerns of philosophy are with the examination of methods and the framing of a broad world perspective. We have called the first type of research *analytical philosophy* and the second *speculative philosophy*. We have distinguished between philosophy and science. Part of the subject-matter of analytical philosophy is science itself. For the scientific method is one of the basic methods of human thinking, and one of the tasks of philosophy is to analyze the way in which it achieves its results, as well as to compare it with other possible intellectual methods. And just as part of the subject-matter of analytical philosophy is concern with the *method* of science, so part of the subject-matter of speculative philosophy is concern with the *total result* of science. The conclusions of science, whatever they may be at any given time, are among those which speculative philosophy must consider in shaping a perspective. Thus speculative philosophy, unlike each of the special sciences that is concerned with one or another specific aspect of the universe, is concerned with far broader theories embracing the sum of their results. But science is only one basic enterprise of the human mind, and the two aspects of philosophy must be defined in awareness of this fact.

Analytical philosophy, then, is examination of the *nature, methods, procedures,* and *foundations* of all human reflection—the latter consisting in the institutions of art, science, religion, and ordinary social communication. Analytical philosophy is concerned with criticism, clarification, and definition.

Speculative philosophy is the formulation of a universal perspective based on a *synthesis* and *interpretation* of what emerges from human reflection in its various forms. Its concern is to unify all the phases of human experience into a comprehensive and meaningful whole. In framing its interpretations, and in testing them, it appeals to observation. This observation, however, is observation in a much wider sense than that of the special sciences. It is to the broadest and most fundamental features of experience that philosophy appeals for verification. And as we have seen, it is possible for different interpretations, like different languages, to be supported by this experience.

It cannot be too strongly emphasized that philosophic analysis and speculation are interdependent. Typical problems that are primarily analytical will be considered in Part Two, whereas those primarily speculative will be considered in Part Three. Very often it is extremely difficult to show where the two are separated, and in the course of actual philosophising a clean-cut separation is rarely made. Though speculative issues will arise in Part Two, they will not be explicitly formulated until Part Three. In the latter, however, we shall be in a position to bring up analytical questions, and the reader will be able to observe how they are interwoven with those of a speculative kind.

# PART TWO

# The Analytical Function
# of Philosophy

❖   ❖   ❖

# The Basic Methods
# of Inquiry

One of the most fundamental problems of analytical philosophy is the discrimination of the basic methods and procedures which can govern human inquiry. The attitude of the medieval philosopher is not that of the nineteenth century disciple of Darwin; the method of Plato is not that of Aristotle; the mystic seeks knowledge by a method radically different from that of the physicist; the method used by the so-called classical economists is opposed to that used by various contemporary economic schools; the totalitarian method is opposed to the social democratic method of investigating and propagating political doctrines. Our task is to formulate these methods abstractly; in other words, so to define them that we shall have clear-cut categories by means of which the above may be classified and understood. In analyzing, we make explicit what in practice is concealed and not critically examined. By so doing we enable ourselves to make sounder judgments, and perhaps to modify a preference the implications of which we may not have perceived clearly.

**What Is a Method?**   If we reflect on the question, How does each of us come by the beliefs which he has, that is, by the opinions which he holds to be true? we find that the answer is far from easy. Very often we think we have actually witnessed what has only been related to us. Our memories commonly deceive us. We imagine we have arrived independently at an intellectual conclusion which has in fact been instilled into us by reading. We hold beliefs, often consciously, about that which we have never observed and never expect to observe; yet we cannot readily say why. We often do not realize that on certain matters we are hypercritical and on other matters thoroughly uncritical, without being able to account for the difference in attitude. We can thus see at once that there are certain *sources* of our beliefs — daily experience, hearsay, tradition, the laboratory, and so on — and certain *attitudes* with which we regard these sources, for instance, blind faith, scepticism, independent and eager examination, and so on. A *method* of inquiry, that is, of adopting beliefs or gaining knowledge or arriving at experience different from that already possessed by us, may be defined as the conscious acceptance of a source of belief and the adoption of a definite attitude in connection with it. Plainly we can hold different attitudes toward the same source, and the same attitude toward different sources. Each different combination means the employment of a different method. It should be noted that in defining "method" we have included the phrase "arriving at different experience" in addition to "gaining knowledge." The purpose of this is to include in the scope of method the enterprise of art. No doubt art is not "inquiry" in the same sense that science is. But we certainly are warranted in saying that the method of the artist in his pursuit is different from the method of the scientist. In so far as the artist manipulates forms in a given medium he is not, to be sure, aiming to arrive at truth, at least in the usual sense of the word; but he unquestionably is seeking to enlarge the scope of his ordinary experience. With this qualification in mind, it will be possible to express the characteristics of the "method" involved in artistic inquiry.

**Common Sense.** Before distinguishing different kinds of methods, it is worth while to mention a concept that serves as a convenient point of departure, that of "common sense." In its non-technical or popular usage "common sense" means "good sense" or native shrewdness, a certain sense of practicality or rudimentary intelligence. To say that a person has common sense is taken to mean something favorable about him.

In philosophical usage, however, the expression has a different and less honorific meaning. It is taken literally, and means "sense that is common," or better still, "beliefs that are common" — common to all men, or arising from overwhelming consensus. What kind of beliefs are these?

All men, whether the highest of creative geniuses or the most completely illiterate and unimaginative animals, call red things "red," hot things "hot," sunny days "sunny." In terms of these objects and qualities, common to all of them, they come to have beliefs in common. The belief that food will satisfy hunger, that water will quench fire, and that the seasons will continue to succeed one another in regular order — such beliefs are derived from the most elementary types of daily experience. No doubt the exact number of such beliefs cannot be specified, and with the development of the human race in its environment over great stretches of time it is highly likely that new beliefs are added to the sphere of "common sense" knowledge. It is probably true also that not all men do have the same number of common sense beliefs, and perhaps that no two men attach precisely the same significance to these beliefs. Nevertheless we may safely say that there *are* beliefs which are universally shared, just as there are physical properties which all men share. And what we mean is that all men, in so far as they do or would fulfill certain biological and social conditions, are influenced by these conditions in essentially the same way. "Common sense knowledge" is the result of this influence. Its source is experience of the most fundamental and pervasive character, the minimal biological, social, and psychological experience of man. All that is necessary for its acquisition is the exercise of the senses and the memory, and the simplest kind of reasoning. But we can hardly speak of an "attitude": common sense knowledge is acquired by us willy-nilly, and not in virtue of any method. It results not from inquiry but from merely living. It is completely uncritical, and there is no knowledge more elementary than it. No matter how widely methods of inquiry vary, the fund of common knowledge remains practically constant. Thus common sense is the starting-point of all inquiry. We may, by the employment of deliberate methods, rise above it; but we can never dispense with it. Let us go on to consider various methods based on conscious choice.

**Faith: Three Senses of the Term.** Any individual possesses a more or less varied group of beliefs. Some of these are common sense beliefs. Others are derived from schooling, from reading the newspapers, from religious counsellors, from political friends, and so on. These beliefs become crystallized gradually into what we call the individual's intellectual makeup. He becomes habituated to a certain outlook and orders the workings of his life in accordance with it. Under such conditions, what will be the natural tendency of this individual's mind? Will it be to look for that which might cause him to doubt his set of beliefs, or for that which will perpetuate his present habits of thinking? Obviously the latter. And the stronger become his habits of belief, the more inclined is he to regard them as correct and as preferable. Thus arises what may legitimately be called conservatism in inquiry. It will be convenient to designate this type of intellectual approach by the term *faith*. In the broadest sense, faith means steadfastness of belief. We may more exactly distinguish three forms which this steadfastness can take.

**Faith as Tenacity.** The first form, a natural outgrowth of the conditions we have just mentioned, is belief *in spite of* evidence to the contrary. It is emotionally more comfortable to cling to the beliefs one already holds than to be troubled by doubts, or to be faced with the need of revising one's habits of thought in the light of new evidence that they are unsound On this attitude therefore one adopts only beliefs compatible with those already held, regarding new evidence with hostility and suspicion; and, when confronted by allegedly new evidence, refusing to interpret it as such. Belief in spite of evidence thus goes hand in hand with the avoidance of evidence. In fact, the avoidance is absolutely essential. For we cannot safeguard ourselves against doubts if we leave ourselves open to their influence. This attitude is often held with regard to political and religious beliefs. Men continue to believe because of the desire to avoid intellectual conflict, because they fear the loss of their stability or complacency, or because, as they sometimes say, it would make them unhappy to believe otherwise than they do. And often, of course, men shun the light of evidence because it might conflict with their material interests or station. Faith in this sense has been compared aptly with the legendary act of the ostrich when danger approaches.

**Faith as the Will to Believe.** When we entertain any opinion, it would seem that there are three possibilities alone that we ought to consider: If there is evidence favoring the opinion, we ought to believe it; if the evidence is contrary to it, we ought to disbelieve; and if there is no evidence pro or con, we ought to remain in doubt. Such an ideal situation is rarely adhered to consistently. We have seen that faith in the first sense is contrary to the second of these alternatives. There is a second sense in which we speak of faith, which is contrary to the last alternative. Faith may be belief, not in spite of evidence, but *in the absence* of evidence. Men dislike a state of doubt. They prefer to believe something and to rest content with that belief. When they choose a belief relating to matters about which they know nothing one way or another, it will very likely be such as to fit in with their religious and ethical needs and desires. Faith in this sense has been the foundation of a good part of organized religion, and has been upheld by theologians and philosophers who have maintained that some things cannot be supported by rational grounds. Thus arose the distinction between "faith" and "knowledge": some things we can never have any knowledge of, but it is justifiable to have faith in their existence. The American philosopher William James (1842-1910) insisted that the right to believe was determined by the will to believe. There is no scientific evidence for or against the existence of God or of human immortality, but we are justified in believing that there is a God and that men are immortal, for these beliefs are the deepest cravings of man. Without them, our moral standards, our hopes and aspirations, collapse. We must respect these basic needs of our human nature. As we shall later discover, James felt that there was a close connection between that which is good and that which is true. We must note, in this second meaning of "faith," that the factor of hope and desire is essential. "Faith" and "hope" are even used synonymously by some philosophers, though this seems unjustifiable; for it is easily conceivable that we should have great hope and small faith, and "hope" by itself does not carry the implications of the will to believe.

**Faith as Expectation Based on Experience.** There is a third sense of "faith" quite different from the two preceding. We speak, for example, of "faith in democracy," "faith in one's physician," "faith in the scientific method." Here faith means belief, not *for lack of* evidence, but *on account of* evidence. It implies expectation that what has been found to be true in the past will continue to be favored by evidence in the future. Thus we mean that instances of failure on the part of democracy, of a physician, and of scientific methods, are only apparent and will in fact be dispelled by future investigation. Certain present facts make our belief more or less questionable, but we have confidence (i.e., faith) that it will ultimately be confirmed. Thus the steadfastness of belief in this sense is of a radically different character from that of the other two.

**Critical Remarks.** To continue to believe in spite of all evidence to the contrary must meet on all sides with condemnation as a method. For it is a frank glorification of the irrational element in human nature, elevating the influence of emotion above that of candor and intelligence. It is a commonplace—though one always worthy of repetition—that whatever progress has taken place in the development of man, particularly in science and art, has been fostered by the attitude of open-mindedness, the tolerance of new ideas and new forms.

Not to be for the extension of inquiry is to be against it, and to avoid evidence is to stifle it. As for faith in the second sense, the "will to believe," the reader will be better able to judge its soundness after discussion of the view known as scepticism and of the nature of truth. It would seem, however, that when we speak of inquiry as concerned with the discovery of truth, we cannot mean by this the promotion of our psychological comfort. Had such an identification ever been accepted, the history of intellectual growth would have consisted in cultivating the art of self-satisfaction rather than in an arduous discipline involving energy and struggle.

In the first two senses of "faith," the source of our belief makes no difference, the attitude being a clearly defined one; in the third, the attitude is different because the source, experience, serves as a guarantee. Possibly "faith" in the first sense ought not to be called a "method" at all, if by "method" we imply an active *search* for knowledge or wider experience. But it certainly is a method if we mean by that term an intellectual policy capable of influencing an intellectual outlook and of determining our criteria of what is true or false, acceptable or unacceptable.

**Authority.** If we ask where men obtain the opinions in which their faith lies, an answer that probably applies to most of them is that it is from some authority or other. The man who is primarily interested in preserving his beliefs is not likely to be the kind of man who has arrived at them in an independent way. Even those who are most willing to discard untenable opinions cannot escape the pervasive influence of authority. The family, the legal code, the state, the church, social custom, and the printed page — all function as authorities propagating opinions that cannot be wholly avoided even by the most critical. In some cases, as for instance the family and the social mores, beliefs are assimilated unconsciously. In other cases, as for instance the state and the church, the authority is consciously looked up to, and deliberately functions as an agency that legislates on truth and falsity, and on desirability and undesirability of belief. In such cases we have an explicit method of inquiry based on definite presuppositions.

**The Authoritarian Method.** The essence of the authoritarian method is that the individual relinquishes, in all but his common sense beliefs, his independent efforts to determine what is true or false. He transfers this function to an institution which lays claim to be in a better position to exercise it. Moreover, the transfer must be a complete transfer. For if the individual may retain the right to test some opinions, which shall they be? Is the individual or the authority to draw the line? Obviously, for either to do so is to annul the force of the other. The method of authority is therefore one which by its very nature cannot tolerate alternative opinion. It should be observed that to preclude independent inquiry is to preclude the questioning of opinions once they are authoritatively laid down, since the questioning of authority implies the employment of an alternative method.

The justification claimed, for authoritarianism is the liability to error of the individual mind. An organized agency especially responsible for the determination of truth is to be preferred to an individual only incidentally concerned with inquiry. Authority goes hand in hand with tradition. In the two fundamental types of historical authority, the church and the state, ecclesiastical and political traditions are invoked to lend the weight of age to dogmas. We hear of "the democratic tradition," "the revolutionary tradition," "the Christian tradition," not as descriptive phrases merely, but as honorific designations. Tradition, it is held, represents that which has stood the test of time. It comprises that which has emerged and endured out of the intellectual strife of the past.

**Critical Remarks.** It may be observed, first, that if the individual is capable of error, it does not follow that authority is incapable of error. But even if it were granted that authority is less frequently liable to error, what justification is there for not tolerating alternative inquiry? For we cannot *in advance* decide on *just which* occasions the individual will be wrong. Consequently we cannot wave aside any objection to authority until that objection is refuted on *specific grounds.* Thus there is a very high probability that on the authoritarian method error must occur; but what is much more serious, every such error is perpetuated, and therefore far more costly than mere error is likely to be. It has been well said that if tradition can preserve wisdom, it can also preserve error and folly. It is supposed that a belief or custom or institution is good if it can survive. But it is possible for the bad as well as the good to survive. It is not tradition that should be venerated — it is *good* tradition; for the two are not synonymous. "Survival" is a biological concept, referring exclusively to biological phenomena; it is not an ethical concept. Moreover, if the authoritarian method is sound, which authority shall it be? For is there not a multiplicity of authorities? If the authority is ecclesiastical, there will be more than one church propagating contrary opinion; if political, there will be more than one state. If there is a single church, church and state may conflict; and so on. There is perhaps no better proof than this of the fallibility of authority, since not more than one of the conflicting authorities can be right. And historical judgment has upheld the independence of men like Socrates against the claims of the state, and of men like Galileo against those of the church. Finally, when authorities conflict it is impossible satisfactorily to resolve the conflict by the method of authority itself. For if we appeal to Authority C to decide between Authorities A and B, C may be disputed by D. If we appeal to E to decide between C and D, E may be disputed by F. And so on without end.

In authority, unlike faith, it is on the source of belief that emphasis primarily falls. Despite the fact that authority is often the motivation of a strong faith, authority and faith methodologically are clearly distinguishable. Beliefs might be accepted on the authoritarian method without our being said to have "faith" either in the eternal incontrovertibility of the belief or the general infallibility of the authority. And strong faith can prevail where a belief is derived not from authority at all but from, say, personal experience or individual speculation. Both authority and faith, however, are essentially conservative methods: they incline to the preservation of what is already established in acceptance, and are hostile to the attitude which questions, examines, or speculates.

**Dogmatic and Expert Authority.** There is a sharp distinction between the authority of church or state and what is sometimes called "scientific authority." In both cases it is the opinion of an organized agency which is accepted or appealed to. But in the former, we are unable to examine the process by which the conclusion has been reached, whereas in the latter we are free to do so and can be prevented only by our own possible incompetency or lack of opportunity. Scientific authority is simply a substitute for the scientific method, and although we do use the word "authority" here we can hardly speak of a "method" of authority. The resort to the opinion of experts is necessary and desirable in a society characterized by highly specialized delegation of functions.

**Intuition: the View of Knowledge as Immediate and "Self-evident."** The objection which very naturally arises to the methods of faith and authority is that they are too rigid. Faith does not permit a sufficiently sharp distinction between true and false, the authoritarian method gives no opportunity for men to exercise their intellectual faculties. Various philosophers have maintained that unless a belief carries conviction to the individual mind, it cannot be said to constitute genuine knowledge. On the basis of this criticism, a third fundamental method of investigation can be distinguished, which we may call the method of intuition. It rests on the assumption that man has a natural capacity for acquiring knowledge, provided that he exercises this capacity properly. There are certain principles the truth of which he knows "intuitively" — that is to say, without reasoning about them, or without undertaking to test them. He knows them to be true by a direct insight, by an immediate awareness. They are "self-evident"; in other words, they need no evidence, they are their own evidence, they guarantee their own truth.

We must emphasize that the term "intuition" (or "intuitive" knowledge) has been used in *many different senses*. Widespread among them is the meaning just given: knowledge that is direct, immediate, and indubitably certain. But philosophers have differed on the *way* in which such knowledge is acquired, or on the *factors* that enter into it. They have differed, for example, on the kinds of principles that are intuitive. Some have cited as intuitive a statement like "A whole is greater than any of its parts"; others, a statement like "Killing is wrong"; others, a statement like "What I now see before me is red." Others have held that the only kind of intuitive knowledge there can be is that devoid of all informational content, exemplified by the statement "Birds are birds." Still others have held the view that intuitive knowledge cannot be adequately expressed in language or any other kind of symbols. We shall have occasion to distinguish these different conceptions of intuition in the course of this study.

Intuitionists have supposed that intuitive knowledge, by virtue of its certainty, must serve as the basis or foundation of all other knowledge. Many have, however, gone so far as to assert that only intuition can properly be called "knowledge." Consider a concrete illustration. Do we not know that there are eight million-odd persons in New York City? Yet we do not know this intuitively, since we must undertake a complex process of gathering evidence for this statement — counting, tabulating, etc. The intuitionist might reply that since we can never be absolutely certain that our processes of counting and tabulating are free from error, or that the number is not changing at any moment, we cannot really be said to *know* that the statement is true but only to associate with it a high degree of probability, which is sufficient for all practical purposes. In intuition, on the other hand, our verification is immediate and self-certifying.

**Critical Remarks.** The method of intuition provides for conviction and satisfaction on the part of the individual as the basis for his acceptance of fundamental truths. It allows him to accept other principles than those which are "self-evident." But the objection at once arises, Who shall determine what is "self-evident"? Does it not seem that the standard of judgment must vary with different individuals, no less than other standards of judgment? If this is so, then the borderline between intuitive truths and non-intuitive truths (if they are to be called such) is hard to draw. Further, how are we to find out whether others regard as intuitive what we so regard? We cannot examine one another's minds, and cannot have one another's feeling of certainty. If an individual protests that he does not see why a given principle is certain, how is he to be convinced by one who does regard it as certain? If the latter furnishes evidence or proof, this is a tacit admission that the principle is not *self*-evident. History, as a matter of fact, shows eloquently how even principles universally regarded as "self-evident" have been demonstrated to be, not merely lacking in "self-evidence" but actually false. Consider, for instance, the "axiom" *A whole is greater than any of its parts.* Modern mathematics has made it clear that this does not apply to quantities or collections that are infinite. Suppose we take the collection of integers which are arranged in the following series:

1, 2, 3, 4, 5, 6, 7, 8, 9, 10, 11, 12, . . . , etc. This series has no end, that is, no last term; it includes an infinite number of integers. Now this collection (or series) consists of other collections (or series). For example, it includes the series of all odd numbers, of all even numbers, of all prime numbers, and so on. Let us take, out of the series of *all* the integers, the series of all *odd* integers, which is part of it. We then have this:

1, 3, 5, 7, 9, 11, 13, 15, 17, 19, 21, . . . , etc. But this series likewise has no last term, and contains an infinite number of integers. It contains *as many* integers or items as the series of which it is a part. And this can easily be seen if we match the first number in the former series with the first in the latter, the second with the second in the latter, and so on. Every number in the former has, corresponding to it, some number in the latter.

Thus the method of intuition allows the *individual* mind *too much* license in discriminating genuine from apparent knowledge. It substitutes a *feeling of certainty* for *proof*. A feeling of certainty varies with different individuals, whereas proof is to be understood as carrying universal conviction. To put the matter into other terms, the intuitive method substitutes a psychological criterion of knowledge for a logical criterion.

Faith and intuition are thus highly individualistic. Faith and authority are extremely conservative. Authority is arbitrary. All three involve to a large extent the human, or subjective, element in determining truth. All three profess infallibility — they provide no means by which their results can be corrected or modified, since they provide no means for detecting error involved in their employment. We must go on to distinguish another method of inquiry, which throughout its historical development has attempted to avoid as far as possible these objectionable characteristics. This is the method of science.

## CHAPTER SIX

❖   ❖   ❖

# The Scientific Method

The term "scientific" is used with remarkable frequency. We daily appraise modes of thought as scientific or unscientific. Peculiarly enough, we sometimes hear, from those who frown upon the results of natural science, that results to which they point are "more truly scientific." In attempting to define "science" and "scientific method," and to compare it with other methods, the philosopher must have an eye to what has gone by that name in the past and to what is involved in the practice of natural science and mathematics today. In so doing he is confronted with a complex, gigantic structure to which full justice can be done only by a detailed analysis. Our purpose here is merely to outline the most general and most distinctive characteristics of the method.

**The Progressive and Public Character of Scientific Inquiry.** There is one outstanding fact about science which is not the case in authority, faith, and intuition, and which must be reckoned with in any ultimate evaluation of the scientific method. This is the historical fact that knowledge acquired by this method has *increased,* has grown and progresses steadily. No one will contest the statement that science has advanced over its state in, say, Galileo's day. To what is this progress due? It is due to a collaboration between many investigators— not in the sense that this collaboration is necessarily conscious, but in the sense that one inquirer can utilize the results obtained by another. We cannot collaborate in the literal sense with Newton or Harvey or Gauss or Darwin. The inquiries of these men (and of countless others), however, have been of such a

kind that it is possible to employ them as means to the further-
ance of inquiry in the present. In other words, the evidence
that science accumulates is *public*. It is open to the scrutiny
of all. If a given scientific result is to be refuted, it must be
refuted by the same kind of evidence. When a biologist experiments in order to test the soundness of a biological theory,
his experiments are such as could be performed and observed
by all who have the requisite training and competence. If the
experimental results are favorable to the theory, everyone must,
in spite of extra-scientific considerations, regard the theory as
more acceptable than it was previously. It is not because the
biologist *says* so (authority); not because of any ethical or
emotional reasons (faith); not because of any feelings of certainty (intuition); it is because the evidence is of the kind
that compels assent. When the mathematician proves a theorem,
the proof is accepted not because he or anyone else however
eminent says that it should be, nor because it seems morally
desirable to do so, nor because of any appeal by the mathematician to our intuition, but because he has actually been able
to deduce the theorem from accepted principles by applying
mathematical rules: anyone who understands can ascertain
whether the theorem has been deduced by the application of
those rules.

**The Rôle of the Individual.** As a result of this rigid
emphasis on evidence of the character described, the emotional
or subjective (or psychological) element is reduced to a mini-
mum in the scientific method. Scientists do, of course, differ
in their mental makeup, and no doubt the personal idiosyn-
crasies of individual scientists are sometimes not so favorable
to the pursuit of scientific investigation as might be wished.
This, however, is a fact about those who practise the method,
not about the method itself. Since it is men who make use of
a method, the scientific, like any other, cannot be free of abuse.
But the nature of science is such that this dependence is mini-
mized. The procedures and rules which have arisen in the
course of its development do not depend upon the personal

characteristics of those who may employ them. Authority and faith obviously do, and intuition at least depends upon personal insight. The arbitrariness of authority, the narrowness of faith, the overemphasis on individual insight of intuition, grow out of the fact that their findings are not of a public character, and are not subject to (since they make no allowance for) criticism and modification. The scientific method is the method which marshals evidence on objective grounds alone. In fact, it might at least plausibly be maintained that evidence based on any other ground is not evidence at all, properly speaking; so that the scientific method might be conceived of as the method which introduces the notion of evidence into human inquiry.

There is one sense in which the individual may indeed play a major part in the development of science. Historically, the great theories by means of which science has advanced have been the product of individual imagination. It is not merely "the scientist" who is the source of scientific ideas, but specifically an Archimedes, a Faraday, an Einstein. Yet in spite of the fact that it has been individuals who have been responsible for the introduction of ideas into science, this cannot be the major factor in the nature of scientific method. For what distinguishes the method of science is the manner in which its theories become transformed into knowledge. And this consists precisely in the process of universal testing that we have mentioned. The individual *introduces* ideas, the scientific community *appraises* them by its objective criteria. As long as an individual contribution remains individual, it can be no part of science. No individual who has come by a fruitful theory could have done so had he not been grounded in the accumulated scientific knowledge which was his heritage and which had resulted in turn from the testing of previous theories. In authority and intuition there is no lack of theories imaginative and sweeping in character. Their status, however, is that of theories which have not been or cannot be tested.

**The Provisionality of Scientific Results.** The scientific method lays no claim to infallibility, and in this respect differs most strikingly from the other methods. This, too, explains its progress. For it manifestly could not have advanced if in any age it had rested content with the results it had obtained. There can be no end to the process of testing scientific theories, improving their expression, and interrelating them with one another. To learn from experimental observation that the facts are not such as a given theory requires them to be, means not a retardation but an advance of scientific knowledge. It is certainly a progressive step to know that of five hypotheses under consideration as interpretations of a phenomenon, only four are henceforth to be considered plausible.

The scientific method agrees with the authoritarian method in recognizing that individual men are extremely fallible. But whereas the latter method transfers the function of inquiry to a *given* man or *given* group of men, who are at best fallible in only lesser degree, the former develops a set of procedures which are the prerogative of no single group. In science, the greater the number of trained men the greater the likelihood of its advance. In authority, on the contrary, the greater the number of trained men, the greater the likelihood of its breakdown; for with the growth of intellectual independence, dissension under so rigid a method is inevitable. It should be clear that, as we remarked previously, those who, lacking scientific training, accept scientific "authority," are far from appealing to the authoritarian method.

**Formal and Empirical Science.** The reader may have suspected already that the type of evidence which a mathematician employs is not quite the same as that employed by other scientists. It is important now to make explicit a distinction between two very different aspects of science: *formal science,* which embraces the sciences of mathematics and formal logic, and *empirical science* (or natural science), which embraces all the sciences called "physical" and "social" — chemistry, biology, psychology, physics, economics, sociology, etc. The term "empirical" means "relating to experience." Formal science asserts nothing about natural phenomena; it is independent of experience, and none of its proofs rest on how facts actually stand.

If we ask the question, What is this or that empirical science about? we answer by pointing to some aspect of the natural world: chemistry is about the physical elements of things and their possible combinations; economics, about the phenomena of exchange and manipulation of material goods; psychology, about the phenomena of individual or group behavior. In other words, each empirical science deals with some aspect of what can be experientially known, and attempts to formulate laws about it. It tests its theories by observing, with the special techniques that it employs, a set of facts.

**The Deductive and Hypothetical Character of Formal Science.** Of pure mathematics and formal logic the same cannot be said. The formal scientist, the mathematician or logician, is not interested in whether statements correspond to the facts or not. He is interested only in the connection — the logical connection — of statements with one another. "Does statement A follow logically from statements B, C, and D?" Or, "What statements follow logically from A?" Whether A is true or not is no concern of formal science. The latter is concerned solely with the question, What are the necessary consequences of any assertions we make? Given any statement at all, its task is to *deduce* other statements from that, or to inquire whether a given deduction is correct. Suppose we were to consider the two following statements:

1. The number of Japanese is greater than the number of Russians.

2. The number of Russians is greater than the number of Chinese.

Both these statements are false. The geographer, as an empirical scientist, would reject them, for he wishes the statements of his science to correspond to the facts ascertained in experience. But the formal scientist does not care whether they are true or false. What he points out is that whoever accepts these two statements must accept another statement, namely "The number of Japanese is greater than the number of Chinese." The latter statement is necessarily implied by the other two. The formal scientist thus regards all statements as assumptions, as *hypothetically* true, and ascertains in accordance with rules and definitions what other statements *would,* in consequence, *have to* be true.

**The Meaning of "Formal."** Why does the third statement above necessarily follow from the other two? Is it because the Japanese, Chinese, and Russians happen to be so constituted that the relationship holds? Clearly not. The real reason for the necessity of the inference is that the first two statements actually assert already what the third asserts. They contain the third implicitly; it makes explicit what is already involved in them. The deduction would still hold good *no matter what* terms we substituted for "Japanese," "Chinese," and "Russians," provided we were consistent in the substitution. If we substituted "lions" wherever "Chinese" occurs, "cigars" wherever "Japanese" occurs, and "Hottentots" wherever "Russians" occurs, the third statement would be "The number of cigars is greater than the number of lions," and it would still follow necessarily from statements (1) and (2), interpreted accordingly. In fact, we can substitute for the original terms "x's," "y's," and "z's," and we get

1. The number of x's is greater than the number of y's;
2. The number of y's is greater than the number of z's;

hence    3. The number of x's is greater than the number of z's.

Here the statements are *neither* true *nor* false. They are not statements at all but mere skeletons, or *forms,* of statements. It is in these forms of statements that the mathematician is interested, and not in what the statements are about, that is, not in their subject-matter. He knows, from the rules of his science, that the inference holds because of the logical form in which it is couched, and not because of the particular terms that occur in it. It is for this reason that we speak of mathematics as a formal science. It is the forms of statements alone that are relevant to the validity of deductions.

Suppose the mathematician is given the statements

I. If A and B are distinct points on a plane, there is at least one line containing both A and B,

II. If A and B are distinct points on a plane, there is not more than one line containing both A and B,

and suppose that a "plane" is defined as a certain collection of lines, while a "line" is defined as a certain other collection of "points" (so that a "plane" is ultimately a collection of "points"). In order to deduce a necessary consequence from I and II, must the mathematician investigate the nature of "points," "lines," and "planes"? Not at all. Whether these expressions are to be understood as referring to anything physical is not his concern but that of the physicist. For the mathematician the above statements are viewed as statements of logical relationships; he is not interested in their empirical or factual meaning (if they have any). Accordingly, before the mathematician performs a deduction, the first thing he does (ideally speaking, not always of course in actual practice) is to express the statements anew, so that all suggestion of factual reference will be eliminated and only the form of the statement (the logical relations involved) will remain clearly exhibited. Instead of a "plane" he speaks of "a class P"; instead of a "line," of "a sub-class of P"; instead of points, of "members of the class P." The following restatements of I and II can then be made:

I′. If A and B are distinct members of a class P, there is at least one sub-class of P containing both A and B.

II′. If A and B are distinct members of the class P, there is no more than one sub-class of P containing both A and B.

From these it follows necessarily that

III′. If A and B are distinct members of the class P, there

is one and only one sub-class of P containing both A and B,

or

III. If A and B are distinct points on a plane, there is one and only one line containing both A and B.

One who is ordinarily confronted with statements I and II ordinarily interprets them in spatial terms and tries to exercise his intuition of spatial relationships in order to see what must follow from them. In I′ and II′ the whole matter of spatial meaning (and therefore of truth and falsity) has been discarded as irrelevant for pure mathematics. A term like "containing," we must note, is used not in a spatial but in a purely logical sense. The mathematician relies, in order to make the deduction, not on intuition (which may or may not help him) but on purely mathematical (logical) relationships. He need never have heard of the fact that the word "plane" is sometimes used to denote something in space in order to have drawn the inference with absolute exactness. And this is shown by the above translation of the two statements.

**Empirical Science and Common Sense.** Common sense, we saw, is the body of knowledge gained through our daily experience and the cumulative experience of the race. What distinguishes the scientific man from the common man? Certainly the basic activities performed by both are the same. Both know that lemons are sour and that a rock sinks in water. But we do not doubt that the scientific man knows *more* than the common man about such facts. In *what sense* does he know more? An answer involves a statement of the fundamental traits of empirical science.

Common sense is knowledge gained through experience *unwittingly*. Empirical science is knowledge gained from experience *methodically*. Common sense is random and accidental; scientific inquiry is purposive and selective. Does this mean that before his scientific inquiry begins the scientist possesses merely common knowledge, and that after it begins he acquires a new and different kind of knowledge which he substitutes for the old? Such an account is in part right and in part wrong. It is right in so far as it implies that there are significant differences between the two. It is wrong in so far as it implies that the two are wholly unconnected or that one is abandoned when the other is acquired.

Common sense is vague. The objects and situations that we refer to are undifferentiated. They are referred to in large masses, so to speak, and without precise specification of the conditions governing them. When we speak of the "earth" we are hardly very clear about its character and its relation to other planets; when we speak of "light," it is vaguely of something affecting vision, not of something defined in terms of waves with frequency of vibration and other properties. "Water" means something which wets us, not a chemical compound. Peculiarly enough, it is largely on account of their very vagueness that our common sense judgments are true. When we say vaguely that the sun rises in the east we are less likely to be convicted of error than when we make a scientific statement, richer in complexity and detail, about the rotation of the earth. Our statement, describing the same phenomenon as does the scientific statement, by its nature makes little pretension to exactness; its "risk" of error is less. The purposes of description and communication for which it is designed are adequately satisfied.

But if common sense is thus essentially reliable knowledge, it is so at the expense of being narrow, static, and unenlightening, and only in so far as our needs are of a rudimentary character. As soon as common sense goes beyond these restricted conditions, it becomes highly susceptible to error — indeed, it ceases to be common sense. We can say on the basis of common sense that the stars twinkle, but not very much more than that about them.

**The Abstractness of Empirical Science.** When the scientist deals with a phenomenon, the things he refers to are, as we have already suggested, the same things everyone else refers to, and often he uses the same name — "sun," "light," "water," "force," etc. It is in his *account* of these things that the scientist differs, often to so great an extent that his reference to them cannot be understood except after considerable study. The language used by the various sciences differs widely in both degree and kind. The language of history and biography (which we sometimes forget are sciences) is certainly different from that of chemistry or mechanics, and is more similar to the language of common sense. In common sense we speak of tables, buildings, stones, and trees; whereas in mechanics we speak of *bodies*. In common sense, it is pulling, pushing, sliding, rolling, breaking, cracking that interest us; but in mechanics *force* is far more fundamental. In other words, the science is primarily concerned with *abstract properties,* with that which all the aforementioned things or events have in *common,* and not with their individual details. The historian, it would seem at first blush, makes no such use of abstractions in his science of reconstructing and interpreting the past. But although it is true that the abstractions of the historian are of a lesser degree than those of the other natural sciences, it is certain that he employs them. In speaking of a "decline of Athenian democracy," a "transition from feudalism to commercial capitalism," a "renaissance of the plastic arts," he is deliberately neglecting this or that detail in favor of an abstract property which will give significance to his historical analysis. In general, then, there can be no doubt that the most evident distinguishing characteristic between common sense and empirical science is the far greater degree of abstractness of the latter.

Why does the scientist use abstract terms — energy, refraction, reproduction, market value, stress, reflex, atomic weight, and so on? The answer is that if he did not he could not formulate his hypotheses. These hypotheses are about properties belonging to classes of things — gases, animals, societies, rocks, stars, immersed bodies. If the scientist did not employ concepts naming properties common to all the individuals comprising a class, he could not generalize at all. The need for abstracting may be made clear in another way. In order to formulate laws about phenomena, the scientist must distinguish certain aspects of a phenomenon from others. In explaining motion, he cannot take into consideration *all* the properties of moving bodies — texture, color, combustibility, malleability, and a host of others. He must abstract the properties *relevant* to motion, and ignore all the others. In formulating the law of gravitation, the color of bodies is irrelevant, but the mass of bodies is important. In formulating the law of the conditioned reflex in animals, the concept of height is irrelevant, but that of stimulus is relevant. Newton, for example, could not have hit upon his principle of gravitation had he been unable to abstract the concepts of mass and distance from all the other properties of bodies, and to perceive that these alone were relevant in the construction of a formula for the motion of bodies with respect to one another.

**The Essential Procedure of Empirical Science.** The purpose of empirical science is to understand the structure and workings of nature. If we had to summarize its essential procedure in the broadest terms, we might do so as follows. As a result of certain observations he has made, or as an outgrowth of knowledge he already possesses, the scientist finds himself confronted with a problem concerning certain objects or facts. He may ask any of a number of questions: "Are there other facts or objects of the same kind?" Or, "What explains the properties of these objects?" In order to *interpret* what he has observed, to see a *connection* among the facts before him and thereby understand their *significance,* he forms a hypothesis (theory), or rather several hypotheses. He must then test these hypotheses, in order to discover the most satisfactory among them. A hypothesis tells him how to *look* at the facts. Each hypothesis prescribes an approach. His testing begins when he inaugurates *systematic* or *deliberate* observation (experimentation), to see which of the alternative prescriptions is favored by facts he had not observed *before* forming the hypotheses. Let us consider an example or two.

**Illustration.** Suppose that in studying American history we concentrate our attention on its economic aspect. We examine periods of industrial depression and expansion. We happen to observe that at a certain period when an expansion of industry took place, increased employment followed. The problem occurs to us: Is this correlation a universal one? That is, does it hold for all such periods? We tentatively adopt the hypothesis that it does. We examine other periods of expansion with deliberate scrutiny of the relation between the two factors; in other words, we are now undertaking *methodical* observation — we are seeking to verify or refute a generalization. After examining as many periods as we can, we conclude (let us suppose) that the generalization is true. It may be that we desire to widen our generalization, to embrace not only American history but that of all modern industrial nations, in which case our observation must be correspondingly wider and more varied. In respect to any hypothesis of a universal nature our verification may become increasingly stronger but can never yield absolute certainty. For there will always remain the possibility that some case we have not yet examined (or one that will occur in future) will be out of accord with the generalization. In the process of experimental verification many problems are involved the discussion of which is beyond our scope. The more complex the generalization, the more numerous the factors which must be taken into consideration and the more precarious our confidence in it threatens to become. Not every hypothesis is a universal or general one. But this kind is by far the most significant, and the kind in which science is most interested. For it is interested not in isolated phenomena but in *laws,* or general patterns, of the universe. Its purpose is not to arrive at an exhaustive catalogue of individual facts but at a system of general principles in terms of which these facts can be explained and rendered more significant.

**"Explanatory" Hypotheses.** In generalizing that increased employment follows business expansion we did not explain why this happens. We could, however, have gone on to explain *why* this holds in a given case (i.e., beyond saying *that* it does), or why it holds in all such cases. Let us illustrate an "explanatory" hypothesis, this time taken from astronomy. When Kepler commenced his studies of Mars, he possessed a great number of records of observations that had previously been made. He knew that at different times Mars was in different places, occupying such-and-such positions relative to the sun and the other planets. The question arose, Why did it occupy those particular positions in succession? In other words, what orbit, if supposed to be that of Mars, would account for the facts observed about it (or in still other words, be such that the observed facts could be deduced from the assumption of it)? These facts were isolated or disorganized so far as Kepler's understanding was concerned, and they were very numerous. He tried different theories, modifying each in turn after it had failed to be substantiated by further observations he made. Finally he arrived at the hypothesis that the orbit of Mars was elliptical. This was capable of explaining all the facts.

**Explanation and Verification.** In what sense did it "explain"? In the sense that from the theory taken together with the data or facts already in his possession he could deduce all the other facts. Even if he had not known the facts in advance, he could have "predicted" them, that is, deduced consequences and then made observations to see whether these coincided with the facts. Given this theory, we know where Mars will be at a given time — we can deduce its position from the supposition of a complete orbit. The theory connects the facts we already know, predicts facts we did not know, and in general, interprets a collection of scattered observations which previously had little meaning for us. That a hypothesis must enable us to deduce from it not merely facts we knew beforehand but facts we do not as yet know, needs great emphasis. This is essential for the process of testing it. Any number of hypotheses, plausible or fantastic, can be devised to explain facts already known. But to predict facts hitherto unknown is another matter. We test an explanation by deducing from it consequences in accordance with the rules of formal science, which is thus seen to play a vital part in empirical science. Among the consequences are some which we can test directly by observation. The more consequences we find to be true, the more likely our hypothesis becomes. If, however, the consequences of a hypothesis are contrary to the facts observed, it cannot be true. For a true statement cannot have false implications. Thus by systematically deducing the consequences of a number of possible hypotheses and checking them experientially we progressively eliminate the hypotheses that are false. From any general hypothesis an indefinite number of consequences can be drawn, and the possibility always remains that at some time one of these may be discovered experimentally to be false. No hypothesis, then, can ever be considered as fixed or certain. This is the more precise way of stating the point already emphasized, that empirical science regards all of its conclusions as provisional, no matter how well verified.

**The Meaning of "Induction."** Reasoning from the truth of the consequences of a hypothesis to the truth of the hypothesis itself — or more broadly stated, reasoning from a limited number of observations to a conclusion that goes beyond any finite number of observations — is sometimes called *induction* or inductive reasoning. Many philosophers have been troubled by what they have called the "problem of induction." How, they have asked, can induction ever be reliable, for surely a limited number of observations will not prove a general theory? This difficulty lies partly in expecting induction to yield what it cannot by its very nature yield, namely, certainty. Some philosophers have held that induction, or experimental reasoning, is as certain as deduction, or purely logical (formal) reasoning. And among those who raise the "problem of induction," though many have expressed doubt that the traditional reasons for the certainty of induction are the proper reasons, they have never questioned whether induction *ought* to be regarded as necessary inference. We may suggest the opinion, in the light of our previous discussion, that if an "induction" ever is necessary, it is not an induction at all but a disguised deduction (in which the conclusions are implicitly contained in the premisses); while if it is a genuine induction it cannot yield conclusions with necessity or certainty. The "reliability" of any induction can be only its success in withstanding the rigors of indefinite scientific testing. The greater the number and the greater the variety of consequences found to be in accordance with the facts, the stronger the induction of the hypothesis that (deductively) implies them.

**The Interdependence of Fact and Theory.** Our discussion has sufficed to show us that facts do not have intellectual significance unless interpreted by a hypothesis or general principle; they do not, as is popularly supposed, "speak for themselves." It has likewise shown us that theories, in order to be regarded as established and as possessing explanatory value, must be verified by facts. We thus find an essential interdependence of fact and theory in the method of empirical science. Theories interpret facts, facts confirm theories. Theories unsupported by facts are baseless, facts uninterpreted by theories are unilluminating and blind. As we enlarge our observation of facts, we modify our theories to fit them; but the modified theories throw a light on these very facts. So the process goes on, in both directions: the expansion of experimentation, the refinement of theory. Each is essential to the other, and each derives a greater value from the other.

**Empirical Science as an Orderly Structure, or "System."** Not only does science seek to explain observed facts, and generalizations about facts, by means of its explanatory theories, but it seeks also to explain *the latter* by means of more fundamental theories. Kepler explained the successive positions of Mars, but we can also explain why the orbit of Mars and in fact the orbits of all planets are elliptical. This was accomplished by Newton, to whom the gigantic hypothesis occurred that the motion of the heavenly bodies and the motion of ordinary bodies on the earth are of essentially the same kind. By means of this insight, formulated in his theory of gravitation, he was able to explain the theories of Copernicus, Galileo, and Kepler. These, in being found to be deducible from the Newtonian theory, thereby become interrelated. They are synthesized by it. In thus unifying and relating theories which belong to the science of mechanics, the Newtonian theory contributes a greater degree of order and coherence to this science. And in comparatively recent times we have seen, in the physics of Einstein, a still more pervasive systematization, in which other branches of physics besides mechanics become interrelated into a tremendous network. Thus historically empirical science has attempted not merely to enunciate as many theories as it can which are experimentally confirmed, but to connect these theories with one another as far as possible into a comprehensive pattern. The connection of these theories is accomplished by mathematical techniques, which ascertain whether certain theories are deducible from others. When we speak of "mathematical physics" or "mathematical economics" we mean an application of mathematical rules to hypotheses of physics or of economics in order to deduce their implications. As we have already suggested, it is this approach to greater and greater degrees of system and order that perhaps distinguishes science from common sense even more than its concern with the rigorous experiential testing of its theories.

**The Place of Insight in Science.** There appear to be certain aspects of science which are not capable of being subject to order and rule. Such, for instance, is the process of hitting upon a theory. Those who in the history of science have contributed fruitful theories did not arrive at them in any prescribed or standard manner. There are no rules for fruitful conjecture or guessing, and science is dependent on the unpredictable element of scientific genius for its major theoretical advances. This applies to formal as well as empirical science. The mathematician is governed by rules in proving a theorem, but there is no rule by which he can perceive the *applicability* of these rules to the proof of the theorem.

This is a matter of insight. In both formal and empirical science, we may, it is true, say that the profounder an individual's knowledge of his science and its results, the better his chance of hitting upon a fruitful discovery. But there is not the least guarantee that he will or when he will do so, or that he rather than another will do so.

**Untestable Hypotheses.** What happens to hypotheses which are introduced into science but which cannot be tested by the ordinary scientific processes? Suppose, for example, the hypothesis of supernatural intervention to explain certain types of psychological phenomena. Is this admissible? We shall have occasion later on (in Chapter XI and Chapter XIII) to consider the status of such views. We may remark here, however, that they are not ruled out of science by arbitrary decree, but only by the adverse weight of scientific history. The history of science shows that such theories have never been instrumental in the promotion of scientific progress, except perhaps in a negative sense, as stimulating the search for an alternative theory. The reason is that they run counter to the public motif of science, and are recalcitrant to the progressive accumulation of evidence. A scientific hypothesis which intrinsically has no promise of ever being *subject to test* really has no more scientific status than a poem. The main difference between the scientific and the poetic imagination is that the former seeks literal corroboration by fact, whereas the latter seeks to enrich personal experience regardless of, and perhaps most often at the expense of, literal truth.

❖   ❖   ❖

# The Rôles of Reason and Experience in Human Knowledge

Since earliest days philosophers have debated and weighed the relative importance of two factors that play a part in our search for knowledge. One is man's power of thought and explanation, the other his power of observation and perception. In the attainment of knowledge (whether scientific knowledge or knowledge of a philosophic or practical kind), is it what the mind contributes that is important, or what the mind receives from the environment? Or if both enter in, which deserves greater emphasis? Is thought more important than observation? Has the mind, by its reasoning power, the ability to discover truth by itself, or is observation of the world of actual fact alone reliable? Is the mind endowed with an "instinctive" capacity for certain kinds of knowledge, or is it fed and supplied only with knowledge from experience, being originally something impotent? These are all different ways of asking the same fundamental question.

**Rationalism and Empiricism.** Those philosophers who stress reasoning or thinking or calculating as the primary and decisive factor in all knowledge have come to be known in modern times as *rationalists,* while those who lay stress on the role of observation or experience or the senses have come to be known as *empiricists.* There are many kinds of both rationalism and empiricism, and few philosophers have been pure rationalists or pure empiricists. Most rationalists assign some function or other to the senses and sense experience, and most empiricists speak of reasoning or thought as an element in knowledge; but it is the way they interpret these that stamps them as of one or the other camp.

74

**Historical Illustrations.** Let us consider some typical historical statements of the two points of view. One of the questions on which philosophers have differed concerns the *origin* of knowledge — whether the mind is in some way equipped with faculties before experience occurs, or whether it begins its operations only after being furnished with "sensations" or "ideas" by the senses. The latter view can, for example, be found in the English philosopher John Locke (1632-1704). He says, in the *Essay concerning Human Understanding:*

> The senses at first let in particular ideas, and furnish the yet empty cabinet, and the mind by degrees growing familiar with some of them, they are lodged in the memory, and names got to them. . . . In this manner the mind comes to be furnished with ideas and language, the materials about which to exercise its discursive faculty. And the use of reason becomes daily more visible, as these materials that give it employment increase.*

And further:

> Let us then suppose the mind to be, as we say, white paper, void of all characters, without any ideas:— How comes it to be furnished? Whence comes it by that vast store which the busy and boundless fancy of man has painted on it with an almost endless variety? Whence has it all the *materials* of reason and knowledge? To this I answer, in one word, from *experience.* In that all our knowledge is founded; and from that it ultimately derives itself. Our observation . . . is that which supplies our understandings with all the *materials* of thinking.†

Locke is not an extreme empiricist. He does not deny that the mind can actively manipulate ideas once it is supplied with them. It compounds together the simple ideas which it "receives" either from the exercise of the senses on outward things — such ideas as sweetness, whiteness, hardness; or from "internal" sense, the contemplation of its own operations — such ideas as perception, doubting, willing. These two sources are the sole sources from which we obtain our simple ideas, which are the materials of all knowledge. All thought can ulti-

---

* Bk. I, Ch. 1, Sec. 15.
† Bk. II, Ch. 1, Sec. 2.

mately be broken down into these atomic elements, which are derived from sense (external or internal).

Compare with this the view of Baruch Spinoza (1632-1677):

> The intellect, by its native strength, makes for itself intellectual instruments, whereby it acquires strength for performing other intellectual operations, and from these operations gets again fresh instruments, or the power of pushing its investigations further, and thus gradually proceeds till it reaches the summit of wisdom.*

Most rationalists have admitted that sense experience is the starting-point of knowledge, for we begin to be conscious at all only when we begin to exercise our senses; but for them it serves merely as the spark that sets off the intellectual machinery. Knowledge is not, as in Locke, built up out of elementary observations, but only given its initial stimulus by observation.

**The Problem of "A Priori" Knowledge: the Rationalist Claim.** We have said that both rationalism and empiricism admit of different degrees and kinds. It is possible, nevertheless, to state what it is that all rationalists hold in common, and similarly all empiricists. The basic claim of rationalism— the minimal claim — is that the mind has the power to know with certainty various truths about the universe which outward observation can never give us. Consider one example. We know, say rationalists, that every event has a cause. Yet how could we know this through experience? If we relied on experience we should have to test the truth of this belief by examining every event to ascertain whether or not it has a cause. Now obviously in experience we cannot examine *all* events, we cannot examine an infinite number of them, for we cannot reach into the entire past and entire future. How, then, *do* we know it to be a truth that every event has a cause? We know it intuitively — it is self-evident, and needs no verification. Experience can suggest and *illustrate* it, but not *prove* it. Absolutely certain knowledge of general principles gained independently of observation has been called by philosophers

---

* *On the Improvement of the Understanding* (translated by R. H. M. Elwes).

*a priori* knowledge, as opposed to empirical knowledge. Rationalists vary in their willingness to call empirical knowledge "knowledge," but all at least hold that we have some knowledge that is *a priori*, whereas empiricists deny the possibility of *a priori* knowledge — unless the term *"a priori"* be interpreted in a way that we shall mention in a moment.

**The Empiricist Interpretation.** There are at least two possible points in reply to the rationalist contention that the belief "Every event has a cause" is known to be true *a priori*. (1) Only by experience can we know that events have causes. It is true that we cannot examine an infinite number of events, but this merely goes to show that we can never know with certainty that such general or universal principles are true. The most we can say is that we have always found a given principle to hold, and that there is every reason to believe it will continue to do so. (2) In one sense we could be said to know with absolute certainty that every event has a cause — but not because of any *a priori* intuition into the nature of things. We would know it to be true in the sense that it would be *true by definition*. An "event" might mean something that occurs or some change that takes place; to say that something changes might mean that it is the outcome of certain conditions, or, in other words, of a cause. Thus there *are* general statements known to be true *a priori,* that is, with certainty yet without empirical testing — but they are not truths about *things* or *facts* at all; they are disguised definitions. When we say "Birds are birds" we need not examine the nature of birds in order to know that this is true. Similarly when we assert "Everything that ascends rises" or "Every object is either round or not round." What we are saying in the latter example is that everything either has a property or hasn't it—which gives us no information about any fact whatever but merely states the condition for the use of intelligible language. Whatever knowledge, then, is alleged to be *a priori* must be of this trivial character; if not, it can be known only through experiential examination, and therefore can never be known with absolute certainty.

**The Rationalist Conception of Knowledge.** The empiricist usually would not reinterpret as tautologous principles alleged to be *a priori* by rationalists. For example, a classical principle held self-evident is that "in all changes of the material world the quantity of matter remains unchanged." Empiricists would hold this to be a statement about fact verifiable only empirically and therefore not "self-evident."

Now the classical rationalist conceives of knowledge as a system of truths based on a solid and unshakable foundation. He is impatient with the acknowledged deceptiveness of the senses and with the tentativeness of everyday human opinion. The foundation of knowledge consists rather of a set of *first principles,* he maintains, — the universal *a priori* principles, known intuitively. From these self-evident first principles other truths can be *deduced,* by the unerring methods of mathematics. So that all knowledge properly so called is arrived at either by intuition or by deduction from truths intuitively known. Experience and observation, classical rationalists like Spinoza and Descartes felt, were extremely useful but only as a stimulus or cue or take-off for the intuition of self-evident, eternal principles. Once the mind is in possession of such truths it can expand its knowledge indefinitely by deduction. The classical rationalists were greatly impressed by the rigor, cogency, and exactitude of mathematics, and attempted to use mathematics and mathematical types of reasoning for the construction of their philosophical systems. The ideal of knowledge that they held to be possible in *any* field and in *any* discipline was a mathematical one. They conceived, however, of the axioms or first principles not as hypothetical assumptions but as truths *surer* and more *basic* than any others. They felt that the foundation must be surer than that which was built upon it — the conclusions. Intuition, moreover, was given a higher place than deduction. For while the latter is free from error, nevertheless each step in drawing a conclusion must be intuitively certified as "logical." The validity of mathematical demonstration was thus not conceived of by the classical rationalists as purely formal in character. (See Chapter Six.)

**Illustration in Descartes.** Perhaps no clearer statement of the rationalist point of view can be given than that of René Descartes (1596-1650). The second rule of his *Rules for the Direction of the Mind* states: "Only those objects should engage our attention, to the sure and indubitable knowledge of which our mental powers seem to be adequate." In comment on this, he continues:

> Thus in accordance with the above maxim we reject all such merely probable knowledge and make it a rule to trust only what is completely known and incapable of being doubted. No doubt men of education may persuade themselves that there is but little of such certain knowledge, because, forsooth, a common failing of human nature has made them deem it too easy and open to everyone, and so led them to neglect to think upon such truths; but I nevertheless announce that there are more of these than they think — truths which suffice to give a rigorous demonstration of innumerable propositions, the discussion of which they have hitherto been unable to free from the element of probability.*

In the third rule he describes the two basic processes of attaining certain knowledge:

> . . . We shall here take note of all those mental operations by which we are able, wholly without fear of illusion, to arrive at the knowledge of things. Now I admit only two, viz., intuition and deduction.

> By *intuition* I understand, not the fluctuating testimony of the senses, nor the misleading judgment that proceeds from the blundering constructions of imagination, but the conception which an unclouded and attentive mind gives us so readily and distinctly that we are wholly freed from doubt about that which we understand. Or, what comes to the same thing, *intuition* . . . springs from the light of reason alone; it is more certain than deduction itself, in that it is simpler. . . . Thus each individual can mentally have intuition of the fact that he exists, and that he thinks; that the triangle is bounded by three lines only, the sphere by a single superficies, and so on.

> . . . We are in a position to raise the question as to why we have, besides intuition, given this supplementary method of knowing, viz., knowing by *deduction,* by which we understand all necessary inference from other facts that are

known with certainty. This, however, we could not avoid, because many things are known with certainty, though not by themselves evident, but only deduced from true and known principles by the continuous and uninterrupted action of a mind that has a clear vision [intuition] of each step in the process. . . . Those propositions indeed which are immediately deduced from first principles are known now by intuition, now by deduction, i.e., in a way that differs according to our point of view. But the first principles themselves are given by intuition alone, while, on the contrary, the remote conclusions are furnished only by deduction.

These two methods are the most certain routes to knowledge, and the mind should admit no others. All the rest should be rejected as suspect of error and dangerous.

Empiricists, while they may differ in their interpretation of the deductive process, do not, of course, reject it. What they do reject is the conception of knowledge as a closed deductive *system,* based on fixed *a priori* principles. And in general, they have tended to distrust the appeal to mathematical reasoning as a model for philosophy.

**Empiricist Conceptions of Intuition.** In this chapter we have perhaps given the impression that intuition as an instrument of knowledge has been exclusively characteristic of rationalism. This is in fact by no means so. Many empiricists have expressed the view that we know certain truths "intuitively." There is, however, a considerable difference in the meaning of the "intuitions" in the two cases. Both do designate knowledge which is allegedly immediate, direct, and certain. But whereas intuition for the rationalist means *a priori* intuition, insight into a universal truth without the aid of experience, for certain empiricists it means the direct apprehension of the simplest truths of sense experience. To illustrate: a typical *a priori* intuition would be the general principle "Every event has a cause" or "The quantity of matter is constant"; a typical empirical intuition would be "The thing I now see is brown" or "I am in pain." The latter are judgments of immediate perception, and empiricists have often claimed that these, being the simplest of all judgments that can be made, are the intuitive foundation of (empirical) knowledge.

It will be clear, then, how strong has been the appeal which the notion of intuition has made to philosophers of diverse schools. Remarkable testimony of this is afforded by the fact that there are certain types of statements which have been called "intuitive truths" by both rationalists and empiricists. Thus, for instance, two of the judgments offered by Descartes in the second paragraph of the preceding quotation — "I think" and "I exist"— have been favorite examples with empiricists. No empiricist, however, as we have already stated, subscribes to intuitively known *general* principles (unless tautological), for these would be *a priori*.

**Reason and Experience in Science.** It would seem attractive to generalize that rationalism is the philosophical point of view which justifies the application of the method of intuition, while empiricism is that which justifies the universal application of empirical scientific method. But this states the case very roughly, and rationalists in particular would differ among themselves and with empiricists as to the justice of these identifications. What we might perhaps justly say is that if the appeal to intuition as a *method* is to be associated with one or the other, it would no doubt be with rationalism; for the notion of intuition plays a far more basic rôle in rationalism than it does (where it is present at all) in empiricism.

But what of the relationship of these points of view to science? Historically, rationalists have been more closely associated with the appeal to mathematics, empiricists with natural science. But to associate empiricism more closely with empirical scientific method involves an interpretation that may itself be either rationalistic or empiricistic in character. Empiricists may of course cite the fact that natural science scrupulously appeals to experimentation in the testing of its theories. Rationalists, on the other hand, may cite the importance of the theories as guides to experience and as factors without which experience would be meaningless and empty. They have indeed urged that the rise of modern science in the sixteenth and seventeenth centuries was due to the imaginativeness and intellectual originality of men like Galileo, Stevinus, Harvey, and Kepler, who by their theories went far beyond what was immediately observable. Galileo at times pointed to the "natural light of reason" as his guide.

**The Possible Synthesis of Emphases within Rationalism and Empiricism.** It seems that neither the extreme rationalist nor the extreme empiricist is correct in his interpretation of natural science. On the other hand, certain emphases within rationalism and empiricism may alike be regarded as correct. The success of modern science has been due partly to theoretical originality together with the application of mathematics, and partly to the faithful submission of the theories to the test of experimental observation. We have seen that neither theory nor experiment is significant alone. They are interdependent. The great merit of science is that it has made this interdependence fruitful. By its theories it has interpreted and organized facts. By appealing to facts it has verified its theories. The greater the number of facts it examines, the greater becomes the necessity of perfecting and modifying theories. But these modified theories explain to us better the very facts which are their support. The more illuminating our theories, the more significant do the facts become. The more exact our experimentation, the more correct do the theories become.

We have defined rationalism and empiricism as differing with respect to their stand on the possibility of *a priori* factual knowledge. It is possible, however, to consider them still more broadly, in the manner just suggested — so broadly as to speak no longer of rationalism and empiricism but rather of a "rational*istic*" or "empiric*istic*" *emphasis*. The rationalistic emphasis would be on the rôle of the intellect and its activity in knowledge, whereas the empiricistic emphasis would be on the corrective and disciplinary effect of experience, and the futility of *a priori* speculation, in knowledge. From this point of view the two become quite harmonious. Throughout the history of philosophy we find attempts to combine the two emphases, even if they are not called by the same names. And this indicates to us the difficulty of making a sharp classification of philosophers into the two camps. In certain cases the attempt to fit a figure into a school proves the inadequacy of mere labels, and a precise historical analysis entailing many definitions and philosophical distinctions is necessary. In actual practice, an empiricist or rationalist outlook is something which emerges from a whole complex of problems which the philosopher tries to answer. Philosophers do not decide that they shall be rationalists, or empiricists, and forthwith proceed to solve problems with that outlook in mind. They first grapple with problems, and the manner in which their approach and method develops determines whether the empiricist or the rationalist temper reveals itself.

**Broader and Narrower Senses of "Reason."** When saying that rationalists emphasize the rôle of reason in knowledge, whereas empiricists emphasize that of experience, we must guard against misunderstanding. The term "reason" may be interpreted in at least three senses.

(1) One of these is illustrated by the contrast sometimes made, as in medieval philosophy, between "faith and reason." Here "reason" is intended to signify merely the use of the mental powers, or speculation, as distinguished from passive acceptance of belief on faith or authority. In this sense there is no implication that reason is superior or inferior to faith.

(2) In a second sense "reason" means the free and exclusive exercise of the intelligence in inquiry. It is intended as synonymous with "reasonableness" or the most judicious employment of the conscious faculties. The use of "reason" in this sense *does* imply an activity superior to any other. It is meant to be contrasted with barbarism, prejudice, uncontrolled emotion, or whatever blindness characterizes faith and authority. It is what philosophers have referred to when they have spoken of the "life of reason."

In these two broader meanings of the term "reason," it is not opposed to "experience" but may include the latter as part of it. Rationalists and empiricists alike have championed reason in these senses. In the second meaning, to employ reason is to be "rational." Not so in the first meaning, however, for there faith might be held equally "rational." "Rational," in any event, is obviously not the same as "rationalistic."

(3) A third and narrower sense of "reason" is the one employed in this chapter to denote the rationalistic emphasis. Here "reason" implies a faculty independent of, or opposed to, or otherwise contrasted with, experience or observation. In this sense, it is sometimes synonymous with "reasoning."

**Extreme Empiricism, or Sensationalism.** There are a number of different ways in which we can divide empiricists. One very important way is on the basis of how they understand the meaning of "experience." There are those who have interpreted this term narrowly, to mean "sensation" or "feeling," the mere reception of stimuli and the corresponding responses by the senses. Such a form of empiricism rules out what is contributed by the imaginative and abstractive capacities of man. Knowledge becomes a passive imbibing of what is poured into us from without, and all mental activity becomes secondary in importance, a mere device for arranging sensations. Thinking is interpreted as a kind of vicarious sensing. Empiricism of this type has sometimes been known as *sensationalism,* or sensationalistic empiricism. Many opponents of the empiricist viewpoint in philosophy have confused empiricism in general with sensationalism. It is important to recognize that many empiricists interpret the concept "experience" much more broadly, so as to include much that cannot simply be reduced to an affair of sense or feeling. Sensationalism is closely associated with a speculative philosophical view called "nominalism," which we shall consider at greater length in Part Three. Nominalism holds that the universe consists solely of individual objects which alone are what we can "experience." A more comprehensive empiricism would find room for the reality of such phenomena as values, ideals, meanings, and relations; of what can be thought abstractly as well as of what can be "sensed."

**What Is "Experience"?** We have been using the word "experience" all along, and it has perhaps not occurred to the reader that the differences in possible interpretation may be important. It is often possible to use an important concept in our discourse without precisely defining it. The reason is that precise definition is not required by the contexts in which it occurs. To give an analogous example — we all use the word "good" countless times, and find it not necessary to define it exactly if at all. This is because when we make such statements as "This apple is good" or even "It was a good play," the context more or less enables us to understand the meaning communicated even though we would ordinarily be hard pressed for a definition that was exact. When, however, we make such statements as "Capitalism is a good economic system," the same word needs considerable analysis if the statement is to acquire intelligibility sufficient for us to be able to test its truth.

It is the business of the analytical philosopher, as we have seen, to define the basic concepts which underlie or are implied in our methods of thinking and communicating. One of the most important of these is "experience." The word is used in many contexts. We say "Experience is a great teacher," "I had a frightening experience yesterday," "He has had long experience as a lawyer," "Natural science appeals to experience," and so on. Let us try to distinguish some different senses of the word in abstract terms, and see into which the above usages fit.

**Experience as Something Accumulated.** When we assert "He has had long experience as a lawyer," there are a number of things we mean to imply. We imply that there has been a development of some kind, and that the development has been more or less gradual and over a period of time. We imply that what has been developed is either greater or less than what may have been developed in another case. In other words, "experience" in this sense is an *accumulation* or *fund* of knowledge, of information, or of skill. It is something which admits of *degrees,* so that one man's experience may be more or less than another's. We ordinarily imply that the greater one's experience the more he has learned or acquired, but it does not necessarily follow that what has been acquired must be more successfully utilized. It is this sense of "experience" that we intend when we speak not only of "my" experience but of the experience of mankind, and it is this sense that we *may* intend when we also assert "Experience is the best teacher." But this last usage might also be interpreted in another sense which we shall distinguish.

**Experience as the Quality of Sensation or Emotion.** When we say "I had a frightening experience yesterday," we are identifying experience with sensation or emotion. Another illustration would be in the statement "I had the experience of sinking rapidly." Experience in these contexts means a psychological reaction. In these two examples the reaction is of an immediate or instantaneous character. But it need not be so. We may say "He had the experience of being cast adrift for ten days" and imply the same meaning of the term. Experience in all these cases is not something which admits of degrees. The factor of development is not implied, nor is that of accumulation. We do not speak of *more* (or less) experience but of *different* experience. Each instance of experience is considered as a unity or single whole. We speak of "an experience." Experience here is something *qualitative.* Sensationalists most often presuppose this meaning, but they also often presuppose the three following meanings.

**Experience as Consciousness.** Sometimes "experience" is taken to mean the whole field of consciousness or awareness. Merely to "be conscious" is "to experience." We speak of what falls "within" our experience or "outside" it. It includes not merely sensing but any mental activity at all. We should note that in most of the other meanings, "experience" of something implies only direct acquaintance with it ("firsthand" experience), whereas in this meaning hearsay, accepted authority, or intuition in any form is equally an instance of awareness.

**Experience as Deliberate Observation.** Everyone is familiar with the usage "Science resorts to experience." *One* meaning this may have is that science employs observation as a means to determining the truth of its theories. We sometimes say, in a rough way, that science does not merely "reason" but that it uses experience — that is, observes. Observation here is of course not simply a passive exercise of sense but a deliberate process. Experience in the second sense above is the occurrence *on a specific occasion* of a psychological response. In the present sense it is a systematic and conscious exercise of a technique of observation, something which is not a mere specific fact occurring at a given time but a policy or habit that may be pursued at any time. In both the preceding and present senses, however, "experience" does have a subjective or psychological connotation. The emphasis is unmistakably on something that involves the exercise of the observer's "mental" powers.

**Experience as the World of Fact.** There are many who would object to the foregoing interpretation of the statement "Science resorts to experience." It is not, they assert, to any faculty of the mind or any process of mental activity that science appeals but to something external and objective, the world of fact or (in a loose and limited sense) nature. The scientist appeals to something constant and uninfluenced by him — a neutral arbiter of the truth or falsity of his hypotheses. In this interpretation the tendency is to emphasize the objective reality that is the source of all occurrences. Experience is something that exists before we do and not something that our conscious activity creates.

**Experience as a Relation or Interaction.** Strictly speaking, the word "experience" cannot be restricted by legislation to one usage. But there are grounds for preferring some usages to others, as being conducive to greater insight and

understanding. Philosophically, we may try to frame a definition that will include the emphases involved in all the established usages. The objection to the two preceding usages is
that, as interpretations, they do not *do justice* to the meaning
of "experience" as it is used in the statement "Science appeals
to experience." The interpretation we go on to state over-
comes this objection and at the same time accomplishes the
synthesis of the various meanings enumerated.

Experience is neither purely subjective nor purely objective, but is rather a relation between the living organism and
its environment. Experience is a process of interaction between these two constituents. The experiencing mind is not
simply a mind but an active, selective, inquiring mind; on the
other hand, experience is not simply the world of fact, but
that world investigated or actively exploited. On this view
scientific activity is simply one kind of such experience—an
interplay between the scientific mind and the scientific environment, between systematic observation and the world of fact.
Thus it is easily seen how we can speak of scientific experience, artistic experience, religious experience, social experience, and so on. And thus it is also seen that experience is not
something opposed to "thought" but something that involves
thought as an integral part of it. This interpretation, as we
suggested, embraces the emphases involved in all the usages
we have distinguished. For experience as an interaction includes within it the factor of accumulated skill or information,
psychological reactions in which the quality of feeling is what
stands out, and of course all consciousness, as well as the
fourth and fifth meanings already mentioned. When we say,
however, that experience includes all consciousness, we must
guard against speaking of consciousness as though it were
something set apart from nature, a view which tacitly or explicitly underlies many philosophies. The present analysis of
the meaning of "experience" goes hand in hand with a definite
speculative outlook, which we shall refer to in Part Three as

"critical naturalism." It will there be seen how a different world-view would influence us toward a different conception of experience.

**The Logic of a Philosophy.** Whether problems of speculative philosophy are attacked from an empiricist or from a rationalist approach makes a vast difference. It should be obvious that the rationalistically inclined philosopher will permit himself greater freedom of speculation than the empiricist, who will be wary of unconsciously admitting *a priori* judgments into his thought. The empiricism or the rationalism of a philosophy might be regarded as the methodology or *logic* of that philosophy. In Part Three we shall have the opportunity to observe the interconnectedness of such a methodology with world-perspectives. But in the succeeding chapters of the present Part also we shall be able to observe how the empiricist or rationalist attitudes underlie other points of view in other problems of analytical philosophy. We should at all times bear in mind the warning previously given against recklessly labeling points of view and ignoring the fact that very different tendencies may exist side by side.

❖  ❖  ❖

## CHAPTER EIGHT

# Problems Concerning the Scope and Extent of Knowledge

Throughout the history of thought certain philosophers have felt troubled by the diverse claims men have made to possess knowledge. In our daily lives each of us often feels quite certain of something being a fact — but not for long. We soon abandon or revise our opinion and adopt a new one which we regard as true no less confidently than we did the previous one. Since this takes place with each of us, we have the spectacle of millions of opinions being adopted and in time changed by individuals, by groups, by nations, even by whole societies; and yet at one time or another these opinions have been put forth as "knowledge."

**When Have We Assurance that We "Know?"**  But not only are beliefs revised by those who entertain them; they are contradicted by other individuals, groups, and societies. And even if we should ignore the great mass of mankind and consider only men who have devoted themselves primarily to studies concerning knowledge and its problems, namely philosophers, we should find even greater diversity of opinion. Amid all this disagreement and change, which beliefs can be said to constitute knowledge?

**Dogmatism and Scepticism.**  The claims to knowledge have been strong ones. We need only visualize the methods of authority, faith, and intuition in practice in order to realize this. The German philosopher Immanuel Kant (1724-1804), of whom we shall have more to say shortly, applied the term *dogmatism* to that point of view which lays claim to knowledge without a critical examination of the methods and principles on which that claim is based. The intellectual systems erected by religious authority and faith are outstanding examples of dogmatism in this sense. Revelation, though held to yield truth, is not to be questioned, nor are sacred texts in general, nor the dogmas developed by theologians, nor the pronouncements of ecclesiastical elders. Among philosophers the dogmatists have been held to be those who accept "self-evident truths" *uncritically,* or who create elaborate chains of reasoning in which conclusions are drawn without analysis of the justification of basic principles. Not all of those who accept intuitive truths are dogmatists. On the contrary, two of those whom we shall consider — Descartes and Kant — have in one or another form been exponents of views called by the name of *scepticism,* which historically has been the attitude antithetical to dogmatism.

In the popular sense of the word, a "sceptic" is one who doubts, or questions what are alleged to be truths. It can be seen at once that there are any number of possible degrees of "scepticism" in this sense — one may doubt very few things, may try to doubt all things, or (in between) may doubt certain *kinds* of opinions. But the term "scepticism" in its philosophical usage means something much narrower than in its popular usage. While in the latter it is sufficient to express doubt on any matter whatever to be called "sceptical," this is not the case in the former. Everyone expresses doubts with regard to various matters in daily life, but not everyone is a sceptic. In the broadest philosophic sense a sceptic is one who for specific reasons questions the validity and conclusiveness of what others regard as knowledge. Scepticism has more and less extreme forms, and manifests itself in different ways. We shall glance at some of these.

**Descartes' Problem.** Descartes raised the question, What guarantee have I that all I have been taught, all I have accepted from tradition, all that my senses tell me, all that I learn from others by daily communication, is true? How can I be sure that whenever I reason, as in mathematics, I may not be in error? In common life we are all familiar with the fact that the senses can deceive us: we imagine we see and hear what is neither to be seen nor to be heard; we mistake one color for another, and one object for another; our sense of sight tells us that the stick immersed in water is crooked, whereas the sense of touch tells us that it is straight. In the case of the senses, we imagine that we usually correct our errors. Why may it not be that in mathematical reasoning we are likewise in error but not so fortunate as to be aware of it? How do we know that we *do* correct the senses? If we can have been in error, how can we ever be sure that we are freed of it? And how much more dangerous still is it to accept beliefs on faith or from authority?

Descartes reasoned that if he were ever to have a guarantee that he did possess valid knowledge, he must, so to speak, try to start with a clean slate. He must probe every single one of his beliefs — doubt all of them, even the belief in his own existence. He would then carefully discern what it was that he could with perfect confidence write on the clean slate, or what might write itself on the slate and defy erasure. From his attempt to place himself in this state of absolute and universal doubt, one of two things would happen. Either he would remain in this state and find no sure way of getting out, in which case a thoroughgoing scepticism would be justified; or, certain beliefs would defy doubt, that is, would prove so compulsive that it would be impossible to doubt them. Descartes soon concluded that the latter was the case, that certain beliefs could not possibly be doubted. First among these was belief in his own existence; for the very fact of his attempting to doubt or think implied the existence of a thinker or subject. Consequent upon this he found it necessary to conclude the existence of God, of other minds, and of the physical or material world. In all this he was guided by that which he found indubitable and clear and compelling to his mind.

**Methodological Scepticism.** In what sense is Descartes a sceptic? Obviously his scepticism is not something with which he ends up but something with which he merely begins. Far from showing that complete doubt is ineradicable, he shows that it is self-defeating. His scepticism, then, if such it can be called, is only a device or method which he employs in order to arrive at the actual refutation of complete scepticism. And the refutation of scepticism takes the form of the view that there are intuitive or self-evident first principles of knowledge, a view with which we have already acquainted ourselves. This scepticism is sometimes called *methodological scepticism.* It serves as a means by which Descartes can gain access to an untroubled exercise of the method of intuition. It does merit the name of scepticism, because in Descartes' view the resort to the device of universal doubt is for each individual the ultimate test by which he can satisfy himself that there is absolute and indubitable knowledge.

**Scepticism as an Attitude: Kant's Critical Philosophy.** More than a century after Descartes Kant inaugurated a powerful tradition in philosophy. In what he called the Critical Philosophy, he undertook a comprehensive investigation of the foundations of knowledge. His main emphasis was that whatever is called by the name of knowledge must justify itself as such. That is to say, we must explain in what sense it is knowledge, what kind of knowledge it is, what its scope is, and what its degree of certainty is. By starting in this critical spirit Kant illustrates an important kind of scepticism — the attitude of unwillingness to accept conclusions unless there are good grounds for them. This *sceptical attitude* has always been as a matter of fact more or less associated with the most searching and penetrating analyses of the great philosophers. It is magnificently exemplified in the Socrates of Plato's Dialogues, who by his method of interrogating and criticizing turned over intellectual problems until all their aspects had been revealed for what they were worth. We have seen that in the practice of empirical science the sceptical *attitude* is exercised to its most fruitful advantage. The scientific method is a critical method *par excellence:* there is no end to its scrutiny of evidence, and its acceptance of a conclusion is always open to re-examination. The scepticism of science is a constructive scepticism. It assumes that knowledge can be attained provided that we adopt rigorous standards and seek to improve them. We shall discover presently what a nonconstructive scepticism is in contrast.

**Scepticism concerning Extra-empirical Knowledge.** There is a sceptical strain of another kind in Kant. In answering his own question as to the conditions and the justification of our claim to possess knowledge, he came, roughly, to the following conclusions. The first question to ask is, What are the conditions involved in conscious experience? Now by experience we do not mean merely colors and sounds and odors, but these things in a definite order and arrangement, that is, as inherently organized and possessing form. Experience is what takes place when materials that we *receive* are received as *structured* in certain ways by the knowing mind. What the experiencer passively receives is the stuff or raw materials of experience; what he "contributes," and what therefore makes actual experiencing possible, is the form or organization which the subject-matter is to assume. The experiencer thus contributes the factors determining the ordered arrangement of experience. What we "receive" does not come to us *before* it is formed or structured; it comes only *as* structured by us as knowers. The very notion of "before" already implies a form of perception, time, through which things can appear to us as earlier and later. The experiencer or knower is *equipped* with a structuring machinery or set of capacities through which he is able to provide form for the raw data given to him. For example, we see colored shapes as existing in space. The colored bulk is the raw material; the property of being arranged in space is a form with which we endow this material. Similarly, it is the knower who contributes, besides time and space, such forms as quantity and cause-and-effect. It is for this reason that we can have *a priori* knowledge (see p. 76) and need not appeal to sense observation for universal and fundamental truths. For such knowledge is derived from those organizing forms which it is our inherent nature to contribute to our ordered experience.

Now according to Kant, the knower, being equipped with certain faculties and capacities and not with others, can have knowledge only of what he can possibly experience. He cannot create the data given to him, nor can he exceed his own powers. Thus he cannot know reality as reality actually is, but only as reality may be reflected in his own conscious experience. Realities like God and immortality are beyond all possible experience, and can therefore never be objects of knowledge. It is in this limitation of the scope of our rational faculties that Kant's doctrinal (as opposed to procedural) scepticism consists. No sooner do we attempt to reason about that which is extra-empirical, i.e., about reality, than we find that we can manufacture arguments for either of two contradictory views with equal plausibility — a fact which proves that all such attempts at knowledge are futile.

**The Kantian Contrast of Knowledge and Faith.** But Kant did not let the matter rest there. While he denied the possibility of knowledge about what transcends experience, he held that we could have faith. What is the meaning and justification of faith in this sense? Man, according to Kant's reasoning, is not merely an animal that knows but one that acts and feels. He has not only scientific but religious and moral capacities. One of his impulses is to seek the truth about experience; but he has other and equally important functions to fulfill — those of duty and conscience and a search for the beautiful. These non-scientific types of experience are the basis of religion, ethics, and aesthetics. How can we understand their occurrence? Only by having faith that God exists, that a moral law governs the universe, and that man is immortal. Where we cannot say anything one way or another on rational grounds, we are justified in interpreting our moral and religious experiences as requiring something more; in fact, we must do so, for our nature demands it. We cannot know the higher realities, but we must have faith that there are such, in order to make intelligible what we find in human nature.

It would seem at first that just as in Descartes scepticism is soon replaced by intuition, so in Kant it is replaced by faith. But there is really no parallel, and Kant's scepticism is really much more thoroughgoing. Intuition, after all, is claimed as knowledge, and Descartes' scepticism is intended merely to have logical value as an approach to knowledge. In Kant, however, faith is ungrounded belief so far as evidence is concerned. So that what he holds to be a justifiable recourse in the absence of knowledge is not a substitute for knowledge or one kind of knowledge called by a different name.

**Historical Illustrations of the Contrast.** The contrast between knowledge and faith is much older than Kant. Faith as an instrument of belief supplementing or even replacing "reason" was an issue that cropped up in many forms throughout medieval philosophy, and sceptical tendencies culminate in the writings of the English Franciscan William of Ockham (c. 1300-1349), who maintained that the existence of God could not be demonstrated. Kant himself it is difficult to label simply "rationalist" or "empiricist" (though his view of *a priori* knowledge would place him in the former camp if a choice had to be made). But it is interesting to note that two of his predecessors, Descartes and David Hume (1711-1776), who definitely can be labeled rationalist and empiricist respectively, alike believe it necessary despite their many differences to draw a distinction between knowledge and faith. Descartes, after asserting that intuition and deduction alone are trustworthy as methods of knowing, immediately adds (continuing the quotation of p. 80 above):

> But this does not prevent us from believing matters that have been divinely revealed as being more certain than our surest knowledge, since belief in these things, as all faith in obscure matters, is an action not of our intelligence, but of our will.

Hume, after an exhaustive attack on the evidence for miracles, nevertheless concludes that the Christian religion

> is founded on Faith, not on reason; and it is a sure method of exposing it to put it to such a trial as it is, by no means, fitted to endure. . . . So that, upon the whole, we may conclude, that the Christian Religion not only was at first attended with miracles, but even at this day cannot be believed by any reasonable person without one.*

Similarly in his *Dialogues concerning Natural Religion,* after sceptical arguments against extra-empirical knowledge, he concludes:

> A person, seasoned with a just sense of the imperfections of natural reason, will fly to revealed truth with the greatest avidity: While the haughty Dogmatist, persuaded that he can erect a complete system of Theology by the mere help of philosophy, disdains any farther aid, and rejects this adventitious instructor. To be a philosophical Sceptic is, in a man of letters, the first and most essential step towards being a sound, believing Christian.†

These statements of Descartes and Hume, and even the view of Kant, which in this respect is built up more elaborately, have been suspected by some critics as weak additions to the philosophers' systems, motivated by the desire to conform with the requirements of organized religion. Whether this judgment is sound would of course demand far more discussion than can be given in this volume. A subject that commends itself to the inquiring reader is whether the distinction between knowledge and faith as made in the foregoing manner is a tenable one. Is faith merely a cloak for ignorance? In invoking the demands of our moral nature, are we deceiving ourselves? If there is a distinction between knowledge and faith, how sharply can the line be drawn?

**Extreme Scepticism: a Fourth Type.** We have considered three manifestations of scepticism: methodological scepticism, scepticism as a critical attitude, and scepticism concerning that which transcends human reason. Let us turn to scepticism of the most radical and extreme character, which

---

* *Enquiry concerning Human Understanding.* Sec. X, end of Pt. 2.
† Penultimate paragraph.

maintains that *all* knowledge beyond that of the most elementary kind is impossible. We may state this in the form of an objection against the validity of the scientific method; for if this method be acknowledged as the strongest available one, an argument against it would be worthy of serious consideration. We may then state the sceptical objection in a more general way, directed against any method of inquiry at all.

**The Argument from Historical Changes in Science.** If we examine the history of science (so the argument might run) we find that in each specific period a given theory is entertained by science as true. Shortly afterward, the theory is found to be inadequate, and is replaced by a new theory. This in turn stands accepted until it is replaced by another, and so on. These theories are, all of them, regarded as "true" and held to constitute scientific "knowledge." But they cannot all be true. A true theory would not be replaceable, for what is true remains true — unless of course what we are explaining no longer remains the same. Thus the theories of science are guesses which are changed after the scientific fashions of the day, but none are faithful accounts of reality. If they have a use, it is the important one of helping to adapt man to his environment by enabling him to predict what will take place and to develop instruments of technology.

**The Argument against Any Method.** Extreme scepticism can be stated also as follows. Of what use is any given method of inquiry? For suppose we employ a method. How do we know it is reliable? It cannot certify itself as reliable, and it must therefore be guaranteed by some other method. But the same objection applies: How do we know that the other method is reliable? We require a method to guarantee it as well, and so on without end — or better, without beginning. We can never be certain that our method of inquiry is sound, and so we never have the right to call results attained by it "knowledge." The objection might be stated in this way: Suppose we attempt to discover the best method of attaining knowledge. In order to do this we must discover a method of discovering the best method, and a method of discovering that too, and so on without achieving anything.

**Critical Remarks on the Latter Argument.** The immediately preceding sceptical argument requires hardly more refutation than is given in the following passage from Spinoza:

> The matter stands on the same footing as the making of material tools, which might be argued about in a similar way. For, in order to work iron, a hammer is needed, and the hammer cannot be forthcoming unless it has been made; but, in order to make it, there was need of another hammer and other tools, and so on to infinity. We might thus vainly endeavor to prove that men have no power of working iron.*

It is a fact that men do have the power of making iron tools, and it is a fact that men do possess knowledge. These facts cannot be abolished by any argument. To assert that "knowledge is impossible" is to adopt an excessively artificial viewpoint and to use the term "knowledge" in a narrow sense. Nor is the fact of knowledge abolished by our inability to analyze the concept of knowledge with perfection, or by the incompleteness of our knowledge. The extreme sceptic looks for something which we should not call knowledge at all. It is as though he were to argue that men are not real because they are not gods. Let us expand on this refutation by considering the former sceptical argument.

**Critical Remarks on Anti-scientific Scepticism.** To represent science as replacing theory by theory in endless succession is altogether superficial. Theories have not been replaced or abandoned; they have been *modified* or *corrected,* for the most part, in the light of new experimental findings. In most cases a new hypothesis may virtually be regarded as the old one in a revised version. When a hypothesis is modified, it is for good reason. Consequently hypotheses in their later form (or different hypotheses, if we prefer to call them that) represent a closer approximation to the scientific ideal. The anti-scientific sceptic forgets that science has a cumulative char-

---

* *On the Improvement of the Understanding.*

acter, and that its predictions do constitute knowledge. What he is looking for is immediate, infallible knowledge; and failing to find it, he concludes that there is no knowledge at all. He confuses knowledge with absolute knowledge, an existing state with an ideal. When we call theories "true" we do not mean that they are exempt from improvement. We mean that they are accepted on the best available evidence. It is possible to eliminate the word "true" in speaking of scientific theories, and speak only of the "best-evidenced" theories. Extreme scepticism is scepticism in a negative or non-constructive form. It is thus at the opposite pole from the critical attitude of science itself.

The confusion just pointed out applies likewise to the general form of sceptical argument. The test of whether a method is a good one is whether or not it actually works out in practice, not whether it can be certified by some other method. The quest for certification can never be satisfactorily completed, because it is a quest for an *infallible* guarantee. If we cease to hunt for infallibility we need no certification by another method. The scientific method, as we have seen, is capable of correcting itself. It is precisely because of its capacity for change that this method is regarded as reliable. That a method is reliable or unreliable cannot be determined antecedently to its use. To attempt such prior legislation, in the manner of extreme scepticism, serves only to paralyze inquiry.

**Further on Methodological Scepticism.** If the hunt for absolute indubitability is fruitless and artificial, it follows that the methodological scepticism of Descartes is likewise fruitless from one point of view. For it starts from the assumption that beliefs which are not absolutely certain do not constitute genuine knowledge, and its effect is therefore to depreciate the value of probable reasoning and probable conclusions. From another point of view Descartes' type of scepticism is of great value; it emphasizes the importance of questioning and criticizing *one's own* beliefs, no matter how fundamental they may be. Such an attitude is harmonious with the critical attitude of science, and serves as a constant reminder to the individual that he is everywhere under the influence of authority and tradition. Historically, the intuitive method of Descartes represents a revolt against authority and a demand that the individual satisfy *himself* of the beliefs he is called upon to accept, regardless of their plausibility. To grasp the full significance of such a demand is to have profited in no small way.

**Outgrowths of Modern Empiricism: Positivism.** Let us recall that empiricism in general is the emphasis that all opinions or theories, in order to be validated, must be submitted to the test of sensory experience. The scepticism of Hume is a direct consequence of his empiricism, and that of Kant is a consequence of his empirical strain. Under the influence emanating from Hume and Kant, and to a large extent also from Hume's own predecessors, Locke and George Berkeley (1685-1753), there arose in the nineteenth century two related forms of empiricism, namely, *positivism* and *pragmatism*. The leading exponent of positivism in France was August Comte (1798-1857), whose major work was produced by 1842. In the last quarter of the century, there was an outstanding Austrian positivist, Ernst Mach (1838-1916), and in the United States at the same time pragmatism was inaugurated by Charles Peirce (1839-1914). Both Mach and Peirce have had a considerable influence on the flourishing of empiricist movements in the present. Positivist and pragmatist tendencies also find numerous applications, and these are especially striking in the recent history of sciences like psychology, sociology, and anthropology; in the philosophy of education; and in certain interpretations of religion. We shall defer discussion of pragmatism to Chapter X, and consider here some characteristics of positivism. The version of positivism we state is that of the nineteenth century. We may also bear in mind that its more extreme tenets are less characteristic of its founders than of their later nineteenth century followers.

**The Positivist Limitation of Inquiry.** Since the eighteenth century the term "metaphysics" has generally been used by philosophers to denote that branch of philosophy which concerns itself with the broadest classes into which we can divide reality, and with the broadest possible theories of the universe. Kant, however, in one of his senses of the term, had used it to designate the field concerned with truths about the realities of God, immortality, freedom, and the soul. His scepticism thus consisted in denying the possibility of metaphysical knowledge. The positivists likewise deny the possibility of metaphysics in this sense. But their position is more extreme than Kant's. To Kant the metaphysical concepts of God, the soul, and freedom of the human will have no specific cognitive value but are of immense moral value as being ideas on which all our practical conduct must ultimately be based. For positivists this value is not attributed to metaphysics, which is held to be a stagnant and useless branch of inquiry. Their use of the term "metaphysics" is for the purpose of labeling theories which cannot be directly tested by sense observation.

**The Positivist Interpretation of Scientific Method.** In attempting to eliminate from fruitful inquiry the concern with metaphysical problems, positivists place a stricture on scientific procedure. Scientific procedure, as distinct from metaphysical, cannot, according to them, admit theories which go beyond what can be tested directly in experience. Science should confine itself either to descriptive generalizations or to explanations which sooner or later can themselves be directly verified just as descriptions can. Positivists differ among themselves on the extent to which they would curb scientific theorizing. Some would hold that a theory about molecules is scientifically admissible (on positivist principles) because sooner or later molecules will presumably be capable of direct observation, while a theory about an ether through which light supposedly passes is to be rejected on the ground that such an entity is not even in principle capable of direct observation, being a mere device used for purposes of explanation. Other positivists would reject both kinds of hypothesis. Positivism in general has been wary of scientific thought which seems incapable of being ultimately reduced to direct observation. In some positivists the conception of science and experience clearly inclines to be sensationalistic. Science is an elaborate and organized instrument for anticipating and controlling sense impressions. Positivists have thus also been hesitant in admitting hypothetical explanation as a function of science and have stressed the value of recording, classifying, and in general, describing.

**Critical Remarks.** An adequate discussion of the merits of positivism would involve among other things a lengthy statement of problems in the philosophy of science. The following considerations will suffice for our purpose.

(1) In so far as positivism rejects any inquiry that does not curb a tendency to probe futile questions it falls into line with the general position of empiricism, which goes back not merely to Locke, Berkeley, and Hume but to the earliest period of philosophy, including men like Protagoras and Aristotle. Positivism has served as a reminder against the dangers of *a priori* speculation. On the other hand, in insisting that theories be ultimately tested by direct experience, positivism reveals its narrow conception of experience and of the process of scientific verification. Its tendency is to use the term "metaphysics" recklessly, and in general to narrow without precise justification the field of speculative philosophy.

(2) The principal question concerning positivism as distinct from empiricism in general is whether in its anti-metaphysical criticism it does not go to an opposite extreme. That it does appears plainly from its circumscription of the field of science. Labeling certain kinds of theory "metaphysical" and therefore inadmissible would hardly seem to be a weighty criticism, and it has certainly had little effect on the actual course of science. The justification of such theories must be found in the rôle they have played in scientific history. The fact is that their rôle has been and continues to be important. Their justification consists in the success with which they en-

able the scientist to predict and control experience. Positivism assumes the somewhat embarrassing guise of legislator to science. We have tried to indicate the dangers of methodological legislation unsupported by history. Many conceptions of scientific *method* are not broad enough to fit the actual workings of *science*. One attempt to embrace what is worth while in positivism and at the same time to do justice to the complexities of scientific procedure is represented, we shall find in Chapter Ten, by pragmatism.

In our discussion of problems concerning the scope and extent of knowledge we must consider, finally, a major twentieth-century effort to provide a new basis for cognitive validity and to show that providing such a basis is the main concern of philosophy. This effort is notable for its claim to have overcome the objections ordinarily raised against the notion of absolutely certain and necessary knowledge.

**The Phenomenology of Husserl.**    According to Edmund Husserl (1859-1938), the aspiration of Descartes to frame an absolute criterion of knowledge, that is, to achieve knowledge which can be justly regarded as necessary and certain, is entirely legitimate. Indeed, only knowledge of this kind is worthy of the name. But commendable as Descartes's objective was, the way in which he set out to achieve it and the means which he employed were sadly deficient. The reason for this failure, Husserl believes, is the absence of a theory of consciousness — of its structure and function. For whatever is known is known only to consciousness (or a conscious being), and in consciousness alone is evidence weighed and its force determined. A critical theory of consciousness in its knowing function Husserl calls "pure phenomenology." (The term "phenomenology" had been used before Husserl, though not in his sense. The meaning of the term "pure" will emerge shortly.) Now if we are going to lay true foundations for a theory of knowing, and to find out what any instance of knowing consists in, we must try actually to find a point at which to begin. Only in conscious awareness of consciousness itself can we do so. But our conscious life is crowded with all kinds of mental activities and all kinds of ideas, thoughts, beliefs, feelings, and images. We are also conscious of encountering "phenomena" or appearances, appearances of existing things and happenings. Amidst all these conscious data and conscious processes, where and how shall we begin?

**Phenomenological Reduction.** In order to determine the nature and possibilities of consciousness, we wish to examine it step by step, unencumbered by its everyday involvements. Shall we, then, try first to obliterate from consciousness everything that is said to be "in" it? That such an attempt, far from being a perfect start, would be self-defeating and futile becomes obvious after a moment's consideration. But on Husserl's view it is also self-contradictory. For he ascribes to consciousness a fundamental property known as "intentionality" (a view which has its roots in medieval thought). Consciousness is intentional in the sense that it is always consciousness *of* or *about*: it "intends" or "means" something. It always has within it an "object" or "datum." What we intend in our conscious thinking or perceiving or desiring may be something that exists in space and time (for instance, a house) or something that does not (for instance, a unicorn). To purify consciousness for analysis, then, cannot be to render it empty — eliminating its processes — but rather to get rid of its previous *commitments*. These are commitments to our "natural" point of view: the beliefs we entertain or presuppose; our ideas about the world "outside" us; the acts and feelings which relate us to what we form beliefs about. The goal of abandoning these commitments is Husserl's "ideal of presuppositionlessness." He admits that it is difficult to attain, for psychological reasons. But the main point is that such presuppositions and present beliefs are to be suspended or set apart; they are to be disconnected from their previous circumstances and reasons; they are to be detached or, in Husserl's phrase, "bracketed." This neutralization of all the data involved in the various interests of consciousness is one phase of phenomenological "reduction." Husserl calls it the "transcendental" reduction. (Using in his own way a distinction made by Kant, Husserl understands "transcendental" to refer to the sphere of consciousness and its powers, and "transcendent" to refer to the sphere of "nature" and the natural, which is to be suspended or bracketed.)

**Two Standpoints and Two Kinds of Experience.**   When we bracket our previous mental commitments we are achieving not merely a stage of consciousness but a new *mode* of consciousness. We are abandoning one way of consciously relating to the world and adopting a radically different way. What we are abandoning is the "natural" standpoint, that which is typical in everyday life and which is shared by historians, psychologists, and scientists in general. In this standpoint, what we are said to experience and take for granted are the events and successions of events, the persons and things, the regularities and uniformities that there are in the natural, spatio-temporal world. This kind of experience, by common consent, cannot yield the necessary knowledge we are seeking. It is based on the gathering of information about what happens to happen. Phenomenology does not appeal at all, therefore, to experience in this sense, and it regards as secondary the knowledge that is called "empirical," such knowledge at best being provisional and unstable.

As opposed to the natural standpoint, the phenomenological standpoint seeks what *must* be true of any object investigated. In so doing, it appeals to an entirely different type of experience — "pure" or "transcendental" experience. This is the direct, immediate scrutiny of an object or datum, ascertaining its relation to intending consciousness and to specific conscious acts. Into this procedure there enters another phase of the phenomenological reduction: we disregard the particular and incidental facts about any datum and seek its essential or indispensable traits —its essence or *eidos*. Pure experience is what gives us access to these essences. It provides us with absolute control over data. The "natural" experiences which have been bracketed can be brought into the sphere of phenomenological scrutiny and treated as pure experiences or pure phenomena. In bracketing, we no longer relate to phenomena as things which we live with and act toward. "Instead of living *in* them and carrying *them* out, we carry out acts of *reflection* directed towards them, and these we apprehend as the absolute being which they are."* Our data now are "absolute experiences." We directly encounter their essence when we discover their place and role in consciousness. The knowledge thus gained is "self-evident" and absolutely free of error. For the knower is no longer a person in the natural stance but a pure ego possessed of complete control over his experience and capable of pure or clarified "seeing."

> Let us suppose that we are looking with pleasure in a garden at a blossoming apple-tree, at the fresh young green of the lawn, and so forth. The perception and the pleasure that accompanies it is obviously not that which at the same time is perceived and gives pleasure. From the natural standpoint the apple-tree is something that exists in the transcendent reality of space, and the perception as well as the pleasure a psychical state which we enjoy as real human beings. Between the one and the other real being, the real man or the real perception on the one hand, and the real apple-tree on the other, there subsist real relations. Now in such conditions of experience, and in certain cases, it may be that the perception is a "mere hallucination," and that the perceived, this apple-tree that stands before us, does not exist in the "real" objective world. The objective relation which was previously thought of as really subsisting is now disturbed. Nothing remains but the perception; there is nothing *real* out there to which it relates.

> Let us now pass over to the phenomenological standpoint. The transcendent world enters its "bracket." . . . We now ask what there is to discover, on essential lines, in the nexus of . . . experiences of perception and pleasure-valuation. Together with the whole physical and psychical world the real subsistence of the objective relation between perception and perceived is suspended; and yet a relation between perception and perceived (as likewise between the pleasure and that which pleases) is left over, a relation which in its essential nature comes before us in "pure immanence," purely, that is, on the ground of the phenomenologically reduced experience of perception and pleasure, as it fits into the transcendental stream of experience. This is the very situation we are now concerned with, the pure phenomenological situation. It may be that phenomenology has also something to say concerning hallucinations, illusions, and deceptive perceptions generally, and it has perhaps a great deal to say about them; but it is evident that here, in the part they play in the natural setting, they fall away before the phenomenological suspension. Here in regard to the perception . . . we

---

* *Ideas* (translated from the German by W. R. Boyce Gibson), Sec. 50.

have no such question to put as whether anything corresponds
to it in "the" real world. This posited reality, if our judgment
is to be the measure of it, is simply not there for us. And yet
everything remains, so to speak, as of old. Even the phenomeno-
logically reduced perceptual experience is a perception *of* "this
apple-tree in bloom, in this garden, and so forth," and likewise
the reduced pleasure, a pleasure in what is thus perceived. The
tree has not forfeited the least shade of content from all the
phases, qualities, characters with which it appeared in this
perception.*

**Pure Seeing: the Absolute Knowledge of Essences.** In
phenomenological "seeing" we are thus concerned with phenomena or appearances—but with "pure" and not "natural" (or
naturally interconnected) phenomena. Pure phenomena, unlike
what are called phenomena in the classical tradition, are not
merely *sensory. Whatever* the object of investigation is —
whether the color of a patch, the nature of memory, the structure of society, the status of natural science, or the idea of a
round square—may be constituted in pure consciousness as a
phenomenon. Knowing the essences or necessary traits of these
phenomena means knowing what is possible and not possible
about them. Scientific knowledge as Husserl sees it may be
regarded as a limited application of such absolute knowledge,
one which explores certain of the possibilities as exemplified
in the natural world.

The essences which phenomenology seeks are essences of
the phenomena "as such." These phenomena are just what they
are. They are not "subjective," not produced arbitrarily and
at will by the knowing ego. At the same time, the phenomena
and their essences are objectively what they are only in so
far as they are meant, as objects of consciousness in its intentionality. Thus the essence of any datum emerges as something
thought, as part of the thinking process; as something meant,
as part of the meaning-process. Husserl emphasizes the shaping
function of consciousness, its "constituting" nature. What is,
is meaningful only in the rôle cast for it by the intending

---

* *Ideas,* Sec. 88. These passages from Husserl's *Ideas* are used with the permission
of the English publisher, Allen & Unwin, Ltd., London. The book was originally
published in 1913; the English translation, in 1931.

consciousness. The phenomenon is controlled, and its essence known, because we can analyze all its relations within consciousness.

Thus Husserl's phenomenology aims to bring together what in the history of philosophy had been contrasted and held apart: it makes necessary and universal knowledge the outcome of "immediate seeing." It reconciles the classical opposition between absolute knowledge and "experience," making the latter, in its pure form, the required *basis* of the former, the sole means of its attainment.

What guarantees the "self-evidence" of phenomenological essences, with due regard for the claim that no guarantees are needed? And what guarantees that pure seeing is perfectly pure and clear? Is it ultimately the ego's awareness of its own meaning or intention, fully controlled and mastered? But can we not be seriously mistaken about the direction of our own consciousness and about what we mean, no matter how critically we set up the conditions? Are we ever able to certify that the world we have bracketed has been effectively bracketed, and that it has not brought into the workings of consciousness its "natural" properties, influencing what we judge to be essential traits? Can the intentionalities of consciousness ever be fully separated from the natural, historical experience of the things that shape the development of consciousness? Is the immediate experience of absoluteness in phenomenological inquiry any more to be prized than the kinds of broad, reliable evidence on which everyday life and prediction depend?

❖   ❖   ❖

## CHAPTER NINE

# Immediacy, Communication, and Language

We consider now another angle of approach to the nature of knowledge. We have seen that some philosophers are strongly inclined to emphasize the conception of degrees as well as kinds of knowledge. Some kinds of intellectual activity are called knowledge and others denied the name; among those which are so called, some kinds are held more trustworthy than others; and so on.

**How Important Is Language in Knowing? Bergson's View.**  One of the most interesting contrasts made between kinds of knowledge, involving at the same time a distinction of degree, is that between knowledge in which language (understood in a broad sense, as will presently become clear) plays a part and knowledge in which it does not. A clearly expressed version of this viewpoint is that of the French philosopher Henri Bergson (1859-1941). According to Bergson there are two ways of knowing anything: "absolutely" and "relatively." The explanation of this distinction may be introduced by an example.

Consider an object moving. Now the ordinary way in which we are said to have knowledge of the motion is by first observing it and then describing it as in physics. We could, for example, say that an object "moves" if at a given instant of time it is in one place and at another instant in another place. We say that a moving object has a certain velocity, that it moves with a certain force, that it meets with resistance by the atmosphere, that the curve of its path is such-and-such. Now in this kind of knowing, Bergson maintains, we are "outside" the object. Our knowledge depends upon the point of view we adopt in observing it and in formulating our description. We describe the motion by means of ready-made abstractions — time, place, force, velocity, etc. In other words, we use concepts, and can only do so in terms of language or symbols. Whatever our linguistic apparatus, whether words, mathematical formulae, diagrams, or any other symbols, it cannot be dispensed with in this way of knowing.

**Points of Difference between Symbolical and Intuitive Knowledge.** We may call the foregoing kind of knowledge *symbolical* or *discursive* or *mediate* knowledge — since on Bergson's view symbols or concepts or theories are instruments which mediate between the knowing mind and the object known. In contrast there is a kind of knowledge which he considers "absolute," which is *im*mediate, direct, and non-symbolical, and for which he chooses to employ the term *intuition* or intuitive knowledge. Intuiting an object or fact consists in our identifying ourselves with the object by an effort of imagination; we sympathize, so to speak, with the pure phenomenon of motion. In doing so, we know the object "from within, as it is in itself" rather than from some point of view.*

Symbolical knowledge, which must always be from some point of view, gives us only part of the object, some aspect or limited phase of it; intuition gives us the object in its *completeness*. The former does not give us the ultimate reality or essence of motion, but merely "translates" it into symbols or concepts; in intuition we eliminate translations or mediations and grasp the original reality. Symbolical knowledge, by multiplying and refining its descriptions and theories, comes closer and closer to thorough knowledge, but by its very nature cannot reach finality; by intuition, on the other hand, we attain certainty and indubitability. Symbolical knowledge is *analytical:* it breaks up the object of knowledge into aspects or elements, each characterized by a concept; but like Humpty

---

* All the quotations are from Bergson's *Introduction to Metaphysics,* translated by T. E. Hulme.

Dumpty the divided reality can never again be recovered in its *unity* or *entirety;* by intuition alone can we know an object as a whole. Further, symbolical knowledge cannot be knowledge of something *unique.* The concepts it employs are abstract and apply not only to (for example) the particular motion with which we are at the moment concerned but to any instance of motion at all — abstract terms apply to some property common to all the members of a class or kind. To intuit something, however, is to know it in its absolute individuality and uniqueness, dispensing with language, which only hinders the penetration to reality. Finally, symbolical knowledge cannot give us the object in its *dynamic, living* character. For the object continually changes, while our abstract concepts do not. These concepts therefore petrify the object and in this respect falsify it: they abstract *it from* the total, living situation in which it is embedded besides abstracting *from it.* Symbolical knowledge gives us "a motionless view of the moving reality."

**Intuition, Symbols, and Empirical Science.** The primary function of empirical science is analysis, so that it is essentially symbolical in character. Bergson conceives the function of metaphysics to be the exercise of intuition. Metaphysics is therefore knowledge of reality in its ultimate and living sense, natural science only of reality as statically and more or less artificially conceived. Metaphysics is "the science which claims to dispense with symbols." But Bergson holds that whatever value empirical science can possess with respect to the pursuit of truth is acquired only if it is based upon metaphysical intuition; else its value consists in its being an adjunct to the promotion of practical or technological ends. We can, according to Bergson, pass from intuition to analysis (symbolical knowledge) but not vice versa. Once we have seized the inmost nature of a given reality we can go on to build concepts and concentrate on different views of it, as though after visiting a town and truly knowing it by intuition or intellectual sympathy we bring back photographs of different aspects of it. But from concepts we can never gain the reality

— from the multiplication of photographs we can approximate more and more closely to the complete town but can never truly know it. When science bases its theories on metaphysical intuition its concepts are influenced by that intuition and are constructed on the basis of it. Once science tries, however, to superimpose "ready-made" concepts upon the real, it forfeits its value. The great classical theories of science sprang from an original intuition. Newton and Galileo built their theories on an insight which came to them in an immediate and illuminating flash.

**The Meaning of Non-symbolical Intuition.** By "intuition" according to Bergson "is meant the kind of intellectual sympathy by which one places oneself within an object in order to coincide with what is unique in it and *consequently inexpressible*."* Intuition in this sense, he holds, entails a reversal of our ordinary method of thinking, which is to perceive things and then graft upon them static concepts by way of description. "The mind has to do violence to itself, has to reverse the direction of the operation by which it habitually thinks, has perpetually to revise, or rather to recast, all its categories." Intuition is made possible when we already have a fund of experience and observation. ". . . We do not obtain our intuition from reality — that is, an intellectual sympathy with the most intimate part of it — unless we have won its confidence by a long fellowship with its most superficial manifestations." Science would be most fruitful if it gathered a great mass of observations and then strove to achieve intuitions or insights, its theories and concepts following. Too often it superimposes static concepts on reality and believes it is achieving knowledge when it is actually committing distortion. When it does base itself on metaphysical intuition its concepts have the serviceable function of connecting intuition with our normal habits of thought. These concepts become the vehicles by which the results of intuition can be profitably utilized and applied in our

* Italics not in original.

understanding of things. Although difficult to achieve, intuition is in itself a simple, that is, unitary or indivisible, act. Bergson says that what he calls intuition is nothing mysterious but a faculty which we all at some time have exercised, as when we have grasped, in an illuminating moment, the meaning of a poem or the essence of a character in a novel.

**Critical Remarks.** Bergson's view has been stated in some detail, because one of the practices which it is desirable for the student of philosophy to cultivate is close attention to the outstanding points of another's thought. Complementary to this, and no less important, is the desirability of detailed critical examination. No matter how attractive a point of view may seem to us, we must *look* for possible difficulties, never relaxing the search for new tests. We should guard, on the other hand, against artificial criticism, purely verbal objection, and the magnification of minutiae.

**Scepticism and Non-symbolical Intuitionism.** It should be noted that, so far as Bergson's attitude toward symbols and analysis, and in general toward natural science is concerned, it is essentially that of the anti-scientific sceptic. Both distrust the complexities and apparent artificialities of scientific thought. Bergson feels that the theoretical formulae of science act as a kind of screen that shuts us off from reality. Bergson nevertheless is at the opposite pole from scepticism so far as his own conception of absolute knowledge is concerned, for he does believe that we can penetrate to the real by direct and unmediated contact. His criticism of science, moreover, attempts to be constructive, advocating less attention to symbolic inventions — which he feels make the screen from reality only denser — and increased emphasis on the insight allegedly resorted to by its founding geniuses, in ancient as well as modern times.

**Insight and Analysis in Science.** The first objection that may be raised against the present view relates to its conception of the place of intuition as the foundation of scientific truth. Bergson seems to imply a situation where Newton (let us say) has a sudden flash of intuition, in which the reality of gravitation is disclosed to him, and then sets about the protracted process of analyzing and theorizing, his analysis and theory being supplementary processes. Now there unquestionably is such a thing as insight ("intuition," if we wish to call it that) in science. It is the spontaneous occurrence of a fertile idea to the scientific man. But it is quite different from the intuition of Bergson. Scientific "intuition" is something *tentative,* it is a rough approximation which calls for formulation and testing on an elaborate scale; whereas intuition in Bergson's sense is an unmistakable and immediate apprehension of the real. No scientist who imagines that he has a valuable insight ever rests content with it: he does not rest convinced of its reliability but proceeds to apply scientific canons, which remove the whole question from the purview of the individual to that of public examination. Bergson's intuition, on the other hand, is essentially something which both originates and remains with the individual mind.

But we can go much further. In many cases, even this temporary element of psychological conviction and feeling of insight may be absent. Scientists have entertained theories deliberately and actually invent them in order to round out the number of possibilities of explaining a phenomenon. When Kepler entertained the theory that the orbit of Mars was elliptical, he did it not as the result of a sudden insight or feeling that it was so, but with considerable uncertainty and with the same patient scrutiny he had given to other theories. And even this was not acceptable until it was heavily qualified, and until laborious analysis resulted in just those qualifications which satisfied observation. Bergson's sharp distinction between the intuitive and analytical phases of knowledge breaks down in actual scientific practice. The insight of the scientist and his formulation of a theory are not two absolutely discrete processes. Nor is there a simple succession of insight first and theory next. We have just seen that the element of immediate insight may be all but absent, but even where it is present it sometimes comes *after* a good deal of theoretical speculation and analysis — and is the direct *result* of it — rather than before it. And clearly it can never precede *all* analysis, for we possess previous knowledge from which subsequent knowledge must start. All we can say is that scientific insight is unpredictable, that, as we have already emphasized above, there is no rule for the attainment of insight at a specified time. When Bergson says that we must start out with observation and experience before we can have intuition, he fails to see that absolutely pure observation is a myth, or if not a myth, is nothing but dumb sensation or feeling. *Meaningful* or *intelligent* observation involves reflection or interpretation. (When we consider pragmatism, we shall find its emphasis to be that, conversely, meaningful reflection involves observation, these two views being interdependent.) But reflection involves symbols or signs which serve as the vehicles by which it can be carried on and which stand for what is reflected about.

**Knowledge and Communication.**    The more general and deep-rooted objection concerns the question whether intuition as conceived by Bergson merits the name of "knowledge." Intuition, he says, is a means of arriving at what is inexpressible in an object. Consequently intuition is private and incommunicable. Only what is translatable into symbols is capable of communication. Now there appear to be a number of properties which we assume that what we call "knowledge" has. We ordinarily want to say that when one individual has knowledge he can convey it to another. We also want to say that one can have more or less knowledge. But these properties do not belong to intuition. If there were some means of conveying an intuition — or, let us say, arousing or stimulating another to intuition — the difficulty would remain as to how we can ever determine whether the intuition in both cases is the same, or in other words, whether the other individual really does exercise the faculty of intuition. Intuition, again, does not admit of degrees: we either have it or not, and there is no sense in saying that we have more or less intuitive knowledge.

If intuition is thus incommunicable and inexplicable, a genuine doubt arises as to whether it constitutes knowledge. Rather, it seems to boil down to one of two things: (1) It may be nothing more than dumb sensation, which is likewise private and incommunicable. When we have a toothache, we can tell someone else *that* we have it, but cannot communicate to him what the ache *is*. We can cause toothache in him, but there is no way of determining whether the ache in both cases is of the same quality. The matter is the same with any other feeling or sensation — whiteness, depression, warmth, calmness, etc. (2) Intuition may be regarded as an *element* in knowledge, something which may accompany or be present in knowledge but which does not constitute knowledge by itself. This alternative is perhaps closer to what Bergson intends, though of course distant from his actual view.

**General Methodological Implications.** In one sense it is arbitrary whether we wish to reserve the term "knowledge" for that which is communicable or extend its application, even, as some have done, to mere sensation. The point is, however, of real importance. The difference is between regarding knowledge as a social product, something that can be indefinitely added to by the community of investigators, or as something which may be possessed exclusively by the individual. There is something strange about Bergson's conception of a "science of metaphysics." How can it be a science at the same time that it "claims to dispense with symbols"? It is by symbols (in particular, language) that we communicate; and if the results of metaphysicians' intuitive inquiries are inexpressible symbolically, no contributions can be made to metaphysics. No metaphysician can utilize or build upon the investigations of another. Such a science consequently could not grow. Not only would metaphysics fail to be a science, but it would not be an art either. For the artist can represent his experience in an overt form, while metaphysical insight cannot be expressed.

Bergson apparently senses the difficulty, and it is for this reason that he distinguishes between "ready-made" concepts and concepts framed *after* intuition, these concepts presumably serving to reflect in some way (if not to "express") its results. But this only tends to undermine his conception of intuition. For if intuition is expressible at all it must be expressed symbolically, and therefore does not differ from symbolical knowledge in kind; if it serves only as a stimulus to analysis, it loses the primary importance originally attributed to it.

**Other Conceptions of Intuition: the Romantic Craving for Immediate Insight.** We have already tried to emphasize the appeal that the conception of intuition has made to various philosophers, and in diverse forms. This appeal is reflected likewise in imaginative literature, not of course in technical expression but in attitudes that lie embedded. Philosophers and poets alike have been impatient with the laborious exactitude and the toils of science. They have craved a way of knowing that should be simpler, more direct, and surer; that should be open to the common man, whereby he, no less than the learned one, might penetrate into the secret of things. We have an extreme emphasis in this direction in Wordsworth, who extols the childlike mind with its native innocence as somehow closer to reality than the mind corrupted by conventions, artificialities, and theoretical formulations.

> Thou, whose exterior semblance doth belie
>     Thy soul's immensity;
> Thou best philosopher, who yet dost keep
> Thy heritage, thou eye among the blind,
> That, deaf and silent, read'st the eternal deep,
> Haunted forever by the eternal mind, —
>     Mighty prophet! Seer blest!
>     On whom those truths do rest,
> Which we are toiling all our lives to find,
> In darkness lost, the darkness of the grave;
> Thou, over whom thy immortality
> Broods like the day, a master o'er a slave,
> A presence which is not to be put by;

Thou little child, yet glorious in the might
Of heaven-born freedom on thy being's height,
Why with such earnest pains dost thou provoke
The years to bring the inevitable yoke,
Thus blindly with thy blessedness at strife?
Full soon thy Soul shall have her earthly freight,
And custom lie upon thee with a weight,
Heavy as frost, and deep almost as life!*

Byron in *Manfred* expresses romantic depreciation of the achievements of science:

Knowledge is not happiness, and science
But an exchange of ignorance for that
Which is another kind of ignorance.†

This derogatory attitude is expressed in more specific and striking terms, and with intense individualism, by Walt Whitman:

When I heard the learn'd astronomer;
When the proofs, the figures, were ranged in columns
    before me;
When I was shown the charts and the diagrams, to add,
    divide, and measure them;
When I, sitting, heard the astronomer, where he lectured
    with much applause in the lecture-room,
How soon, unaccountable, I became tired and sick;
Till rising and gliding out, I wander'd off by myself,
In the mystical moist night-air, and from time to time,
Look'd up in perfect silence at the stars.††

The proofs and charts leave him profoundly dissatisfied. Much talk of the stars, yet no stars! Silent, peaceful contemplation, with its incommunicable immediacy, discloses infinitely more, albeit untranslatable into formulae — a reality deeper and more interesting. The revolt against the analyzing intellect as an instrument of distortion may be summarized by another quotation from Wordsworth:

One impulse from a vernal wood
May teach you more of man,
Of moral evil and of good,
Than all the sages can.

Sweet is the lore which Nature brings;
Our meddling intellect
Misshapes the beauteous forms of things —
We murder to dissect.

---

*Intimations of Immortality, viii.
†Act ii, Scene 4.
††From *Leaves of Grass*.

Enough of Science and of Art;
Close up those barren leaves;
Come forth, and bring with you a heart
That watches and receives.*

**Mysticism.** One of the most interesting forms intuitionism may take is *mysticism,* the view that there is a reality
hidden from the ordinary channels of knowledge which can be
revealed only to an individual mind in certain moments of insight. Reality is conceived of as underlying common experience. The mystical, revelatory experience is so absolutely
indescribable as to be hostile to all attempt at ordinary expression. Mystics of the religious kind have attempted to manifest their experience in the form of prayers or adulatory ad-
dresses. In this respect mysticism is similar to but more extreme than Bergson's intuitive insight, which according to him
can be scientifically utilized. Both are essentially non-symbolical, and mysticism may even be called anti-symbolical. But
mysticism and Bergsonian intuition differ in two very significant respects. (1) The latter is intuition which takes place in
ordinary experience. For Bergson experienced time or dura-
tion is something that enters into every one of our intuitions.
Mysticism, on the other hand, is not only intuition of what is
extra-empirical but of what is often alleged to be timeless or
eternal, of something which ordinary experience is impotent
to reveal. Mysticism has frequently been associated with some
individualistic form of theism, and one of its claims has been
that it is the sole means of penetrating to the essence of God.
(2) The other point of contrast is that mysticism is in a definite sense "anti-intellectualistic" whereas Bergsonian intuitionism is not. The mystical experience requires more or less an
abandonment of or escape from reflective inquiry. Intuition
in Bergson's sense, on the contrary, is a process of the most
conscious and intense intellectual activity, involving according
to him a violent reversal of the ordinary direction of thought.

---

*From *The Tables Turned.*

**Critical Remarks on Intuitionism in General.**  Intuition as an independent and allegedly superior form of knowing represents the hunt for a royal road to knowledge. We have in part suggested that this desire to seize *more* than is acquired by scientific means, to pierce to reality by a method free of complexities and circuitousness, misconstrues the fundamental properties and purposes of knowledge. The point is well stated by George Santayana (1863–1952):

> Knowledge is not eating, and we cannot expect to devour and possess *what we mean*. Knowledge is recognition of something absent; it is a salutation, not an embrace. It is an advance on sensation precisely because it is representative. The terms or goals of thought have for their function to subtend long tracts of sensuous experience, to be ideal links between fact and fact, invisible wires behind the scenes, threads along which inference may run in making phenomena intelligible and controllable.*

Knowledge, then, does not consist in becoming identical with its object, or in being swallowed up with it in a blind union, as the philosophical mystics and those who like Wordsworth and Whitman have mystical tendencies suppose, but in ordering, interpreting, anticipating, and controlling our experience. Intuition, with its all-or-none emphasis, and a demand for an instantaneous penetration to the nature of things that would be miraculous if it could be achieved, fails to meet these requirements. In demanding more it achieves less, as the history of the growth of knowledge seems to testify.

**Art and Intuition.**  We have spoken of intuition as essentially non-communicative where all the senses of this term have had to do with claims of knowledge. We often speak, however, of intuition, and indeed of a type of knowledge, in connection with the realm of art. The artist is said to achieve the character of his work intuitively in that he allows a sense of or insight into what is artistically desirable to guide him. Whether in poetry, music, the dance, sculpture, ceramics, archi-

---

* *The Life of Reason*, Vol. I (*Reason in Common Sense*), Ch. III.

tecture, painting, tapestry, or any other art, the treatment of the subject-matter is ultimately governed by some intuitive perception. We say "ultimately" because in perhaps the majority of cases the treatment is the result not merely of spontaneous magic but of extended planning, analysis of forms, working and reworking, choosing and discarding—literally of reasoning and experimenting. But the final product is determined to be successful by a sense of fitness or felicitousness, not by its conformity to a single standard that rules out all others. The work of art is not true or false. One work of art does not refute another, or verify another. The spokesmen for what we call "schools of art" often do, no doubt, berate one another. The criticism, however, is not, or in most cases does not intend to be, that a given type of artistic standard is "false" but that it is "bad," that is, inferior with respect to a given purpose or the general purpose of art.

**Does the Artist Communicate?**    It seems quite certain that in a sense the artist communicates when he expresses himself in an overt medium. Some, like Benedetto Croce (1866-1952), have maintained that what essentially distinguishes the artist is the occurrence of the artistic intuition, not the fact of his expressing it in a medium. We do not, however, call "artists" men who in no outward way express their "creations." In what sense is there communication? The work of art conveys no *literal* meaning—no fact or law is asserted, and the work is not true or false. No bundle of information is communicated by the work *itself,* though we may doubtless derive valuable information from facts *about* it. What is communicated is some phase of the artist's experience, or better, of the world as experienced by the artist. This communication is not necessarily conscious or purposive; it takes effect when the work of art is observed or is capable of being observed by the spectator. We do not need to relive the artist's experience in order to be imaginatively enriched. What is communicated is adapted into our own experience. The work of art communicates not by stating but by suggesting or evoking. In science what is communicated must result in the same response by all, one that is the criterion of our being said to understand. But in art, unanimity of imaginative response, even if it could be established and determined to be such, is not of primary importance.

**Philosophy and Language.** Philosophers have long differed over the problem of the rôle of language in the quest for knowledge. The general position that language is an impediment to knowing, that it obstructs or distorts or is basically inadequate for genuine understanding, is by no means rare in the history of philosophy. To a certain extent this position is reflected in the everyday and seemingly innocent view that such-and-such a reality is "indescribable" or "indefinable." Some philosophers have thought of language as a natural enemy of knowledge; others have thought of it as a barrier only to the deepest and most fundamental characteristics of the world; still others have thought of it as merely a precarious and tricky part of the business of knowing, but as subject to control. A common position is that only certain *kinds* of language obstruct knowing. But this position divides sharply into opposing positions. One is that figurative and literary language is the chief enemy, and that literalness and precision alone count in the attainment of knowledge. The other is that linguistic literalness and restrictiveness is an impoverishing and oversimplifying force in the struggle for human expression.

Proceeding from a quite different orientation, certain philosophers hold that, properly speaking, knowledge is possible only *because* of language — because formulation is possible; that we cannot be said to know what we cannot express in language. Reflecting this essentially Greek view, some have affirmed a basic identity of language and rationality. Among those who, taking this type of direction, regard language as natural and inevitable in human experience, the tendency has been to *interpret* the nature of language and its functions rather than to extol or disparage it. Actually most philosophers have been concerned less with the rôle of language as such or as a whole than with this or that way of speaking, this or that method of linguistic expression, this or that type of obscurity or ambiguity or vagueness.

**The Linguistic Movement in Recent Philosophic Thought.** In recent decades an extreme form of language-consciousness has arisen, mainly among English and American philosophers. The leading figures of early modern British philosophy — Hobbes, Locke, Berkeley, and Hume — had transmitted a firm emphasis on the importance of linguistic clarity and on concern with linguistic usage. They stressed, in Locke's words, both the "imperfections of language" itself and the "abuses of language" by its users. The British tradition of closely attending to the rôle of language and usage was greatly augmented by the work of G. E. Moore (1873-1958) and of Bertrand Russell (1872-1970), a teacher of Ludwig Wittgenstein. Russell and Gottlob Frege (1848-1925), both major figures in the modern theory of the relation between logic and mathematics, also strongly influenced the study of the relation between logic and language. So far as philosophers of the twentieth century are concerned, none has had a greater influence on the development of "linguistic philosophy" or "linguistic analysis" than Wittgenstein (1889-1951), some of whose views on language and meaning will be outlined in the next chapter.

Among those who are counted as "linguistic analysts" there is of course considerable difference of approach and practice. Most of them appear to assume that, whether we are dealing with the meaning of a philosophic concept or the solution of a philosophic problem, we are dealing basically with a body of terms and statements. Accordingly, attention to the rules and procedures of the language involved, and concern with the level and type of such language, is a paramount philosophic obligation. To deal with a problem is equivalent to clarifying our ways of talking about that problem and showing how it arises in discourse. Similarly, to be clear about the kinds of existence there are in the world is to be clear about the ways in which we talk of them. It is not unusual to hear this type of approach criticized on the ground that it is not the "topic itself" which is being analyzed but discourse *about* the topic. The whole issue is a large and intricate one. But to proceed philosophically by examining discourse about what we are concerned with is not without precedent. Aristotle, for example, often investigates the kind of being that something has by investigating the ways in which it is talked about — the *varied* contexts in which it is to be found. The difference in approach, however, seems to be that for Aristotle the analysis of linguistic usage is the *beginning* of a problem, whereas for the linguistic analysts it is the heart of the problem and sometimes its solution. Otherwise stated, this difference is between the tendency to think of language usage as the way into a problem and the tendency to think of it as the way out of a problem.

Thus far we have dealt with questions about the relation between language and *knowing*. We have yet to deal with questions about the relation between language and *meaning*. It is evident, therefore, that language need not be studied in terms of meaning alone. And from another point of view, as we shall see, *meaning* need not be studied in terms of *language* alone.

## CHAPTER TEN

✦   ✦   ✦

# The Problem of Meaning

Questions relating to inquiring and knowing cannot be separated from the problem of meaning. Sometimes it is not whether a view is true or false that is the major issue but whether it is at all intelligible or meaningful. The problem of determining a standard of intelligibility is obviously of tremendous importance. In this chapter we shall first be concerned with the view known as *pragmatism*, and then consider other ways of approaching the problem of meaning. Perhaps no philosophic doctrine has been so variously interpreted and so often misinterpreted as pragmatism. In fact, there is not one but many kinds of pragmatism, of which we shall distinguish the most important and influential. We have suggested that pragmatism is a form of empiricism, and that it has something in common with the other form of empiricism that we have mentioned, positivism. We shall for the most part leave it to the reader to discern these affinities in detail. Pragmatism originated in the United States and received its principal formulations at the hands of the American philosophers Peirce, James, Dewey, and Mead. Since the last three were influenced (directly and indirectly) by Peirce, who was the founder of this point of view, it will be best to examine first what it is in his formulation and what he intended its purpose to be.

**Pragmatism as Experimentalism; Genuine and Pseudo-Problems.** Philosophers have often reflected on their methods, and have sometimes been impressed by the fact of controversy and the lack of a standard by which to lessen disagreement. Charles S. Peirce (1839-1914) was struck by the historical fact that certain intellectual problems are solved over a period of time whereas others appear to be no nearer solution now than when they were posed hundreds or even thousands of years ago. "Is there a God?" "Are mind and matter essentially different from one another?" "Is there an immortal soul?" — these questions are still in the forefront of speculative philosophic discussion. The fact of unsolved problems had likewise impressed the classical empiricists and Kant, but with Peirce a new question is raised. Is the fault *with us,* or with the *problems themselves,* that they remain unsolved? Are they unsolved or are they insoluble? According to Kant, these problems — the "metaphysical" problems, relating to the universe as a whole, God, the soul — are insoluble because of the limitation of our intellectual powers. Peirce asks in effect, If certain problems are absolutely insoluble, in what sense are they "problems"? A problem which is a genuine one should be, *in principle* at least, capable of solution. If it is not, in what sense can it be said to be significant? Peirce thus introduces the factor of the *meaningfulness* or *significance* of a problem. Certain problems may have been insoluble because of something wrong with *them,* because they are not genuine problems at all but pseudo-problems. Problems, so-called, relating to what transcends possible human experience preclude the conditions of their own solution. It is not because of the limitation of man's cognitive powers — who is to decide where these limitations begin?—but because the cards are stacked, so to speak, from the very outset, that he cannot solve them or fruitfully approximate a solution. To speak of that which is absolutely unknowable, as Kant does, is not to speak of anything meaningful. For if it is impossible to know anything at all about it, how can we speak of it? Something absolutely "unknowable" is absolutely indefinable, and is quite evidently devoid of intelligibility.

**Literal Meaning and Psychological Meaning.**   The pragmatism of Peirce is primarily the formulation of a rule specifying under what conditions the language we use is meaningful. The answers to problems are given by sentences, and sentences consist of words. To show when words and sentences have meaning and when not is to show when problems have meaning, that is, when they are soluble. But before stating the conditions laid down by Peirce, it is necessary to point out just how far he intended his pragmatism to go.

When we speak of the "meaning" of a word or statement, we refer to something that can be interpreted in two different ways. Let us illustrate by an example. Suppose we say, "One hundred armed battleships are approaching the shores of the United States." This has "meaning" in two senses. In one sense we ordinarily say that "the meaning is different for different individuals" or that the statement "means" different things to different people — some may be terrified, some overjoyed, some expectant of certain acts, some indifferent; and in general, no two individuals would be said to have the same response precisely, nor if they did could we test the similarity, since we cannot inspect the quality of one another's feelings. But in another sense, a *literal* sense, the "meaning" of the foregoing statement is the same for everyone who understands the English language: the set of facts which it refers to is the same set of facts for all, and anyone who chooses to ascertain whether the statement is true or not can undertake an investigation which would terminate practically in the same way that another would, *regardless* of his emotional reaction or personal feelings.

The first kind of meaning may be called *psychological* meaning, the second *logical* or *literal* meaning. In the latter we are concerned with the objective content of a word or statement, and not with individual reaction to it. We are concerned with what can be made intelligible to all and not with private differences. When we sometimes speak of, for instance, "poetic meaning" it is not the literal meaning that we refer to but meaning in a psychological sense, in which different images may be called up by association and different spontaneous responses may occur in different minds. Now the pragmatism of Peirce is interested only in logical or literal meaning, because he believes it is this type of meaning alone that is concerned when we ask whether problems have meaning. The solution of a problem is a contribution to knowledge and so far as the advance of *knowledge* is concerned it is only logical meaning that is relevant. A solution to a problem is *no* solution if it is not a solution for everybody.

Peirce emphasized that although to many men certain concepts may *seem* clear, they may in fact be logically meaningless. Thus the mere fact that men *use* the term "soul" or "God" does not *necessarily* imply that these terms are intelligible — they may or may not be, depending upon the way they are defined. We are likely to be misled by the familiarity of the words we use into believing that the ideas they stand for are perfectly intelligible. Many a person who confidently thinks he knows what he means is unable when the test comes to explain himself with any degree of *logical* coherence or clarity.

**The Experimental Standard of Definition.** The pragmatism of Peirce maintains that in order to make sure of using meaningful language it is not sufficient merely to *define* the words we use. Thus the meaningless term "abracadabra" may be defined as "hocus pocus," but it remains meaningless. It is the *kind of* definition we offer that is important. According to Peirce, a definition must enable us to become acquainted in experience with what the word stands for, if it stands for anything (for words like "if" and "and" do not stand for anything in the usual sense). The word "mammal" is a meaningful one because its definition enables us to examine or identify certain specific characteristics which can be distinguished from any other set of characteristics. This would not be the case if "mammal" were defined as "a glorious manifestation of eternal providence." This definition gives us no direction as to how we can *experimentally identify* the type of object defined. The purpose of the experimental emphasis is to point out that definitions must be publicly intelligible. We saw how the procedure of the scientific method achieves universal or public agreement. Peirce's pragmatism consciously employs the scientific method as its model in formulating the rule of significance for terms in general. To define terms experimentally is to use a means by which we can communicate meanings without ambiguity. Thus if anyone maintains that he does not understand the meaning of a term, we need only describe the experimental conditions which define this word, and thereby establish a standard of agreement and of universal understandability. It is in this way that the pragmatic rule of Peirce is designed to achieve clarity. Terms are to be defined by relating them not merely to experience but to public experience. We can imagine the benefit of pragmatic definition if we try to picture a situation in which such words as "democracy" and "freedom" are defined clearly enough for us readily to identify the state of affairs correlated with them.

**The Requirement of Scientific Verifiability.** The pragmatic standard of Peirce can be stated for theories or opinions as well as words. Traditionally the criterion of significance is whether a statement is made up out of "clear and distinct ideas," or whether it "conveys a distinct thought." But how are clearness and distinctness to be understood? Can they be measured? The fact is that they are only psychological criteria, confusing familiarity with logical intelligibility. What may be clear to one is not necessarily clear to another. The criterion of Peirce attempts to substitute an objective standard of intelligibility.

It might seem that we could state the standard for sentences by saying that a sentence is significant if it consists of pragmatically defined words arranged in correct grammatical order. But this is not correct. For statements like "Galaxies appointed melancholy brothers" or "He divorced his husband" meet that requirement and yet are generally acknowledged to be meaningless. We may say, then, that a factual statement is a significant one if it is possible to collect evidence for it — in other words, if it is possible to investigate its truth or falsity. For a statement to meet this standard means that it can be investigated by the scientific method. As in the case of scientific statements proper, it is not essential for us actually to know that a statement is true or false but essential only that it be possible to take steps leading to such knowledge. In other words, meaningful statements must conform to the standard of scientific verifiability. Some statements, as we have seen, are directly, others indirectly, verifiable.

Pragmatism points out that the meaning of a statement consists in the sum of its verifiable consequences, rather than in the psychological reaction that it arouses in us. Two statements may contain in part different words, yet their meaning may be the same, because they have the same factual consequences. On the other hand, the only way of distinguishing the meaning of two opinions which appear to be verbally similar is to exhibit their consequences and observe the different facts implicitly referred to by each. The purpose of Peirce's pragmatism was precisely to overcome verbalism in intellectual matters by supplying objective criteria of distinction.

We are now able to say what it is that makes a problem a significant (or soluble) one. A problem is significant or genuine if the possible answers to it are verifiable, that is, if it is capable of scientific investigation.

**The Broad Conception of Experience and Verification.** When we say that a problem is "capable of scientific investigation," that a statement is "verifiable," that a term is "experimentally defined," we can give these expressions a narrow or a broad meaning. We have already ruled out an *extremely* narrow or *sensationalistic* interpretation by saying that the pragmatism of Peirce endeavors to set up as standard the broad canons of science — this in opposition to the narrow canons of positivism, which distrust indirect verification and are inclined to restrict "experience" to sense-experience. But we must also on Peirce's pragmatism avoid another narrow interpretation, which takes the terms "experiment" and "experience" to refer to physical experiment and physical experience alone. This narrow interpretation would render "unverifiable" any theory which deals, for instance, with the general course of history or of civilization or of the nature of man's relation to the universe as a whole — any theory, in short, of speculative philosophy. Peirce's conception of experiment allows for the verification of such theories. The complexity and difficulty of the process is immeasurably greater but is of essentially the same kind. In a given science, say psychology, the facts verifying psychological theories would be specific instances of behavior by the individual organism. In a general theory of civilization, on the other hand, the verifying "facts" would include not merely these but psychologically accepted *theories* as well, or a combination of facts and hypotheses of psychology *and* physics *and* biology, and in general the entire set of scientific results. The kind of facts serving as evidence for speculative philosophic theories is thus of a far broader and more complex character than that serving as evidence within a given science. Yet the process of verification may be called "scientific," for while we are no longer concerned with verification in a *special* science, we can employ the scientific *method*. The pragmatic standard of Peirce thus requires that *all* hypotheses purporting to be about fact be verifiable, but avoids a narrow conception of verifiability.

**Kantianism, Positivism, and Experimentalist Pragmatism.** Experimentalism differs from Kantianism (to sum up) in its rejection as unintelligible of the conception of an unknowable extra-empirical reality; and from both Kantianism and positivism in its introduction of the factor of meaning or significance in the analysis of knowledge, as well as its more exact conception of experience and scientific method. It differs from positivism in its discrimination of speculative theories as verifiable or unverifiable, as opposed to indiscriminate lumping together of all speculative theories as "metaphysical" in an extra-empirical sense; in its more liberal interpretation of science and its avoidance of legislation on scientific method; and in its substitution of a specific criterion of the intelligibility of theories as opposed to the vague positivist criterion of their "usefulness" or "fruitfulness."

**Pragmatism as Practicalism: the View of James.** Most people associate the conception of pragmatism with William James; and it is true that the form which James stood for has been far more influential than any other. James's original intention was to elaborate on the pragmatism of Peirce. But the manner and phraseology in which he formulated his view resulted, consciously or unconsciously, in something quite different. According to James,

> The pragmatic method . . . is to try to interpret each notion by tracing its respective practical consequences. What difference would it practically make to anyone if this notion rather than that notion were true? If no practical difference whatever can be traced, then the alternatives mean practically the same thing, and all dispute is idle. Whenever a dispute is serious, we ought to be able to show some practical difference that must follow from one side or the other's being right.*

James, conceiving of pragmatism as a manifestation of the empiricist attitude, interprets this attitude in the following terms. The pragmatist

> turns away from abstraction and insufficiency, from verbal solutions, from bad *a priori* reasons, from fixed principles, closed systems, and pretended absolutes and origins. He turns towards concreteness and adequacy, towards facts, towards action and towards power. That means the empiricist temper regnant and the rationalist temper sincerely given up. It means the open air and possibilities of nature, as against dogma, artificiality, and the pretence of finality in truth.†

**The Meaning of "Practical" in James and Peirce.** Perhaps the essential point of difference in the two types of pragmatism considered thus far is that for James the word "practical" has a looser and more popular meaning than it has for Peirce. The general pragmatic emphasis is that statements are significant if they have "practical" consequences. But this may mean (1) that they have consequences capable of experimental investigation, or (2) that belief in these statements influences human conduct. The first meaning defines the standard of Peirce, the second that of James. For the former the terms

---

* *Pragmatism,* Lecture II.
† *Ibid.*

we use should be defined by means of a scientific procedure with which they are associated; for the latter what is important is that the terms we use should be capable of affecting our behavior. Thus on Peirce's principle, to speak of "purpose" or "design" in the universe, or of "God," is to speak of nothing, significant *unless* these terms are capable of being experientially defined in accordance with scientific standards. For James, however, it would appear that such terms need not be thus defined in order to be "pragmatically" significant.

> . . . Any one who insists that there *is* a designer and who is sure he is a divine one, gets a certain pragmatic benefit from the term — the same, in fact, which we saw that the terms God, Spirit, or the Absolute, yield us. 'Design,' worthless tho it be as a mere rationalistic principle set above or behind things for our admiration, becomes, if our faith concretes it into something theistic, a term of *promise*. Returning with it into experience, we gain a more confiding outlook on the future. . . . This vague confidence in the future is the sole pragmatic meaning at present discernible in the terms design and designer.*

> Other than this practical significance, the words God, free-will, design, etc., have none. Yet dark tho they be in themselves, or intellectualistically taken, when we bear them into life's thicket with us the darkness *there* grows light about us. . . . Pragmatism alone can read a positive meaning into [them], and for that she turns her back upon the intellectualist point of view altogether.†

Thus when we are confronted with a speculative problem, say that of materialism versus spiritualism, the difference in meaning of these two theories is determined not by their different experimental consequences but by their different effects upon our personal experience and conduct.

> Here then, in these different emotional and · practical appeals, in these adjustments of our concrete attitudes of hope and expectation, and all the delicate consequences which their differences entail, lie the real meanings of materialism and spiritualism. . . . Materialism means simply the denial that the moral order is eternal, and the cutting off of ultimate hopes; spiritualism means the affirmation of an eternal moral order and the letting loose of hope. Surely here is an issue genuine enough, for any one who feels it; and, as long as men are men, it will yield matter for a serious philosophic debate.††

---

* *Pragmatism*, Lecture III.
† *Ibid.*
†† *Ibid.*

The foregoing quotations reveal clearly that for James the discussion of the nature of meaning is placed primarily on a psychological basis, whereas for Peirce it is on a logical basis.

**Critical Comparison of Experimentalism and Practicalism.** *The Place of Emotion and Will.* In James pragmaatism becomes a revolt against "intellectualism," the use of the intellectual and logical faculties in inquiry. He feels that emotion and faith, the "will to believe," are important factors. Thus for him the meaning of two views is different according as they make different "emotional appeals" to us, or as our conduct is modified by one or another of them being believed — these are the "practical consequences" in James's wide use of the term. The pragmatist turns "towards action and towards power," away from logic to fact, away from abstractions to concrete experience. James revolted against "intellectualism" because he tacitly identified this with rationalism, with the *exclusive* or the *predominant* emphasis on the intellectual powers. He fails to take into consideration the fact that there is an intellectualism of another kind. This intellectualism emphasizes that experience without interpretation or abstraction is blind and unintelligible, whereas intellect disconnected from experience is barren and meaningless. Peirce's experimentalism is intellectualistic in this sense. His purpose was to extend the method of science to all inquiry whatever, including that of speculative philosophy. This intellectualism rigidly excludes emotion and the "will to believe" from inquiry. For James a philosophic controversy is a genuine or significant one if the conflicting issues arouse conflicting hopes or expectations in the hearts of the respective proponents. For Peirce the existence of such emotional responses may be interesting enough from one point of view but is utterly irrelevant to the determination of the problem's significance. The fact that men are psychologically affected by a controversy is no proof that the controversy is logically intelligible. History teaches that men have been profoundly affected by magical incantations, nonsense, pseudo-problems, and personal bias, and that they have have differed vehemently where their respective opinions have been logically identical. Such differences, psychological in character, are variable and accidental, and cannot be the basic factor in a theory of meaning.

*On "Experience."* In their attempt to relate abstractions to experience, Peirce and James conceive of experience differently, and by this time we need hardly state the point. For the former it is public experience that counts; for the latter no distinction is made between this and experience more or less sensationalistically conceived, from which it follows that meaning may vary with different individuals. Peirce's experimentalism offers an impersonal criterion of meaning; the pragmatism of James does not. For the former it is society and communication that are the foundation of meaning; for the latter it is the individual mind and its power of association and anticipation. For James feeling, sensation, or emotion, is important as such; for Peirce it is only the vehicle by which we use symbols to communicate.

**Pragmatism as Dealing with the Knowledge-Situation.** Thus far we have looked at pragmatism as a theory which discriminates between significant attempts to gain knowledge and meaningless pretensions to knowledge. Pragmatism can also be formulated from another angle. If we undertake to inquire into the actual conditions under which what we call knowledge takes place, by formulating and understanding these we can obtain a standard by which to judge whether claims to knowledge are valid. This would be an investigation of the knowledge-process or -situation. Of course, the advance charge can be made by anti-pragmatists that in so doing we arbitrarily call such-and-such knowledge and attempt to describe this while ignoring all else. The reply of the pragmatist is that the instances of "knowledge" chosen for analysis are universally recognized as such. They are, first, what is called knowledge in everyday activity, as when we are said to know how to cure a disease, to know the structure of an automobile, to know why water freezes; and second, what has been called knowledge throughout the history of empirical science.

**Instrumentalism: the Experimentalism of Dewey.** The account of the knowledge-situation that we shall state is in its fundamental features common to Peirce and John Dewey (1859-1952) and we explain here the approach and version of Dewey, sometimes called *instrumentalism*.

**Reflective Thought as a Means to the Solution of Problems.** On one very influential tradition in philosophy, a certain basic distinction is supposed to underlie all sound speculation. This distinction is between nature on the one hand and the mind which *knows* nature on the other. Nature consists of objects and events. The mind knows nature to a greater or lesser degree when it has "true ideas" of these objects and events. We shall consider such a view in Part Three. Suffice it here to point out that the view of Dewey proceeds from an entirely different general outlook. The human mind is conceived of not as something radically distinct from all other phenomena but as part and parcel of nature itself. Consequently knowledge is something which falls within nature as a natural activity, one among other activities, such as the rotation of the earth, the birth of a child, the overthrow of a government, an earthquake, and walking. Since it is a natural fact in which human beings are involved, knowledge takes place within human experience, where by "experience" Dewey means the complex network of interaction between man and his environment, defined in Chapter VII above. At what stage in human experience does the knowledge-getting activity begin?

According to Peirce and Dewey, it is when we begin not merely to think but to think reflectively. Reflective thought properly so called takes place when a *problem* confronts us, when disturbances in our environment make us uncertain about our future course of action, about the meaning of what we are doing.

**Ideas as Instruments.** Thus reflective thought begins for a man walking in the woods when he is confronted with the problem of getting out, and for a scientist when he is confronted with the problem of why human tissue dies, or why there are tides in the surf. In one case we have a daily environment, in the other a scientific environment. The "action" about which the man in the forest is uncertain is that of taking a path that will result in his emerging; the "action" about which the scientist is uncertain is the prediction of events and the observations which he should perform. Now knowledge is something that consists, as we say, in possessing true ideas or hypotheses. How shall we interpret these ideas? In the light of the aforementioned set of conditions, they function as devices by means of which we attempt the solution of the problem in which our inquiry originated. They are, in Dewey's terminology, *instruments* or *means* which we employ in order to attain an end — this end is knowledge, or the resolution of the problematic situation. They are "working hypotheses" in a special and definite sense — tools by means of which concrete problems are solved. Ideas (theories, beliefs) are not entities somehow carrying with them a mysterious property called truth, our job being somehow to search them out. They are each of them relative to a specific problematic situation. In other words they do not, when meaningful, arise in a void.

We may put the point somewhat differently. According to Dewey, the end that we achieve is intimately tied up with and its character is influenced by the means we employ in achieving it. In other words, the kind of knowledge we attain is partly determined by the way we attain it. Knowing is not a process of hunting for objects which come labeled "objects of knowledge." In trying to solve problems in our environment, we manipulate that environment; we experiment. When we make a discovery, what we discover does not present itself ready-made; it is the result of our experimentation or knowledge-getting, our testing of theories. It is something with which we have entered into a relation — the knowledge-relation — and it is not the same thing apart from the relation that it is within it. Thus a disease is not the same as a disease experimentally analyzed. In knowing, we select certain aspects of a thing, consider it from different points of view, consider its relation to other things, and so on. So that the character of our knowledge is in part something determined by our activity. For had our selection been different, our attention differently directed, our knowledge would not have been the same.

**The Implication of Instrumentalism.** It is thus clear that for Dewey experimentation is an essential part of the knowing process, and it is clear also that the term "experimentation" is to be interpreted broadly. We get to know by *acting*, by *testing* our ideas, by working them out. Knowing is *one kind* of doing. The consequence of this should likewise be clear. What is not an idea or theory arising in a problematic situation of our environment — whether it be the social, scientific, political, aesthetic environment, or any other phase of human experience — is not, for Dewey, an idea that can terminate in genuine knowledge, but is rather of the kind that engenders and perpetuates verbalism and fruitless controversy.

**Different Aspects of Meaning-Theory.** Many philosophers are inclined to associate "meaning" with words and word-combinations, that is, with language as language is commonly understood. On this view, when thoughts or ideas are said to have meaning they are regarded as formulated in language. But there is a tradition within the history of philosophy which sees the matter differently and for which meaning cannot be limited in this way. In this tradition the emphasis is on "symbols" or "signs," a category which includes words. Some signs are thought of as "natural" signs (for example, clouds are a sign of rain — clouds "mean" rain; or, smoke is a sign of fire). Other signs are "human" signs or symbols (for example, a weathervane is a sign of the wind's direction; a traffic light is a symbol of a certain legal regulation; a common noun is a symbol of a certain class or type of things). In this approach, language is treated as one form of signifying or symbolizing. There are linguistic symbols and non-linguistic symbols. Indeed, the notion of language itself has often been construed as embracing much more than words, and the conception of a "language of nature" or "language of God" appears from time to time in the history of philosophy. Some philosophers, like Peirce and Dewey, whose views on the relation between language, thinking, and meaning we have considered in the preceding pages, have also developed theories of meaning in the more comprehensive sense — "general" theories, as they are sometimes called. Such theories may attempt to show how meaning depends on basic conditions of man and nature — e.g., social institutions, history, biological activity, communication, patterns of child development, physical behavior, or the nature of consciousness. Some important general theories of meaning are those of Josiah Royce (1855-1916), George Herbert Mead (1863-1931), Alfred North Whitehead (1861-1947), and Ernst Cassirer (1874-1945).

The two additional conceptions of meaning which we shall sketch in the remainder of this chapter are those of Cassirer and Wittgenstein. Cassirer's is of the comprehensive type, concerned with various forms of symbolism, of which language is held to be one, while Wittgenstein's focuses on language.

**Cassirer's Conception of Symbolic Forms.**    A glance at the philosophy of symbolic forms may be of special interest because of its historical and anthropological aspects. According to Cassirer, the kinds of meaning and value men find in the world reflect the processes of human civilization. When we speak of human civilization and levels of culture we are speaking of the way men make things, the way they name and express things, the way they try to predict their environment, the way they seek out and defer to gods or powers. In other words, human civilization consists in such fundamental activities as art, language or speech, science, and religion or myth. These activities provide men with the major types of symbols through which the world makes sense to them or by which it acquires special kinds of significance. Since these activities constitute what is distinctive of man, Cassirer defines man as "the symbolical animal." Each of the activities has its own structure, its essential character; and accordingly, Cassirer calls them "symbolic forms."

The symbolic forms — art, language, myth, science — are ways in which men see the world; more precisely, ways in which they cultivate the possibilities of seeing and understanding it. We must also recognize that these forms shape and determine what it is that we call the world; in a sense they provide different worlds for men to see and understand. Cassirer finds much significance in the historical growth of science, art, myth, and language. It is not primarily (as in Kant) man the abstract knower that helps to shape the world and make it accessible, but man in his various communicative and institutional roles, in his capacity as a cultural being. If meaning, then, is to be grasped in terms of experience, such experience cannot be regarded as merely private or individual, and much less as merely sensory, but as consisting in the life and history of peoples, civilizations, and traditions. For even the most valuable and unique experience of an individual yields meaning only within the context of common life.

**Myth, Science, and Language.**   In Cassirer's works on the philosophy of symbols, the relations among the various symbolic forms are intricate and detailed. His conception of these forms is not the same throughout his thought. At times he seems to imply that each of the forms is as fundamentally human and as humanly important as any of the others. At other times he seems to imply instead that myth and art are more primitive than science, and that science represents the kind of symbolic interpretation most characteristic of advanced civilizations. The difference of viewpoint is between that which conceives of *each* form as having a primitive stage and an advanced stage, and that which conceives of some *forms* as primitive and others as advanced. Whether terms like "primitive" and "advanced" have any other meaning than—or *should* have any other meaning than — "early" and "late" is a controversial question.

If we consider as basic Cassirer's view of the symbolic forms as varying ways of producing and finding meaning, then, for example, myth and science are not opposed to each other in the sense that myth is crude knowledge and science accurate knowledge. They are not opposing ways of aspiring to the same goal; their goals are different. Myth seeks to grasp something in experience which it deems to be of great importance, and to subordinate everything else to that *selected aspect*. Science aims, on the contrary, to achieve explanations which bring various aspects of experience *together*. Myth isolates or separates something (a force, an event, an idea) and seeks to intensify the experience of it. Science seeks to interconnect occurrences or states of affairs which thus far have been thought of as separate. Myth has a dramatic function, science an analytical and systematic function.

Language is closely associated with both mythical and scientific meaning. In its mythical mode of expression it pinpoints and intensifies experience through names. For mythical consciousness, Cassirer believes, the god is the name and the name is the god. In its scientific and logical dimension language promotes the process of reasoning by its marvelous flexibility and its capacity for abstraction. For Cassirer, we must remember, language *as such* is a way of seeing and rendering the world. It is the experience of the world as divided, patterned, and identified by the processes of naming and describing.

**Wittgenstein's Conception of Language.**    Wittgenstein's views fall into an earlier and a later period. The work of the earlier period (mainly the book *Tractatus Logico-Philosophicus*) influenced the school known as "logical positivism" or "logical empiricism." The work of the later period (mainly *Philosophical Investigations*) influenced the school of "ordinary-language analysis," one of the leaders of which was J. L. Austin (1911-1960). But the general influence of Wittgenstein's views has been much more widespread. One of his dominant interests, both early and late, is in the question of how a philosophic emphasis on language can help to solve philosophic problems and to clarify the ways in which we think about the world. In the earlier period, this interest leads him to explore the possibility of model languages—languages which would be so constructed as to eliminate the vagueness and confusion inevitable in the everyday means by which men express themselves. Such languages, as his followers later showed in detail, would be artificial structures as distinct from cultural languages which have grown up in the course of time among peoples. While an artificial language would have to be much more restricted in its range and application, it would also be much more precise than any natural or cultural language. It would aim at clarified discourse rather than spontaneous expression. It would show how economy and exactitude could be achieved in place of sprawling, chaotic formulations. Such a language would find its own model in mathematics, with postulates, definitions, restricted vocabulary, and rules of procedure. Its norms and logical grammar would guarantee that we knew what we were talking about and would prevent lapses into ambiguity or meaninglessness. It would be made perfect by agreement, and its statements would be logically connected with one another.

The later Wittgenstein departs from this standpoint. He feels that "ideal languages" with fixed rules and completely determined procedures, legislating what is and is not permissible, achieve precision of a sort, but only of a sort, and at a high cost. They are false to language as it is spoken and written in the many activities of life. They are not representative of the innumerable forms in which language can be manifested. And consequently they do not do justice to the varied ways in which the meanings of language arise.

**The Language-Game and Language Games.** Wittgenstein comes to believe that the best avenue to the understanding of language is the "everyday," "ordinary" speech that men use and cannot help using. How should we proceed, then, if we wish to find the relation between language and meaning? We select typical instances in which people use language: a doctor and a patient, a mason and his helper, a teacher and students. These are not language systems. They are language situations. In various ways they may differ from one another. But in each of them certain devices are to be found by which meanings are arrived at, even if vaguely or without definite boundaries. Wittgenstein calls these situations "language games," and speaks of language as a whole as "the language game." Helpful as he finds the analogy of the game to be, he refuses to define "game" in any formal manner. He is convinced that formal definitions tend to deny the ever-present plasticity in language-conduct and in the conduct of games. There are rules in both, but the rules may be changed or even made up as we go along. When we speak of the language game, we are speaking of "language and the activities into which it is woven." Some language games, as indeed some non-language games, are very simple, others very extended and complicated. But the meanings to be found in each are indigenous to it, even if it is quite similar to other games. The concept of game is broad enough to apply to artificial or formal systems: they too are language games. We are deceived, however, when we ask what is *common* to all language games. We should rather feel our way among what we ordinarily call games to see the ways in which they are linked and related to other games. Wittgenstein seems to equate the "meaning" of a word with its "use." And he sometimes speaks of "moves" in a language game rather than "assertions" or "expressions."

**Philosophy as Linguistic Therapy.** According to Wittgenstein, philosophers are prime offenders in the "misuse" or unclear use of their language. They are unaware of the kind of game they are playing—in itself perhaps no great crime—but think they have the keenest awareness and are excessively confident that they are making sense. And they struggle, generation after generation, to deal with the same problems. So strongly does Wittgenstein feel about this entire matter that he conceives the main function of philosophy to be the elimination of linguistic confusion, the "uncovering" of "nonsense." On his view of what philosophy ought to be, "the philosopher's treatment of a question is like the treatment of an illness."[*] Thus the philosopher solves a problem when he shows that it is no longer a problem; when he exposes "the bewitchment of our intelligence by means of language."[†] The philosopher must "bring words back from their metaphysical to their everyday usage."[††] He must "uncover the bumps that the understanding has got by running its head up against the limits of language."[†††]

---

[*] *Philosophical Investigations* (translated from the German by G. E. M. Anscombe), Sec. 255.
[†] *Ibid.* Sec. 109.
[††] *Ibid.* Sec. 116.
[†††] *Ibid.* Sec. 119.

This last formulation is as good a point as any to suggest some questions which may reveal why Wittgenstein's work has been so provocative and controversial. Are there, indeed, "limits of language"? Is such a conception not more surprising for a view like Wittgenstein's than for almost any other view of language? If there are such limits, and especially if we know what some of them are, why should we have been so cautious as to stress the indefinite flexibility of the language game? And why should "metaphysical" words be "brought back" to their "everyday usage"? Did they come from everyday usage? Is not a metaphysical viewpoint itself a language game, with its own usage and its own meanings, just as a scientific theory or a mathematical system is? Are we not obliged to acknowledge the language situation of special inquirers as well as laymen? Are we clear about what is to be understood by the term "use"? Can we speak readily of any use as a "misuse"? If so, on what basis? Is not ordinary or everyday language itself *one kind* of language game? Do we actually want to say that it is the *ideal* language game—if we have resolved to respect the integrity and the inherent meanings of *all* games? Is the "ordinary" or "everyday" something absolute? Should not the ordinary be regarded as itself relative to a situation or context—such as ordinary number-theory or everyday mechanics? Finally, is the notion of "game" helpful in the understanding of all forms of language, or indeed of more than a very few? Does it shed light on the nature of language as occurring in Darwin's *Origin of Species,* in the Book of Isaiah, in *Hamlet,* or in the Constitution of the United States? Is a game in these language situations significantly like a game in more familiar and ordinary senses? Or has the notion of game gradually been stretched beyond recognition of what most people *are* willing to call "games"?

❖   ❖   ❖

## CHAPTER ELEVEN

# What Is Truth?

Meaning and truth are not the same thing. If a statement is significant, this does not necessarily imply that it is true. This distinction seems simple, but it is not accepted by all philosophers, as the student who goes on to study the history of modern philosophy will discover. According to some philosophers, for example, when we have expanded the *full* meaning of an idea, we have thereby determined its truth. Let us now turn to a consideration of some of the attempts that philosophers have made to define "truth."

**The "Correspondence" Theory of Truth.** One of the most widespread conceptions has been the so-called correspondence theory of truth. According to this, truth consists in the *agreement* of our thought with reality. A belief is called "true" if it "agrees" with a fact. Or, stated otherwise, a belief is true if the ideas contained in it *correspond* to objects as they are in fact. This view has not merely been held by many philosophers but seems to conform rather closely to our ordinary common sense usage when we speak of truth. The flaws in the definition arise when we ask what is meant by "agreement" or "correspondence" of ideas and objects, beliefs and facts, thoughts and reality. In order to test the truth of an idea or belief we must presumably *compare* it with the reality in some sense.

**Critical Remarks.** (1) In order to make the comparison, we must know what it is that we are comparing, namely, the belief on the one hand and the reality on the other. But if we already know the reality, why need we make the comparison, since we are assuming ourselves to be in possession of the truth? And if we do not know the reality, how can we make the comparison?

(2) The making of the comparison is itself a fact about which we have a belief. We may believe that the given belief agrees with the fact which it refers to. But the question then crops up, How do we know that our belief in this agreement is "true"? On the correspondence theory we would say that it is true if it agrees with the agreement, if it corresponds to it. But if we believe that it agrees with the agreement, how do we know that *this* belief is "true"? It must agree with the fact that the previous belief agrees with the original fact of agreement. And so on in infinite regress.

(3) Do our beliefs "agree" or "correspond" with facts in the sense that they *copy* them or *resemble* them? It might perhaps be said with some plausibility that our belief that a fire occurred is "true" if our idea of the fire occurring resembles the actual occurrence, though this way of putting the matter suffers from many difficulties. But what about a belief that a given poem is beautiful? Does our belief resemble the "beauty" — the fact of "being beautiful"? If it is true that Plato is a better philosopher than John Doe, does this mean that our belief of this resembles "betterness"? And between what is there a resemblance when we hold the view that man is an intelligent animal? We might argue that our idea of a person we know acting intelligently in a given situation actually corresponds to the fact of this person's having acted intelligently in that situation. The belief, however, concerns not this or that man, not any *particular* man, but man in *general,* man as a class. If we wished to retain the correspondence theory, we should at least have to make a clear distinction between a belief corresponding to or resembling a concrete, specific fact and one corresponding to a fact in this very different sense.

**The "Coherence" Theory of Truth.** Partly as a result of difficulties in the correspondence conception and partly for other reasons, another traditional view arose, propounded principally by rationalistic philosophers. A belief is true not because it agrees with fact but because it agrees — that is to say, harmonizes — with the body of knowledge that we possess. The conception of agreement with fact is replaced by that of *consistency,* consistency being a logical property concerning the relations of ideas with one another. It is maintained that when we accept new beliefs as truths it is on the basis of the manner in which they cohere with knowledge we already possess. This does not necessarily imply that all the knowledge we claim to possess can never be abandoned (though adherents to the view would disagree here, some insisting that what is abandoned cannot have been knowledge in the first place). But if part of it *is* abandoned when a new belief is accepted, it is because the new belief coheres better with the great bulk of our experience and knowledge than does the part abandoned. Thus it would be held that in the history of science theories have been chosen as "true" because they have been the theories which have best supplemented the main body of scientific knowledge. It cannot have been because of their verification by "fact"; for more than one theory, indeed an endless number of different theories, can be devised to explain the same set of facts. Thus the Ptolemaic theory of the solar system was abandoned in favor of the Copernican not because it failed to "agree" with all the facts, for it explained as much as the Copernican did, but because the latter, as Copernicus himself said, was "simpler," more elegant mathematically, and a more harmonious addition to the body of science than the former.

There are numerous elaborate arguments in favor of the "coherence" definition, and it is impossible for us to consider all of them. But the following objections may be cited as carrying force with and meeting with acceptance among many philosophers today.

**Critical Remarks.** (1) Even if the element of agreement with fact *were* entirely eliminated and attention to the relationship among ideas alone *could* be achieved, this would hardly be a sufficient guarantee of *factual* truth. For it is possible that a system of beliefs should be perfectly consistent and yet that each of these beliefs should be false. We have seen this in discussing the nature of formal science. We have seen that beliefs may be deduced from one another in perfect consistency depending solely on the observance of *formal* relationships between them. In fact, we may have a consistent deductive system in which there is neither truth nor falsity. Thus coherence or consistency can never by itself suffice for the establishment of truths of fact. The coherence theory would be justified only if pure mathematics alone constituted knowledge, if we were concerned only with *formal* truth.

(2) There appears to be a certain amount of plausibility to the coherence view where complex scientific theories are concerned. When, however, we take an unpretentious statement like "Jim loves Joan" or "Smith is the mayor of Boston," it is difficult to see how these can be true except as referring to something which is not just another statement or idea but what we all call a fact. To consider the consistency of these statements with other statements already accepted by us is an important factor in estimating their truth; often we accept statements as true because they follow from other statements which we know to be true. But if statements are inferred from other statements, then the *other* statements, or statements from which *they* are inferred, must be verified by reference to fact. In the case of many scientific theories, since we are not describing simple facts which we can directly observe, there is no question that the element of convention or expedience plays a relatively greater part in their acceptance. But here again, it is the ability of a theory to predict facts that *can* be observed that constitutes its adequacy and that is the final determining factor. For if elegance and convenience alone counted, then certainly mythology would have been substituted for laborious

theoretical speculation.. A theory is accepted not only because it can explain all facts already observed (for it is true that an infinite number of theories can meet *this* requirement) but because consequences (predicting facts as yet unknown) can be deduced from it which will be capable of subsequent verification. This requirement of conforming to *future* observations can certainly not be met by every theory. To invent a theory to fit the facts after they have been examined is easy — but the procedure of empirical science involves much more than that.

**Pragmatic Theories of Truth.** Pragmatic theories of truth were formulated with the conscious intention of avoiding objections to which the preceding theories are susceptible. We shall consider two forms of the pragmatic conception. One represents the views of James and the British philosopher F. C. S. Schiller (1864-1937), the other those of Peirce and Dewey.

**Truth and Value: the "True" as the "Useful."** Schiller starts with the assumption that when we judge a belief to be true we are *evaluating* it. Just as we evaluate certain things as good and bad, pleasant and unpleasant, beautiful and ugly, so we evaluate the things called propositions or beliefs as true and false. Thus truth is a form of value. What is meant by the terms "true" and "false"? According to Schiller, these are terms which mean, respectively, that a proposition is *useful* or *useless*. When an individual declares a belief to be "true," this means that the belief in so far as it is entertained by him fits in with the sum total of his interests. Sometimes the individual will pronounce a belief to be true and subsequently retract this judgment. This means, on Schiller's view, that in the course of time the belief has proved useless and is therefore rejected, that is, called false. Now valuation is a psychological act. But this does not mean that the determination of what is true and what false is an individual matter. On the contrary, what come to be accepted as truths are the results of social intercourse. Since man is a social being, truth is a social product. Individual truth-valuations are altered and corrected under social influences, until certain beliefs are accepted generally. It is not the mere making of the valuation that is important but the *sustaining* of it. A truth may start as entertained by a minority of one, but it cannot be a truth if it remains in that state.

> The use-criterion selects the individual truth-valuations, and constitutes thereby the objective truth which obtains social recognition. . . . Truth is the useful, efficient, workable, to which our practical experience tends to restrict our truth-valuations; if anything the reverse of this professes to be true, it is (sooner or later) detected and rejected.*

Schiller calls his pragmatism *humanism,* because of his emphasis that all theories and beliefs can be neither meaningful nor true unless some human value is inherent in them. He sums his view up thus:

> As regards the psychical fact of the truth-valuation, Truth may be called an ultimate function of our intellectual activity. As regards the objects valued as "true," Truth is that manipulation of them which turns out upon trial to be useful, primarily for any human end, but ultimately for that perfect harmony of our whole life which forms our final aspiration.†

**Critical Remarks.** Objections against this conception of truth must take their starting-point from a consideration of how vague the term "useful" is.

(1) Does Schiller mean that the true is the "useful" in the sense of being applicable technologically, or of affording some practical social satisfaction? If so, then to say that Sophroniscus was the father of Socrates, or that the amoeba reproduces by binary fission, would not be to speak truth, for neither of these truths affords such utility or satisfaction. It would appear, from the immediately preceding quotation, that for Schiller those beliefs which ultimately make for human happiness are true, while those which do not are false. But the his-

---

* *Humanism,* Ch. III, Sec. III
† *Ibid.*

tory of human frustration and misery shows that what men desire to be true, or what if true would make them happy, is thwarted by facts. That a fearful war rages is true, but hardly conducive to the harmony which we seek.

(2) Is a belief "useful" in the negative sense that it causes us no intellectual inconvenience to accept it, or that there is no particular reason why it should not be accepted, or that it fits in well with what we already regard as true? But there was no intellectual inconvenience at one time in regarding the earth as the fixed center of the universe, nor was there any particular reason, socially or otherwise, why it should not have been accepted, nor was it inconsistent with the existent body of knowledge.

(3) Is a belief "useful" in that it is in some sense *simpler* than an alternative belief, or that it facilitates mental labor? Schiller says that "what decided the rejection of the Ptolemaic epicycles in favor of the Copernican astronomy was not any sheer failure to represent celestial motions, but the growing cumbrousness of the assumptions and the growing difficulty of the calculations which its 'truth' involved." But it could not have been *merely* this consideration which was the reason for the truth-valuation. For if it were, then a more simple and socially intelligible theory than the Copernican could have been found; in fact, a simpler theory in some sense than any theory now accepted by science can always be found. And in general, as we have already remarked in discussing the coherence theory, if it is elegance and simplicity and poetical richness that we desire, fiction should replace science.

(4) Does the fact that the bulk of society prefers a given belief mean that it is true? There certainly is no contradiction in saying, and it is easily conceivable, that a single man may entertain a belief that is true while the rest of society regards it as false. To hold that social acceptance is the criterion of truth is to base the criterion of truth on historical accidents. It confuses an accidental occurrence with a logical method. It is

not the *fact* of social acceptance that is important but the *ground* or *reason* of acceptance. If it should be the case that a minority of one always contradicts the judgment of society, the question which side is right depends on the kind of *methods* respectively employed, not on the force of numbers.

**The True as the "Workable."** James to a considerable extent shares the view of Schiller. He holds that ideas are true if they "work"; that "ideas (which themselves are but parts of our experience) become true just in so far as they help us to get into satisfactory relation with other parts of our experience, to summarize them and get about among them by conceptual short-cuts instead of following the interminable succession of particular phenomena." Truth, as for Schiller, is one kind of goodness (value). "The true is the name of whatever proves itself to be good in the way of belief, and good, too, for definite, assignable reasons." What is *true* for us is what it is *better* for us to believe. Again, " 'The true,' to put it very briefly, is only the expedient in the way of our thinking, just as 'the right' is only the expedient in the way of our behaving."

There is latent here a conception of truth more exact than Schiller's conception of it as the "useful." James was influenced by Peirce and Dewey as well as by Schiller. For them it is not sufficient to say that truth is a special kind of goodness or satisfactoriness. We must specify what kind of goodness it is.

**The Reinterpretation of "Agreement" or "Correspondence."** Our sketch of Dewey's conception of significant knowledge prepares us almost at once to state his conception of truth, based on the view of Peirce and stated by him in an original manner. Truth *is* correspondence or agreement or accordance with reality in *some* sense, but a sense quite different from the usual one which starts out, as we saw, with the separation of ideas from facts, or of mind from nature. The difficulty of the traditional view of "agreement" with reality can be seen from Dewey's illustration (already cited) of the man lost in the forest. Suppose this man "compares" his idea with the reality, in order to see whether it is "true," that is, whether it is the idea of the proper way to get out. With what reality should he compare it? If he compares it with what falls within the ken of his observation, that reality comprises no more than the situation of his being lost, and an idea of it alone cannot help him. The reality of which he needs to form an idea must comprise much more than this. It must include a total environment, consisting of the path out and of numerous other things. But if so, it is obvious that with such a reality he cannot compare his idea, in the ordinary sense of "comparison." It is not something given to him ready-made for comparison. The only kind of comparison he can make is to use the idea

> as a working hypothesis, as a plan of action, and proceed to *act* upon it, to use it as a director and controller of one's divagations instead of stumbling blindly around until one is either exhausted or accidentally gets out. Now suppose one uses the idea — that is to say, the present facts projected into a whole in the light of absent facts — as a guide of action. Suppose, by means of its specifications, one works one's way along until one comes upon familiar ground — finds one's self. *Now,* one may say, my idea was right, it was in accord with facts; it agrees with reality. That is, acted upon sincerely, it has led to the desired conclusion; it has, *through action,* worked out the state of things which it contemplated or intended. The agreement, correspondence, is between purpose, plan, and its own execution, fulfillment; between a map of a course constructed for the sake of guiding behavior and the result attained in acting upon the indications of the map. Just how does such agreement differ from success?*

**Truth as Success in Inquiry.** The hypothesis (idea), then, "agrees" with reality in the sense that it is a successful solution of a problem. We determine this "agreement" by experimentation (in Dewey's words, "through action"). It is in *this* sense (in the sense that it is a means or guide to the solution of a problem) that the "true" hypothesis is good or satisfactory, that it "works" or is "useful." As Peirce once pointed out, an idea is not called true because it is satisfactory — it is

---

* *Essays in Experimental Logic,* Ch. VIII, Sec. II.

called satisfactory because it is true. Truth means scientific success, or as we ordinarily say, "verification," with all that this term implies. It is what emerges from the critical employment of the best method that we can develop. It *is* a social product, not in the sense that a majority happens to accept a given belief, but in the sense that no belief can be called true unless it is capable of compelling the universal assent of those who understand. Thus we call the belief that the earth is one among planets and not the fixed center of the universe "true," not because it was always believed by a majority, but because all who subscribe to the method of science would be brought to this view if they persisted in the exercise of the method.

This theory of truth appears capable of absorbing what is best in the traditional correspondence and coherence theories, as well as the emphasis on the factor of value. It acknowledges that agreement with fact is essential, but redefines "agreement." It acknowledges that consistency and harmony with previous knowledge is essential, but insists that this cannot be the exclusive element in truth. And it holds that truth is a value, but attempts to specify unambiguously the sense in which it is.

❖   ❖   ❖

# The Concept of Value

When discussing the "truth-value" of a belief we emphasized the meaning of the first rather than the second word in this expression. In speaking of truth-value we are referring to a kind of goodness, as we are when we speak of the economic value of gold, of the religious value of ritual, of the moral value of charity, of the aesthetic value of a poem. Thus there are various kinds of value (or forms of goodness): what is good in one respect may not be good in another. In reacting to the objects and events of our environment we do not merely describe them but evaluate them, and in fact for the common man as distinguished from the scientist, the latter function is performed far more frequently than the former. His world is not simply one that is, but one that is good and bad. Some philosophers indeed hold that we cannot describe anything without thereby evaluating it in some respect. One of the important tasks of analytical philosophy is to define the concept of value. Here we shall ask what "value," in *general,* means. In Part Three we shall limit ourselves, in accordance with the purpose of speculative philosophy, to ethical, religious, and aesthetic values, which are central in determining man's broadest perspectives. But the reader must note that the present discussion is not wholly understandable apart from the later one, and a number of conclusions at which we arrive now will take on their full meaning only afterwards.

**The Status of Values.** Philosophers have often asked questions of the following kind in the following way: Do values belong to things, or do we endow things with value?

To use the customary terminology, are values "objective" or "subjective"? Do the values of a diamond belong to it in the same way that the quality of hardness does, or does the diamond lack value until it is given that property by human experience? Is a work of art good because of qualities it would possess independently of our judgment about it, or because for one reason or another it has come to be *regarded* as "good" by men?

**The Subjectivist Interpretation.** Those who oppose the view that values are objective usually argue from the fact of our experience that standards of value are relative: they vary with different cultural groups and even with different individuals. For certain groups a given work may represent the highest in artistic value, for another its value is nil, for still another it may represent an abomination. What is sincerely regarded as good by one individual is with equal sincerity regarded as bad by others. To the man in the forest on a cold night flint takes on a greater value than diamond. The subjectivity of values contrasts with the objectivity of other qualities. The squareness of a block of stone is the same for all societies and all individuals, for the man in the forest and the man at home, for the philosopher and the savage, for the ill and the hale.

**Values as Objective Qualities.** Those who argue for the objectivity of values maintain that it is not the value which varies but the different groups or individuals. Their environment or circumstances or biological constitution may prevent them from discerning those qualities called values, just as blindness prevents a man from discerning colors and color-blindness prevents him from discriminating them. A creature who could distinguish only one spatial dimension would not necessarily attach the same meaning to squareness, yet this quality is not on that account held to be subjective. If values are relative, why is a painting by Raphael generally preferred to one by Bill Murphy, even by Bill Murphy himself? Why do we call

Miss A *pretty* and Miss B not? Why do we regard milk as having greater "value" for health than gasoline? If values were subjective we could call any painting or any type of food valuable that we wished; but the fact is that we cannot do so. Our choice is restricted.

The values with which philosophers have been most concerned are moral values. The question whether types of conduct which are called "wrong" or "bad" are *always* wrong or bad, and those called "right" or "good" *always* good or right, is traditionally tied up with the question whether values are objective properties or phenomena of a subjective character.

**Critical Remarks: the Relational Status of Values.** Many philosophers have come to see the inadequacy of both the foregoing extremes, and indeed of putting the whole question into such simple terms. The question, Are values subjective or objective? seems to assume that they must be either purely subjective or purely objective, and that there is no other possibility. But a view widely accepted today is that value is neither exclusively a property of objects or acts, nor exclusively created by human beings. It has both a subjective and an objective *aspect*. The diamond, for example, is not valuable *in itself;* it must be valuable *to* someone and *in some capacity*. But on the other hand, its qualities are not created *by* us; for it is not we who make the diamond hard and brilliant. Both the objective qualities of the diamond and the human act of valuation are necessary in order that a value-relation or value-situation should arise. It is easily conceivable, of course, that our taste should be different and the diamond cease to be valuable. Tastes and conventions differ among different groups and individuals, and they do influence valuations. Yet is is not *purely* taste or convention that determines the character of the valuation. That we *select* certain qualities is wherein the human or subjective factor consists, but that it is *such* qualities and not others that govern our selection is the objective factor. Two persons may value opposite qualities, but it is because these qualities are what they are in each case that they are valued. We do not create the qualities that we value.

To alter the example: the value which a musical composition is said to have is dependent on its being valuable for someone or some group; but this does not mean that the individual or group can decide arbitrarily what they will or will not value. Milk would not be of biological value except to some organism, but this organism does not create the properties which make the milk biologically valuable to it. The existence of value depends upon a relation between the object valued and those who do the valuing, and neither by itself is sufficient.

A "value" itself is not a quality or a thing that can be separated or isolated in the sense that a ball or a house can. The term applies to a relatively complex situation or relation. A value, as we have already indicated, is always a value-*relation* or value-*situation*. This consideration is important. For if we lose sight of it we tend to think of values in far too simple terms, as many do who think it sufficient to ask simply whether values are "objective" or "subjective," or who speak of "a value" as though it were something we could naïvely locate somewhere in space.

We have not yet specifically defined the term "value," in the sense of saying what *kind* of situation or relation is involved whenever we say that something is good or right. We now turn to this problem, and consider three points of view.

**Value and Pleasure.** An opinion which has appealed to many is that a thing is good for someone if it promotes his pleasure, bad if it causes him pain. Thus the value of a painting consists in the pleasure that we (ultimately) can derive from it. Obeying the law is better than not doing so because ultimately it is more conducive to pleasure than is violation of the law. Similarly, the taking of medicine is a good, because although the immediate act of taking it may be painful, it is a means of yielding greater pleasure in the reward of health. The working of kind acts toward others derives its values from the pleasurable satisfaction that we derive therefrom. And so on.

**Critical Remarks.** We may first raise a question by means of an illustration. We say that a real estate lot has economic value — it is a good economically if not otherwise. But where does the element of pleasure enter? We might say that the owner of the lot derives potential pleasure from possible sale. But when we say of something that it is economically valuable we do not refer solely to its relation to one individual — we mean something much broader; and in the case of the lot, this would be clear if we supposed the owner to be the government. Nor do we necessarily mean that the lot is valuable because it can be used pleasurably; for it may have value as a garbage dump. Looking at this theory from another point of view: If a man refrains from a theft which would make no difference to the owner but would increase his own pleasure, we nevertheless regard it as "right" that he does refrain. Again, when the martyr goes to the stake to be burned, his act may have immense moral value, but certainly neither he nor the posterity of his age derives "pleasure" from it. To hold that either does is to use the term "pleasure" in an unjustifiably broad sense. One might perhaps say that the martyr derives satisfaction, in some sense, from his act; else he would not consciously perform it. But it cannot be called pleasurable satisfaction in any case. A tendency among proponents of the present theory is to stretch the sense of the term "pleasure." To stretch the term to meet every case is to prove the theory by making it a definition, which of course can be done for any theory whatever. It appears clear, however, that the term "pleasure" ought not to be used to cover such diverse cases as the judgment of a painting, the sensation of eating, and the act of self-sacrifice.

It is possible to state the present view in two versions, one reflecting an objectivist and the other a subjectivist emphasis. According to one, the value resides in the object or act which yields pleasure; according to the other, the value is identical with the feeling of pleasure. These emphases are not important for our purpose, and the foregoing objections apply indifferently.

**Value as Indefinable.** A second conception of value is based on the assumption that it is incapable of definition. This view has been linked with the name of G. E. Moore. It is substantially as follows.

All concepts (or notions, or meanings) may be divided into the complex and the simple. Complex concepts are all capable of being defined, for when we define one we employ simpler concepts to explain it. Thus the concept "horse" is definable, because it refers to something capable of being *analyzed into parts*. If we took the concepts used to define the concept "horse," which are simpler than it, and wished to define *them*, we would do this by using simpler concepts still, until (theoretically) we would come to concepts that are absolutely simple, and these would be incapable of definition, for there would be nothing simpler to explain them by. An example of an absolutely simple concept is redness. We can *show* someone what the quality redness is by pointing to something red, but we cannot *explain* what it is, because it is a perfectly simple quality not further analyzable. It is true that we can describe the physical conditions under which redness occurs — the kind of light vibrations and eye-action which accompanies it. But it is not this which we perceive, it is the *quality* of redness. We can explain to a blind man what a horse is, but not what redness is. He either knows it or does not know it, and never can if he is congenitally blind.

Now according to Moore, goodness or value is exactly the same kind of quality as redness — absolutely simple. It belongs to certain things or situations just as redness belongs to certain other things. Either we perceive the value of something or we do not — there is no way of explaining it to us. The reason why we so often attempt to define wherein the value of things consists is that all things which have value have other properties *also*, just as all objects which are red have other properties and are not merely red. In our attempt at definition what we do is confuse the value with these other properties. According to Moore, when it is said that all good things are pleasurable (or that "the good is pleasure") we cannot mean that "good" *means* "pleasure"; this is nonsense. What we mean is that good things *also* have the quality of being pleasurable (which may or may not be true). It is as though, in saying that an orange is yellow, we meant that "an orange" *means* "yellow"; what we can intelligibly mean is that the quality of being an orange is associated with another quality, that of being yellow.

**Critical Remarks.**   Since the property of goodness, which belongs to certain objects, is held to be indefinable, several questions at once present themselves. Is this property the same for all men, so that they should all agree that certain objects are good, just as they all agree that certain objects are red? But it is a fact that the agreement in the one case is infinitely less than in the other. Is the wide difference of opinion on what is and is not good due to the fact that the conditions under which men make their value-appraisals differ, just as, if some of us habitually wore blue spectacles we should not agree with others as to what is red? If, in a given group or society, the majority agree on what is good, how shall they convince a dissenter? If he honestly persists in calling certain things bad which they call good, would it not follow that the two sides cannot hope to have ethical discourse in common, since goodness can be pointed to but not explained or described? There are two major objections to Moore's view.

**How Are Values Tested?**   On this view, first of all, it is impossible for anyone ever to be in error on matters of moral conduct. For there is no way of analyzing what a person calls right or good in order to show him that it is in fact wrong or bad. There is no *test* for value. Suppose, further, that a person tells us he perceives the value of an object. Since he cannot in the nature of the case communicate a reason, we cannot know whether he does or not, or whether, if he does, the ob-

ject is valuable for us both in the *same respect*. Now this is in
direct conflict with the facts. If we could not set up standards
by which to convince one another of ethical matters, then anything could be good for anyone at all, no two persons might
have the same ethical standards; all would be equally acceptable, and a chaos of values would result. But the fact is that
we *do* set up standards, that people *are* often convinced, that
disagreement with a standard *is* often based upon a *reason;*
and in general, far from there being a chaos of values, there is
widespread uniformity (though whether this is for better or
worse is another ethical question).

If the property of goodness has the same status as the property of redness, then it is surely capable of test. If a person
cannot distinguish the color orange from the color red and
maintains that they are the same, we can convince him that
they are different by proving that the light waves in the two
cases have different frequencies of vibration. Moore would
reply — But the man still cannot distinguish the color red from
the color orange; he knows that they are associated with other
qualities that differ but does not know wherein *they* differ.
This seemingly foolproof reply rests on a confusion which it
is of the greatest importance to grasp. This will be clear from
the following point.

**Sensed Qualities and Known Qualities.** In the second
place, how does Moore determine which qualities are complex
and which perfectly simple? Is the quality of beauty absolutely simple (and hence indefinable)? Is tallness? Is heavi-
ness? Is vindictiveness? How do these differ from redness
and goodness?

Moore's confusion arises from his failure to distinguish between qualities in so far as they are *sensed* or *felt* and qualities
in so far as they are *known* or *understood*. If we consider
qualities from the former standpoint, that is, from the standpoint of their being subjectively experienced, then *all qualities
alike* are perfectly simple. For each feeling — the feeling of
no matter what — has a uniqueness, distinctiveness, and indi-

visibility of its own. As felt, all qualities are incommunicable, unanalyzable, and indefinable; we cannot define a *feeling,* but only a *word* or *expression* or *concept.* As a subjectively experienced whole, a horse is no more definable than redness. It is not "a solidungulate perissodactyl mammal of the family Equidae and genus Equus" that we *sense;* what we sense is the horse.

On the other hand, in so far as qualities are *known, all* are definable and analyzable (though for purposes of expedience, and since we must stop somewhere, we may *leave* certain qualities undefined). And here we may return to the example of the testing of red and orange. The physical analysis of a color is precisely what we mean by knowing it. What Moore would have to mean in holding that the man is still unable to "distinguish" red from orange is that he is unable to *sense* the difference. But he may nevertheless *understand* the difference. For as we have in detail tried to emphasize throughout this Part, understanding and knowledge relate not to private sensation but to what is communicable and public. What applies to redness applies to any other concept, including that of value.

**Value and Preference or Desire.** A widespread theory since ancient times is that things are good if and only if we desire or prefer them. "We do not desire a thing because it is good," says Spinoza; "it is good because we desire it." Here again there are objectivist and subjectivist emphases. Some might emphasize the experience of desire; others the object desired. But all agree on the inseparability of the two factors. This view has obvious advantages over the others. It avoids the identification of the valuable and the merely pleasurable, holding that we may desire what brings no pleasure, and it is thus able to account for the value of the martyr's act. Such an act is good because it is preferred and not because it is pleasurably anticipated. This view also does justice to the facts of relativity in values: value standards vary with the varying preferences and desires of different individuals and groups.

**Critical Remarks.** There are, however, objections against this view in the preceding formulation of it. May not something be desired or preferred and yet be bad? The drug addict desires heroin; yet we say that it is not good but bad for him. A person may desire to marry another; yet it certainly makes sense to assert that his choice would not be good. On the other hand also, may there not be things which are good but which we do not desire? If a man does not despite all warning prefer to take medicine or be operated upon, we could still say that such a course would be good for him. And so on. Now there is no doubt that wherever there is desire there is *some* value, namely, that which arises from the immediate gratification of the desire. The taking of the drug, the occurrence of the marriage, have an immediate or temporary value which cannot be ruled out of existence. But this is hardly sufficient to warrant our calling the event in question "right" or "good." In other words, we cannot divorce an act or object from the consequences which ensue upon the commission of the act or the possession of the object, so far as its value is concerned. We judge values to belong to interconnected situations rather than to the immediate satisfaction of our impulses or cravings. This point will be stressed again in Chapter XVII.

**"The Desired" and "the Desirable."** There appears to be an important element of truth in the coupling of value and desire. But a number of philosophers have recognized the necessity of improving the foregoing formulation of their interrelationship. The good, it has been pointed out, is not that which we *desire* but that which is *desirable,* not that which we prefer but that which is preferable. The drug addict desires something that is not desirable for him; the sick man does not desire what is nevertheless desirable. In this way of putting the matter, we take note of the relevance of consequences in our valuation. But the problem only begins — for what is the meaning of "desirable"? It is easy to become confused here. We might, for example, define "the desirable" as "that which we ought to desire"; and we might define this in turn as meaning "that which it is good to desire." But this lands us in a circular definition, for we have already defined "the good" as "the desirable." The occurrence of such predicaments in the history of ethics — in far less obvious form, of course — no doubt motivated Moore in concluding that value is indefinable.

There are various promising possibilities. We might say that the desirable is what we would desire if we were aware of the consequences of our choice. This is perhaps not broad enough, for while it would explain in what sense an act like the taking of drugs is undesirable, it would not explain in what sense a real estate lot is something (economically) "desirable." We might suggest that the desirable is what satisfies a given interest. Thus the interest of health is not satisfied by the taking of drugs; the interests of housing, garbage dumping, etc., are capable of being satisfied by the lot. We do not, however, wish to enter into an exhaustive analysis, but merely to raise questions connected with a conception of the meaning of "desirable." May a thing be desirable for society and undesirable for an individual? Can the interests of the individual be segregated from those of society? May an individual have genuinely conflicting interests, so that what is desirable relative to one interest is undesirable relative to another? Is there such a thing as the "most desirable" end or purpose of man, or of society? Our discussions in Part Three may serve to throw light on some of these questions, and to stimulate others. Perhaps the point that should impress itself uppermost in the mind of the reader is that the philosopher who ceases to ask questions and to look for new complications has ceased to be a philosopher.

# PART THREE

# The Speculative Function
# of Philosophy

❖   ❖   ❖

# The Supernaturalistic
# World-Perspective

In turning our attention to speculative philosophy, we shall be concerned, as we have already explained, with attempts to formulate an all-pervasive or comprehensive interpretation of the broadest phases of human experience. Some of the theories we shall consider are of a very special character, but of a kind nevertheless which relates ultimately to the formulation of a world-perspective. Throughout the course of discussion we apply the tools of philosophic analysis developed in Part Two, in order to help define important concepts and to characterize important types of speculative thinking.

**What is Supernaturalism? The Concept of God.** Supernaturalism, the world-view held by so many millions of people today, is older than philosophy, but is not the oldest of reflective philosophical theories. In its broadest sense, as the term implies, it is the view that there is a being (or beings) in some sense higher than or superior to what we call nature. So defined, it would not apply to the belief, held chiefly among primitive peoples, in magical agencies or "souls" manifesting themselves within natural objects, a view known as *animism*. Nor is it to be used without qualification as synonymous with the term *theism*, or belief in a God or gods. For the term "God" has been and is sometimes used in a non-supernaturalistic sense. Supernaturalistic theism has for some peoples meant belief in a system of deities governing the various phases of nature or human life. But among philosophers it has generally meant that there is a unitary being distinct from nature and standing in definite relations to nature.

**The Attributes of God.** Belief in God as a supernatural being is often bound up with a number of other beliefs. First, God cannot be part of nature, though nature may or may not be (supernaturalists differ here) part of God's being. Second, God is responsible for the existence of nature: God cannot be supposed to have come into being, the predicates of space and time being inapplicable to him, whereas nature must derive its being from God. Third, God is more powerful than and better than nature. This last follows from the second. For if nature and all values in nature emanate from God, power and value must belong to God at least in a higher degree. Most supernaturalists ascribe to God not only greater power and greater goodness but perfect power and perfect goodness. God is said to be eternal and infinite — infinite in power, goodness, and knowledge; eternal in that for him there is no time.

**Anthropomorphism.** It is necessary to point out the differences between the conception of God embodied in traditional religion, for instance in the older Hebrew conception, and that of philosophers and philosophic theologians. The former is *anthropomorphic* as well as supernaturalistic; that is, God is endowed with attributes which characterize man. Thus in ancient literature and in a good deal of popular organized religion to this day, God is held to be capable of wrath, jealousy, vengeance, and displeasure. Philosophers have usually tried to avoid such anthropomorphism, realizing that it is the product of the crude attempt to envisage a supernatural being pictorially. In a sense, however, any attempt to relate God to human affairs involves some anthropomorphic element. Thus the assumption that God responds to prayer, that he participates in and influences human relations, that he rewards and punishes, in short, the assumption on which much of organized supernaturalistic religion is based, is inevitably anthropomorphic. Some theologians avoid this conception by supposing that God's relation to human affairs consists not in specific participation but in the consequences for the universe as a whole of his infinite goodness and his omnipotence.

**Minimal Supernaturalism: "Deism."** There are other supernaturalists who hold a purely impersonal or non-anthropomorphic belief in God, namely, that although such a being is the creator of nature, he does not interfere with the course he has fixed for it, and is indifferent to human affairs. This view, originating in ancient philosophy, is in modern times often known as *deism*. The term "deism," however, is misleading, because it is likely to be confused with a view of the same name which is far closer to the traditional supernaturalistic assumption of divine intervention in human affairs, but which differs in maintaining that truth about God can be arrived at by the natural powers of the mind (rationalistically) and need not be accepted merely on faith as "revealed" truth. In this latter sense, "deism" (developed chiefly in eighteenth century English philosophy) reflects the doctrine of "natural" religion. In the former sense, "deism" is sometimes distinguished from "theism," asserting that God transcends nature (is completely "outside" it) not only in his being but in his activity; though the student will do better to regard it less confusedly as simply one form of theism.

**"Miracle": Two Senses.** By a "miracle" is ordinarily understood an event resulting from a supernatural act that suspends a law of nature. In this sense non-anthropomorphic or deistic supernaturalism excludes belief in miracles. In a wider sense of the term "miracle," however, meaning anything inexplicable in natural terms and humanly incomprehensible, all supernaturalism rests essentially on the concept of miracle; for such matters as creation of nature are held by all supernaturalists to be absolutely beyond human inquiry and understanding. A "miracle" in the first sense, that is, a specific supernatural intervention in the natural course of events, is also a miracle in the broader sense; but belief in the latter (e.g., in a supernatural creation) does not necessarily imply belief in the former.

**The Idea of Revelation.** The success or failure of supernaturalism as a philosophically tenable world-view obviously
depends on whether it can be shown that "nature" is not all-
inclusive; or positively stated, whether the hypothesis of God
is supported by evidence. There have always been many who
maintain that evidence for the existence of God is not to be
assembled in the same manner as evidence for other hypotheses.
It is something that concerns faith rather than active inquiry,
fidelity of belief regardless of all arguments to the contrary.
"Faith," in religions like Judaism, Christianity, and Islam,
means "faith in revelation," that is, in God's manifestation of
himself to those whom he divinely inspires to record his Word
— in the Ten Commandments, for example. We must presumably refrain from asking, What evidence have we that the
inspired writers were *supernaturally* inspired? or, Regardless
of how they came to be inspired, what assurance is there that
what they record is *true?* or, By what kind of test could we
ever *identify* an inspiration as a "supernatural" one? Faith in
revelation means unshakable belief that God has revealed himself and therefore exists. Throughout philosophic history
there has been conflict among supernaturalists regarding the
proper approach to belief in the supernatural. On the one hand,
there are those to whom faith alone is sufficient; on the other,
those who consider philosophical reasoning sufficient; and in
between, those who, like St. Thomas Aquinas (1225?-1274),
consider both as requisite (with varying emphases on the one or
the other) and as complementary. Supernaturalistic philosophers, as distinguished from theologians, have usually been
dissatisfied with the first of these approaches, and have attempted
to construct specific arguments to justify their position.

**The Argument for a First Cause (the "Cosmological"
Argument).** One of the oldest arguments amounts essentially to the assertion that nature — the realm in which physical, biological, social, and psychological events take place —
requires an explanation. Just as within nature we attempt to
explain all things, so we must explain nature as a whole. But

we cannot explain nature by employing the concept "nature" alone, just as we cannot explain, for instance, why the earth moves by referring to the earth alone. Thus we must explain it by appealing to the concept of something *super*natural. Nature could not have brought itself into being; it must have had some cause. Or the argument is sometimes stated in this manner: Any event whatever must have had some cause, it is a contradiction to say that anything brings itself into existence. But by the same reasoning, the cause is itself the effect of some previous cause. And so on back, in the case of each preceding cause. Now this chain of causes must have had a beginning. There must consequently have been a first or ultimate cause, itself uncaused, responsible for the initiation of the series of events. This series of events is nature, and the first cause, God.

**Critical Remarks.** (1) The foregoing argument assumes that every event must have a cause. Now to say that every event *has* a cause is one thing; but to say that every event *must* have a cause is something very different. For this means that to say that some events are causeless is to say something contradictory. But although the assertion that an event occurs by chance may be *false,* it is not *self-contradictory*.

(2) The argument as usually stated further assumes that the series of causes (granting that every event has a cause) *must* have had a *beginning*. Here again, if this means that to deny such a statement is to become involved in a contradiction, it is an unwarranted assumption. Whether a series of causes *did* have a beginning is one question; but it is certainly not *necessary* that it should have had a beginning. Mathematics shows us that the *notion* of a series without a first term is at least *consistent*. Thus in the series . . . . -5, -4, -3, -2, -1, 0, 1, 2, 3, 4, 5 . . . . each term alike is preceded and succeeded by one integer, yet it has neither a first nor a last term.

(3) The argument fails to give an adequate reason why, though every cause must allegedly have had a previous cause, the "first" cause is excepted from this rule. To say that the

rule applies only to natural events is simply a restatement of the same point; for the question still remains, Why may we assume that the supernatural requires no cause and is its own cause? The usual answer is that the supernatural is something incomprehensible — we can know that there must *be* such, but we cannot know *what* it is, we cannot know anything *about* it. The argument falls back on the presupposition of an unknowable reality with miraculous properties (in the sense defined above). We shall have occasion later to examine conceptions of an unknowable reality in other world-views that do not appeal to the concept of miracle, and to indicate, as we have indeed already done in Part Two, Chapter X, their incompatibility with a scientific attitude. Here we need only point out that the reply to our question is not a consistent one. For to assert that the first cause is *different* from natural causes *is* to assert something *about* it, something very significant. Difficulties of this kind indicate that an appeal to faith is sooner or later inevitable for supernaturalists who appeal to argument.

**The Argument from Order in Nature (the "Teleological" Argument).** The cosmological argument tries to show that the very *existence* of a natural world implies a creator. The so-called teleological argument, perhaps the most popular of all, tries to prove God's existence from the *character* of the natural world. The argument may be stated in two different ways, the first of which is more general than the second.

(1) Nature, it is asserted, is not a mere chance collection of events, a mere jumble of accidents, but an orderly affair. The planets move regularly in their orbits, planted seeds grow uniformly into complex structures, the seasons succeed each other in order. Everything conforms to pattern, is governed by law. Now this gigantic order of nature cannot have ordered itself in this way, nor can it have been a huge accident. It requires the existence of an intelligence responsible for it. The presence of a pattern or structure necessitates our assuming a designer or architect whose purpose it was to create this.

(2)   The most cursory examination of things suffices to reveal that everything fulfills some function or other. Everything has its "purpose" in the total scheme of nature, whether animate or inanimate. But certainly it is fantastic to suppose that every object in the universe consciously chose for itself a function to fulfill. The only alternative is to suppose that the respective functions were planned or designated for the various objects; in other words, that their co-ordinated activity reflects a single universal mind.

**Two Meanings of "Purpose."**   The first of the two foregoing forms of argument asserts that nature itself is the *result* of an intention or purpose. The second asserts that nature is the *instrument* by which a goal or result is achieved. For the first, nature is an *end,* for the second, it is a *means* to an end; but in either case it is maintained that nature reflects supernatural intelligence or purpose. Hence the application of the broad term "teleological" or purposive, from the Greek *telos,* meaning "end" or "fulfillment." Now it is important to note that the term "purpose" has at least two uses, both of which are implied in the two forms of the argument. (a) It sometimes means the *will* or *intention* to achieve some end or goal. We say, in this usage, that Smith's purpose in traveling was such-and-such; that God's purpose in creating was such-and-such. (b) It sometimes means the *end* or *goal* itself. We say, the purpose of an axe is chopping, the purpose of a ship is sailing, the purpose of using a bed is comfort. We leave it to the reader to discern the presence of both these usages in each of the forms of the teleological argument.

**Critical Remarks.**   (1)   First a general point relating to either form of the argument. Even if it be granted that nature is arranged as the first assumes, or in addition that everything in nature "works toward ends" as the second assumes, it would not *necessarily* follow that only a supernatural agency could account for this. Again we must point out that there is no self-contradiction in the denial of this necessity. But — so a counter-objection might run — if the existence of a supernatural being does not necessarily follow from these assumptions, would it not be a highly *likely* or *well-grounded* conclusion? We must turn to the assumptions themselves in order to answer this.

(2) Let us take the second form of the argument. Here an important distinction has to be observed. When we say that the "function" of a stone lying in a given place is to divert a current of water, we *may* interpret this as the result of design. But we can also interpret it as due to wholly natural causes. On such an interpretation no object has an *absolute* or *single* "purpose" under all circumstances. If a random stone is to be spoken of as having a purpose or function, this is not something with which the stone is intrinsically endowed or antecedently equipped; it is determined only *after* the stone is found to function within its environment in a definite way. But the same stone may function in many other ways, depending on the character of that environment; and it cannot therefore be said to have "a" function without qualification. Its function will be a relative and not an absolute one. Thus the assumption of a single purpose on which this teleological argument rests is far from being the only interpretation of the facts. Many would go further and say that it is more an expression of faith than a statement of fact. And it is confronted by the task of explaining the relation between a natural and a supernatural realm, while the alternative suggested is not.

(3) We may now consider the assumptions of the first form of the teleological argument, which are the really basic ones. Nature, it is maintained, is "orderly" and not "disorderly." But how significant is this assertion? If nature were "disorderly," would not that situation constitute merely a *different* order? Strictly speaking, it is self-contradictory to speak of nature as possibly lacking order. Any situation, any arrangement among existing things constitutes some kind of order. There can only be situations differing *relative to human adaptation* and human expectation. Now we do, of course, dis-

tinguish between *chance* in the universe and *law*. The former is a state in which we cannot predict definitely what will occur in the future when we are acquainted with what has already occurred; while the latter is a sequence of events always repeated under the same conditions, enabling us to predict. But a chance order of nature is not less "orderly" than an order of law or repeated sequence. Again, if we regard our very same world from another angle, there is a sense in which its diversity is far more prominent than its uniformity. If the seasons succeed one another according to topographical and meteorological patterns, on the other hand a specific daily state of a given area seems entirely spontaneous; if there are laws governing stellar events, on the other hand there seems no rhyme or reason to the specific distribution of the stars in the heavens; if, in general, all facts occur in accordance with law, each fact on the other hand is unique, specific, and brute. Thus, if objectively speaking there can be neither greater nor less order in nature, the argument that the character which nature has requires us to assume an extra-natural architect collapses. Either any order necessarily requires us to assume this, or no order necessarily does. To maintain the former of these alternatives is simply to restate the cosmological argument.

**The "Ontological" Argument.**  A third traditional argument, first fully stated by St. Anselm (1033-1109), is quite different from the other two. It may be rendered as follows. Let us, instead of speaking of "God," speak of "an absolutely perfect being." Now if we consider the very *meaning* of this notion, we find that what it refers to *must exist*. For by an absolutely perfect being we mean one that is complete or possesses all possible properties; and this includes the property of existence. The idea of absolute perfection being non-existent is self-contradictory; for not to exist is not to be absolutely perfect — an absolutely perfect being that was only a fiction would be robbed of a basic element of its perfection or completeness. Now any other concept whatever can be conceived without being conceived as existent; but of the concept "absolutely perfect being," the very *definition* implies the existence of such a being.

**Critical Remarks.** This argument has a superficial plausibility. Yet few can accept such a mode of proof. The conclusion does indeed follow from the definition of "absolutely perfect being." But this makes the argument merely a tautology or restatement of a definition. It amounts to the assertion "If something has existence as one of its properties, it exists." Though this is absolutely true, it proves nothing factual or positive. For the statement "*If* something exists, it exists" does not necessarily imply the statement "Something does exist." The ontological argument has, moreover, the embarrassing consequence of assigning to God undesirable as well as desirable properties.

The ontological argument, it is interesting to note, is later employed by a naturalist, Spinoza. Spinoza uses the term "God" to designate the all-inclusive system of the universe. He holds (in the manner of the ontological argument) that God or the universe necessarily exists. It is in the nature of the universe to exist. To suppose it not to exist is to suppose something self-contradictory.

**The Rationalistic Character of the Traditional Arguments; Kant's Analysis.** Not only the ontological but the other two arguments are based on a rationalistic methodology. The reasoning is not supported by empirical or observational evidence but consists in deducing the consequences of principles alleged to be *a priori,* that is, "self-evident" or necessarily true — for example, the principle that every series must have a first term, that order in nature presupposes an agent responsible for it, that "absolute perfection" must exist. Empiricist philosophers have always emphasized that reasoning by itself is insufficient for the *discovery* of any existent circumstance; that the only way of showing that something *exists* is to appeal to the realm of fact, which can be investigated and described. To this Kant added a striking demonstration that if we remain within the domain of *a priori* reasoning about what transcends all experience, we can construct equally plausible arguments for each of two contradictory theses. For in such a procedure our concern is no longer to marshal facts but to marshal ingenuity. What transcends experience can be neither proved nor refuted.

**Two Interpretations of the A Priori.** We saw (p. 94) that Kant *does* believe in some *a priori* knowledge. It will pay to digress for a moment in order to distinguish between the kind of *a priori* knowledge he believes we have and the kind he shows to be futile. The former is (allegedly) knowledge which we know to be certain without appealing to experience, but which is *about* experience; which cannot be *proved* by experience because of its universality, but for which we can assemble *illustrative evidence* in experience. The latter is (allegedly) knowledge which we know to be certain without appealing to experience, but which is about something *beyond* or deeper than all experience; which can be neither proved nor illustrated by experience. Kant's justification for maintaining the former kind lies in his theory of the organizing structure which makes conscious experience itself possible. This has already been alluded to (Part Two, pp. 94-5).

**The Argument from Man as a Moral Being.** It will be recalled that by means of his distinction between knowledge and faith, Kant holds it possible to entertain belief in the existence of God while denying that *knowledge* of God is possible. We shall not repeat his reasoning here, but we must repeat the basic assumption which underlies it, namely, that belief in God (and in "immortality of the soul") is necessary if we are to understand man's moral experience. Men *are* creatures with moral interests and moral values; they act as well as think — indeed, they *primarily* act. Now moral values cannot be explained, they cannot be made intelligible, unless they are associated with the notions of God, immortality, and "freedom of the will." Thus these notions, although they lack a *cognitive* value (they are not elements in proven knowledge), have an all-important *practical* (or moral) value in explaining and guiding conduct.

This point of view has been stated in divers forms since Kant's time, with differing special emphases. In general, the moral argument for the existence of God bases itself on the assumption that "reality" is not exhausted by a realm of things and of facts but contains also a realm of values and ideals, not only moral but aesthetic and perhaps other values. We can explain facts in terms of nature, but not values; electricity and gravitation, but not beauty and goodness. This higher "realm of values" must in turn have been derived from a supreme source, one which invests our conduct with significance and purpose.

**Critical Remarks.** The Kantian contrast between faith and knowledge is not perfectly consistent. For to assert belief in God's existence is already a claim to knowledge of *some* kind. No belief can be absolutely isolated or divorced from other beliefs which either imply or are implied by it. And to assert that the ideas of God, immortality, and freedom of will make moral distinctions intelligible is to assert something that has immense cognitive significance. This becomes clear when we ask what the reason is that *only* these ideas endow morals with significance. If we know enough to exclude any other hypothesis as the foundation of ethics, it would seem that we do know something positive about God. Kant's denial of the possibility of transempirical *a priori* knowledge returns to plague his most ingenious efforts to maintain the theistic hypothesis.

The moral argument reaches its conclusion only through a separation of the spheres of fact and value which is by no means a necessary one. Facts and values may instead be regarded as *both* aspects of nature, and indeed as intimately connected or even inseparable. Instead of supposing with the moral argument that ethical values cannot possibly be explained in natural terms, and drawing the inevitable conclusion that a supernaturalistic basis for ethics is the only one, we can conceive of moral standards and moral distinctions as one phenomenon among others within the natural situations that we call instances of human behavior.

The sharp distinction between fact and value implied by supernaturalism goes hand in hand with a sharp distinction between body and soul (or in general, matter and mind). Matter is the realm of things and facts, mind that of values and ideals. Matter is perishable, mind is immortal. And so on. In Chapter XV we shall examine this theory, and a little later in the present chapter we shall have more to say about the kind of moral theory that supernaturalism implies.

**The Claim of Mysticism.**    Just as there are philosophers dissatisfied with the processes of analysis and discursive knowledge who place greater reliance on immediate and direct insight or intuition, so there are those who, applying this general attitude to the problems of supernaturalism, distrust all argumentation and all authority as well, in favor of an alleged immediate insight into the reality of the supernatural. By no means all mystics have interpreted their mystical experiences as evidence for a *supernatural* reality. Among those who have, the number of non-philosophic or lay mystics is relatively large, and includes many who were subsequently canonized as saints. There are also many who look to the insight of mystics as supplementary to, rather than as opposing, theistic argumentation.

**Critical Remarks.**    There is no need to doubt the mystic's veracity when he tells us of a remarkable experience. That he has *had* an experience of a peculiarly personal and overwhelming character may be admitted. But certainly the *interpretation* of this experience is open to question. Since the evidence which it is supposed to contain is something private, we should, if we accepted the supernaturalistic interpretation, be placing credence in the report of an excessively small number of persons, most of whom in addition are bred in a theological atmosphere and most of whom are under a strong emotional stress. That their environmental influences on the one hand, and their psychological makeup of deep desires, hopes, and prepared anticipations of divine revelation on the other, may be the major factors which color their interpretation, as opposed to a dispassionate examination of their experience, in the manner in which a man dispassionately analyzes a dream he has had, cannot be overlooked.

**The Argument from Alleged Miracles; Hume's Analysis.** It has often been maintained that there is empirical evidence for supernaturalism in the form of miracles, which have been recorded in the past and recent past. Miraculous powers have been reported to belong to those later canonized as saints, or to occur in connection with mass prayer and various religious exercises. This type of contention was dealt with very thoroughly by Hume. He pointed out that, in the first place, the testimony of miracles is historical testimony, like any historical document, or report by word of mouth. As such it is open to at least the same doubts that other historical events are open to, and at the very best can gain second-hand acceptance. Now it is far more probable, if we take this historical view, that men are credulous and governed by emotion than that the laws of nature have been suspended. We know from experience in ordinary affairs and in courts of law that the veracity and the observational power of men are far from perfect; and we know that their fabrication in religious matters is proportionately greater. So that as testimony, the evidence for miracles is slim indeed.

But in the second place, according to Hume, there is a far greater objection. Even if the events called "miracles" can be shown to have occurred, there is no way of proving that they are supernatural in character. For whatever occurs, there is a *possible* natural explanation for it. Let us test Hume's point by an example. Suppose that a cripple begins to walk immediately after visiting a shrine. It is possible to explain this fact by citing as causes the physico-chemical bodily changes that often result from a high pitch of emotional intensity and anticipation. Whether in a given case such a hypothesis is correct or not, it at least has the merit that it can be *tested,* while the supernaturalistic explanation cannot be — it must be either believed or disbelieved. We have seen reason to conclude in cases where a given natural explanation is inadequate that it is far more satisfactory to regard ourselves as thus far ignorant of the correct explanation and to continue scientifically trying others than to resort to the supernaturalistic explanation. The latter is always easy, and if we resort to it in one case, why not in all other cases where we encounter obstacles to explanation? There is no specific criterion — except the subjective criterion of pious judgment — by which we can distinguish "supernaturally caused" events from all others. But why is the growth of a seed less wonderful than the cripple's sudden ability to walk? If in the history of science men had resorted to supernatural explanations every time difficulties of explanation cropped up, there would be little science to speak of.

We may state the difficulty in another way. By what criterion are we to recognize a miracle as such, that is, as supernaturally caused? Events do not come with the label "miracle" stamped on some of them. Since "event" is by definition "natural event," what test could possibly establish a given one as having "supernatural" origin? Since a natural explanation is always a possibility, the criterion would seem to be wonder or surprise or perplexity. But these are subjective criteria which depend upon and vary with education, expectation, and emotion.

One final objection strikingly reveals the difficulty in the concept of miracle. To assert that an event is a miracle is to assert that no possible natural explanation can be a correct one. But to assert this means to rule out *in advance* an infinite number of possible explanations — not only without testing them, but without even knowing what they are. Whatever other advantages such a contention may have, it is methodologically absurd.

**Lay Arguments.** (1) Of those who, as members of the great organized religions, accept the hypothesis of the supernatural, perhaps the larger number do so on authority and faith, built up and strengthened from infancy. There are many, however, who have reflected on this hypothesis, and have come to accept it on other grounds. One of the widespread lay arguments is that I (a given individual) have the "feeling" that there must be some guiding force which governs the universe and has planned it, for all things could not have "just come about." `Such an argument must be accorded due respect, and the sincerity and unbiassed judgment of those who advance it must be recognized. But it has little standing, philosophically speaking. The history of human opinion is testimony to the fact that the sincerest of men have believed in witchcraft and demonology. To rely on the judgment of personal intuition is to rely on something governed far more by psychological impulse, however well-intentioned, than by reason and patient analysis.

(2)   Sometimes it is held (and by many other than laymen) that belief in the supernatural is an "instinct" in man, which can indeed be more or less suppressed by various environmental factors. Against this, two replies are in order. First, if it were an instinct, all men would possess it. But we know that most men come to have the belief through training and indoctrination, and that many assert ardent disbelief. If it were instinctive it would manifest itself much earlier, more forcibly, and more pervasively than it does, especially since environmental factors tend to favor its development rather than to suppress it. On these scores it can hardly be compared with the "instincts" properly so called: rage, love, feeding, etc. But secondly, even if it were an instinctive belief, that would constitute no proof of its truth. Such an "instinctive" belief could hardly be classed with others so called as beliefs of "common sense," beliefs socially transmitted by the basic conditions under which the human race subsists, for it relates to no data of common experience. But even the common sense beliefs, as we have seen, are notoriously vague. And in general, if we should see fit to cling to whatever we feel most inclined to believe, we should not need to pursue scientific inquiry.

**Supernaturalism and Moral Values.** We have seen the rôle which an appeal to moral values plays in arguing for the existence of a supernatural being. It was held that the existence of moral values implies the existence of God. But now, instead of asking, What kind of being must exist if we assume that there are moral values? let us ask, What kind of moral values must we adhere to if we assume that there is a supernatural being?

**Moral Standards as Based on Divine Will.** The assumption that supernaturalism is the only possible basis for morality is far more widespread among the masses of men than among philosophers. In fact, it is the most widespread of all theoretical beliefs and the one which comes into greatest play practically. It underlies the greater part of organized religion, and teaches that the ideas of good and evil, rightness and wrongness, virtue and vice, derive their meaning and force ònly from the command of a final arbiter of all conduct, God. Moral standards are determined by God's Will, expressed in his Word — in Western religion, the Ten Commandments, the teaching of the Hebrew prophets, the teaching of Christ and of St. Paul, and, many would add, the interpretation of all this by the Church. What significance, it is argued, could be attached to human conduct if there were no standard higher than those created by men? For if we had only human standards, what judge is to decide between standards that conflict? If nature alone comprised the whole of reality, and all acts were measurable only by natural standards, what justification would there be for saying that one natural standard is any more "right" than another? Within nature alone every act would be as morally correct (or incorrect) as any other, since all acts would merely have the status of natural events, and natural events are ethically neutral. In a blind, brute nature, since all things must ultimately perish, what is done by human beings would not matter one way or the other. Without an absolute, supernatural standard, universal license would prevail.

We shall defer consideration of this viewpoint and of the alternative to it until pp. 212 and 252-3 and Chapters XVI and XVII in general.

**The Problem of Evil.** In most supernaturalistic philosophy God possesses, as we have had occasion to point out, the attributes of benevolence and omnipotence, and man is an agent morally responsible for the acts which he performs. (The latter assumption is essential to any viewpoint for which the ideas of praise and blame, approval and disapproval, punishment and reward have meaning; for if an individual is not regarded as responsible for his actions, the application of these appraisals is nonsense.) With these assumptions, supernaturalists have been troubled since ancient times by the so-called problem of evil (suggested though not explicitly posed as far back as the Book of Job). One way of stating this is as follows. The universe contains not only good but evil. Now if God is omnipotent, it was within his power to create a universe without evil. Since he did not do so, he is responsible for the existence of evil as of everything else, and is therefore not benevolent. If, however, we start by assuming that he is benevolent, and that it was not within his power to prevent the existence of evil in creation, he cannot be regarded as omnipotent. Thus if omnipotent and capable of abolishing evil, he cannot be benevolent; and if benevolent, he must be lacking in power. But the denial of either attribute is a denial of the perfection and divine prerogatives of a supernatural being.

**Five Attempts at Resolution of the Problem.** There appear to be at least five major courses which supernaturalists have taken in the light of this difficulty. (1) The adoption of a deistic or non-anthropomorphic position. But this entails shelving the conception of supernatural reward and punishment, and is actually an abandonment of the position that supernaturalism alone is the basis of ethical values. (2) The denial that evil is a "reality." Just what meaning such a denial has is not clear. Even if evil were an "illusion," the *character* of this illusion would in no way be changed, and suffering, pain, cruelty, and war would not thereby be abolished. A dream no less than a waking event is real, though in a different sense of the word, even if it is not shared by more than one individual. For if in dreaming, this individual experiences pain, the pain is not abolished by the fact that it occurs in a dream; its character is the character of pain. So that whether we call it a reality or an "illusion," evil remains evil. It is worth adding, however, that this denial of the reality of evil, if it will not bear philosophic analysis, has nevertheless had great practical significance. Sociologically considered, human attitudes toward what is ordinarily considered evil have been tremendously influenced by the doctrine that the facts are not what they seem. (3) The view that while evil exists, it is relative to man alone, and that the universe "as a whole" is not evil but good. Just what it means to say that the universe "as a whole" is good or bad is, again, far from clear. But this point need not be pressed, because the present answer quite obviously fails to solve the problem. It can still be argued that God being omnipotent could have chosen to create a universe that was good not only as a whole but in all its parts. (4) The position that the whole difficulty in the problem of evil is a difficulty only to our finite minds but not to that of God. The "ways" of God are held to be incomprehensible to man, and it is maintained that even though we are confronted by what seems to be an irresoluble difficulty, recourse to faith is always open to us. This answer is essentially the one suggested by the Book of Job to similar perplexing difficulties. As this answer achieves its end by abandoning the method of the intellect, so any reply to it must also be on methodological grounds. Perhaps in the light of what we have said in Part Two, it is necessary for us here only to describe the situation accurately. We may say, then, that faith in intellect is abandoned for faith in faith; or less paradoxically, that faith in the sense of confident expectation based on past experience here gives way to faith in the sense of hostility to the very possibility of evidence. Active inquiry has yielded to the method of tenacity. If this method can justify our saying that apparent evil is ultimate good, it can equally well justify our saying that apparent good is ultimate evil. (5) The position that the existence of evil is not a denial of God's benevolence because the presence of evil enhances the good that exists. Though there is evil, the good by which God supplants it is in so far a greater and richer good. "He judged it better to bring greater good to pass out of evil." That human beings more strongly grasp the significance of a good when it is contrasted with or succeeds an evil, is a truth of experience. But so far as the problem of evil for supernaturalism is concerned, the present argument in a sense reduces to the preceding one. For the question may still be asked why the nature of goodness could not have been such (God being omnipotent) that it did not have to be supplemented or intensified by evil, and the answer would still seem to be that this must remain a mystery to our finite mind.

**An Alternative Statement of the Problem.** The problem of evil can be stated in another and perhaps more forceful way. God created man as a responsible moral agent, and men are subject to divine punishment or reward according as their actions do or do not conform to divine will. God, however, being responsible for creating man as a fallible animal, is responsible for man's wrongdoing. Since by his omnipotence and omniscience he was able to avoid a creation with such consequences, and is able to avert specific acts of wrongdoing, wrongdoing exists by his will. This means that he lacks perfect goodness, and that reward and punishment reduce to a game or divine sport. If, however, wrongdoing exists in spite of his will, he lacks complete power. So that, again, benevolence and omnipotence become incompatible attributes of God. In this way of stating the problem, by substituting "wrongdoing" for "evil," answer (2) could no longer be attempted. For to deny that wrongdoing is "real" makes a travesty of reward and punishment.

**The Empirico-Pragmatic Difficulties of Supernaturalism.**
In carrying further the empiricists' criticism of the traditional
theistic arguments Kant emphasized that they exceeded the
bounds of all empirical evidence and that therefore the whole
subject-matter, whether argued pro or con, transcended the
jurisdiction of the human intellect. We saw in Chapter X of
Part Two that the empiricist development of this strain after
Kant culminated in experimentalist pragmatism, a critical
method of clarifying our meanings. Pragmatism sets limits
not as Kant did to the province of the intellect but to the way
in which we may meaningfully employ language, and warns us
that to remain in the realm of abstractions which are unconnected with the world of common experience is to border on
unintelligibility, however intelligible our arguments may *seem*.
Let us now apply pragmatic criticism to the concepts which
we have been discussing.

**Example: Meaning of "Absolute Perfection."**     Consider,
for instance, the ontological argument. In addition to the difficulties already pointed out, another arises, namely, What is
*meant* by "absolute perfection"? Perhaps a fairly coherent
significance can be attached to the expression "perfect government" or "perfectly rigid body" or "perfect blueness," in
terms, say, of a limiting or ideal state of a property already
empirically discernible in an object or situation. But to speak
of perfection *as such* is very different, and the conception of
something absolutely perfect, perfect in *every* respect and not
in any *specific* respect, is not readily intelligible. It is so vague
that whatever properties we do assign to it are assigned either
arbitrarily (without any definite criterion) or out of purely
subjective preference. Whether a concept of this kind *could*
be satisfactorily qualified to cohere intelligibly with the rest of
our knowledge need not be discussed by us; but it is certain
that before *some* further clarification is introduced, the argument remains not much more than an ingenious bit of verbiage.

**Example: Meaning of "Eternal," "Infinite," Etc.** The
same objection applies to the conception of the traditional at-

tributes of divinity: "omnipotence," "omniscience," "eternality," "infinity." Does the "infinity" of a divine being mean that it occupies all space and lacks boundaries? It is surely not this crude pseudo-naturalistic notion that is intended. Is God "eternal" in the sense that he exists forever, or that he is "outside time"? If the former, then he is comprehended by the province of "nature"; if the latter, in what manner does he affect that which *is* in time? And so on. A pragmatic analysis raises the question whether, in asserting that "God is eternal and infinite" we are asserting any more than we would if we said that "x is y and z." One difference is that the former expressions are familiar expressions, so familiar that we never bother to analyze them. But we have warned (Part Two, pp. 128-9, 135-6) against the confusion of psychological familiarity with logical intelligibility.

**Example: Meaning of "Outside Nature," Etc.** We have called attention to the obscurity of the assertion that nature "as a whole" is good or bad. The idea of goodness or value would seem to relate to human affairs. Undoubtedly we cannot forcibly restrict the usage of a given term, but we can say that the usage *is* a different one, and we can ask *what* that different meaning is. But further, consider the usage of the term "nature." What is meant when it is said that God is "outside nature"? We cannot mean spatially outside, as outside a box; for the realm of space relates to nature itself. And when the cosmological argument refers to nature as having a "beginning," and the teleological argument refers to nature as requiring an architect, are we not speaking of nature as though it were a specific, manipulatable object? The term "nature" is not the same kind of term as "house" or "star"; it does not *designate* in the same way. A term which collectively represents all possibilities and all actualities cannot very well be associated with the property "having a beginning." This tendency of using the term "nature" as though it represented a given object, and the tendency also of conceiving it anthropomorphically in the manner of a huge organism (whence the ascription of "goodness") are difficult to avoid, but this does not render them the less objectionable. In general, a supernaturalistic philosophy must reply positively to the foregoing queries. If it contents itself with saying that such-and-such is *not* what it means, without saying what it *does* mean, it will never give a satisfactory account of the relation between a natural and a supernatural realm.

**Methodological Conclusions.** It might be urged that if the arguments for supernaturalism do not conclusively prove their points, they at least render them more probable than alternative views. Does not the hypothesis of the supernatural enable us to explain more than any other does? Now whether such a philosophy is preferable to a naturalistic or to some other philosophy will depend on which best enables us to solve our intellectual problems in coherent, well-balanced, orderly, objective manner. A comparison of the supernaturalistic with other world-perspectives in detail would require previous discussion of the others. But the supernaturalistic theory has two fundamental disadvantages. First, it suffers from the pragmatic difficulties mentioned. It may be superior poetically or mythologically, but not logically. Second, it does explain more — but this is its very drawback. It explains *too much*: it can explain a world of chance as well as a world of law, an evil society as well as a good one. For since, by definition, nothing is outside the power of the supernatural, any kind of universe and any kind of fact within the universe can be attributed to its will and explained as an effect of its action. But a theory which can explain *anything,* explains nothing. Since *everything* can serve as evidence for it, nothing in particular can.

To insist on retaining the supernaturalistic hypothesis is to adopt ultimately some form of faith, which is content to asseverate *that* there is a supernatural being, without being able to say *what* it is. This involves the anti-empiricist or anti-pragmatic assumption that we can speak significantly of what we hold is intrinsically beyond the possibility of human knowledge. Whatever one's final evaluation of such an attitude may be, whether it be held superior to the scientific attitude or not, that it *is* not a scientific attitude should be clear. The proportion of desire, hope, emotion, and will that enters into and governs it is inimical to scientific objectivity. To adapt the words of an eminent philosopher of the recent past, we are always faced in our philosophy with two very different modes of approach to inquiry: we may reason in such a way that our conclusion determines what our reasoning shall be, or we may reason in such a way that our reasoning determines what our conclusion shall be. The latter approach alone is that of the scientific method. Too often in the examination of the supernaturalist thesis, we proceed by trying to find evidence for what we have antecedently resolved to accept, and we are blinded, naturally, to evidence which is unfavorable. The sounder way is to decide that whichever conclusion the total evidence confirms is the conclusion we shall accept.

❖   ❖   ❖

## CHAPTER FOURTEEN

# Materialism and Its Implications

Let us recall our discussion of "common sense" at the very beginning of Part Two. Now, if we were to ask ourselves whether there is a world-view involved in common sense before it is elaborated and corrected by theoretical inquiry, and what that world-view is, it would not be easy to answer. For common sense, as we saw, is not a system; it is essentially unsystematic, and therefore does not embody a comprehensive outlook.

**What is the World-View of the "Common Man"?** But on the other hand, this mass of rudimentary knowledge is not chaotic, either, and it is possible at least to a certain extent to say what the broadest presuppositions are of the pre-philosophic, uncritical mind in Western society, influenced in the main only by the broad features of the environment and the elementary reflective situations of conscious life. Perhaps they add up somewhat in this way:

We regard ourselves as having a "body" and a "mind." We regard some bodies, our own and other animal bodies, as "living" in the midst of a much wider physical world. We assume that when certain things happen, certain other things will happen; and we assume further that *whenever* things of the first kind happen, things of the second kind will. We suppose that the physical world controls us to some extent, and that we to some extent can control it. We speak of our "will" as influencing many of our bodily actions, and we assume not only that the "mind" can thus "cause" the body to act, but also that certain conditions of the body cause certain states of mind.

**Problems Confronting Philosophic Speculation.** Speculative philosophy, in trying to understand these relationships better, and to formulate and correct them, must necessarily ask many questions and introduce many new ideas concerning them. What is meant by "mind," and in what sense if at all does it "interact" with the body and the material world in general? Does mind represent a supernatural force, or can it like the material world be explained as an aspect of "nature"? What grounds have we to assume that future events will occur in the same way that past events of the same kind have been observed to occur? In its attempt to answer these and innumerable other questions, speculative philosophy appeals to the scientific, the religious, the aesthetic, the moral, and the personal experience of the human race. It seeks to extract both from common sense and deliberate reflection whatever it can that is of interpretative value. In Chapter XIII we offered one approach, which interprets human experience as justifying belief in a reality ultimately beyond its comprehension and sharply distinguished from a realm of nature. The further implications of this view will emerge as we go on to consider other approaches and their implications.

**Materialism: One Version of Naturalism.** As its name implies, *naturalism* is a view antithetical to supernaturalism, though, as we shall see, it is not the sole alternative. We shall distinguish two versions of naturalism, a narrower or extreme version and a broader or more liberal version. We shall call the former *materialism* and the latter *critical naturalism*. An important warning is necessary concerning this usage. There are a number of philosophers who are *called* or who *call* themselves "materialists" who would on our usage better be called "critical naturalists." These philosophers, still following the fashion of the nineteenth century, when the distinction was temporarily obliterated, use the terms "materialism" and "naturalism" interchangeably or synonymously. But historically speaking, there is no doubt that naturalists do fall into two readily distinguishable groups, and that the name "materialism" has for the most part been applied to the narrower naturalists, while no special name has been applied to the other group only because its members up to the present century have been few in number. This is not to imply that the similarities between materialistic naturalism and critical naturalism are less important than the differences between them. We shall consider the former version in this chapter, and the latter in Chapter XVI, after which the similarities and differences may be surveyed by the reader.

**The Historical Affinity of Materialism and Physical Science.** If we accept the traditional view that philosophy as a conscious discipline originated with the Greeks in the seventh century B. C., which there is little reason to deny, then naturalism is the oldest of philosophies. Naturalism questions the existence of forces or events other than those which can at least in principle be scientifically investigated. Unlike the supernaturalist, the naturalist assumes no intrinsically unknowable reality in the universe but only the fact of nature remaining always to be further explored and the fact of natural limitations to present knowledge. As supernaturalism has usually gone hand in hand with authority, faith, and intuition, so naturalism has usually been associated with the development of natural science. Most naturalists have inclined to materialism, and most of the early Greek materialists were what we today would call astronomers and physicists. But much more than in ancient times, the development of modern science since its renascence in the post-medieval period has been largely responsible for the stimulation of the materialist viewpoint. This is very different from saying—what does not happen to be the case—that most of the outstanding physical scientists have been materialists, or that the development of physical science has in turn been stimulated by materialistic philosophy. A considerable degree of mutual influence was, it is true, achieved in the nineteenth century.

If the development of modern science has spurred on materialism, it has spurred on many other philosophies as well; and in fact virtually none of the philosophies that could be called scientific philosophies have been materialistic. Materialistic philosophies have been attracted to physical science, not because of any intrinsic affinity between the two, but because they have seen in it the best buttress to naturalism and an anti-clerical moral philosophy. It is important to observe this historical fact that materialism has functioned more as a means to a naturalistic moral philosophy than as a clear-cut theory of the universe. It enables us to understand how various philosophers with a tendency toward naturalism have unconsciously embraced the more extreme form as a reaction to anti-naturalistic moral emphases.

**The Thesis of Materialism; Classical Statements.** Naturalism excludes what is not scientifically investigable, and calls the domain of possible investigation "nature." Materialistic naturalism goes much further. It offers a very limited definition of what nature consists in. Nature and the physical world are one and the same. And by the physical world is meant the collection of facts, events, and things that have space, time, and motion as their sufficient and fundamental defining characteristics. Nature is the sum of all events and things that are quantitatively measurable. In thus defining nature, materialism asserts that what is "natural" or "real" is "material" or physical in character, despite the fact that it may appear to us to be otherwise. In the terms of the classical exponents of materialism, everything that exists is resolvable or reducible ultimately into "matter." Matter, motion, space, and time — these concepts suffice to yield a fundamental interpretation of human experience. Whatever is to be called "real" is a concrete physical object that can be given a date in time and a locus in space. The principles of materialism were first formulated by the Greek philosophers Leucippus and Democritus in the late fifth and early fourth century B. C. Maintaining that all things could be reduced by scientific analysis into their material constituents, they believed further that matter had ultimate constituents, atoms; so that although the universe appeared to contain more than what was physical or material, atoms and empty space were all that existed "in reality." Everything else was the product of a subjective, artificial, human way of looking at things.

Democritus says:

> [By convention sweet is sweet, by convention bitter is bitter, by convention hot is hot, by convention cold is cold, by convention color is color. But in reality there are only atoms and the void. That is, the objects of sense are supposed to be real and it is customary to regard them as such, but in truth they are not. Only the atoms and the void are real.]*

After Aristotle had formulated ideas conflicting with materialism, Epicurus in the late fourth and early third century returned to the principles of Democritus. Epicurus' materialism is given elaborate exposition by his disciple of the first century B. C., the Roman poet Lucretius. Lucretius states the materialist thesis that what we call "mind" and "soul" are ultimately material.

> . . . The nature of mind and soul is bodily. For when it is seen to push on the limbs, to pluck the body from sleep, to change the countenance, and to guide and turn the whole man — none of which things we see can come to pass without touch, nor touch in its turn without body — must we not allow that mind and soul are formed of bodily nature? Moreover, you see that our mind suffers along with the body, and shares its feelings together in the body. If the shuddering shock of a weapon, driven within and laying bare bones and sinews, does not reach the life, yet faintness follows, and a pleasant swooning to the ground, and a turmoil of mind which comes to pass on the ground, and from time to time, as it were, a hesitating will to rise. Therefore it must needs be that the nature of the mind is bodily, since it is distressed by the blow of bodily weapons.†

A succinct and vigorous statement is furnished by the seventeenth century English materialist Thomas Hobbes (1588-1679):

> The world (I mean not the earth only . . . but the "universe," that is the whole mass of all things that are) is corporeal, that is to say body, and hath the dimensions of magnitude, namely length, breadth, and depth; also every part of body is likewise body and hath the like dimensions, and consequently every part of the universe is body, and that which is not body is no part of the universe.††

---

*A later author's restatement. See Bakewell, *Source-Book in Ancient Philosophy.*
† *On the Nature of Things,* Bk. III, Bailey translation.
†† *Leviathan,* Ch. 46.

All that exists is body, all that occurs is motion.

One of the most popular books of the nineteenth century, Ludwig Büchner's *Force and Matter,* is instructive as a summing up of the case for materialism, based on the scientific research then current as well as on the pronouncements of philosophical materialists in past centuries.

> Thinking can and must be regarded as a special mode of general natural motion, which is as characteristic of the substance of the central nervous elements as the motion of contraction is of the muscle-substance, or the motion of light is of the universal ether. . . . The words *mind, spirit, thought, sensibility, volition, life,* designate no entities and no things real, but only properties, capacities, actions of the living substance, or results of entities, which are based upon the material form of existence.*

**Mechanism.** We found that supernaturalism interprets the universe as in some sense teleological or purposive, though it is not true that all teleological interpretations must be supernaturalistic. When we speak of a "teleological" interpretation of the world we usually mean, not one which admits the existence of teleology or purpose in some sense, but one which supposes it to be the fundamental or pervasive character of the universe. Now materialism, in its opposition to an approach of the latter kind, adopts a position opposite in the extreme, one which denies even the limited existence of purpose. Historically, this materialistic position has taken two forms: one, the assumption that the universe is in part a chance universe (that is, to some degree without law in the sense of repetitive sequence); the other — and this is the most common form by far in modern times — the assumption that the universe is perfectly mechanical or machinelike, implying not only that it is governed by law but that we can explain everything about it by the laws of the science of mechanics, or any similarly limited number of physical principles or laws. A machine, we must remember, operates on a very few principles. It operates, not purposively but with blind regularity. And the *pattern* in which it operates does not *vary.*

---

* *Force and Matter,* Chapter on "Thought."

This point of view is known as *mechanism* or mechanistic materialism, and it is sometimes used as simply synonymous with "materialism." In order to understand it more fully, let us turn to an important piece of philosophizing by the Greek philosopher Aristotle (B. C. 384-322).

**Aristotle on "Efficient" and "Final" Causation.** If we consider the various phenomena that go to make up nature, we find that some kind of change is always taking place. Some changes are merely spatial changes — changes by objects of their positions. Others are chemical changes, for instance, change of color by a liquid. Still others are changes that consist in *development* of some kind — the development of a rainbow after a storm, the development of a tree after the planting of a seed. Now Aristotle was particularly interested in the last, developmental change. If we take an object that changes in this way, we can ask, What makes it become what it is? and, Into what kind of thing is it changing? To answer these two questions, Aristotle distinguished two kinds of explanation. Let us take, for instance, the seed and consider how its growth is to be understood. In one sense, the reason is the physical and chemical actions producing the growth which constitute the means and conditions for its taking place — e.g., planting and rainfall. This Aristotle called the *efficient* "cause" or reason — some agent or event or set of conditions without which the phenomenon would not take place. But in another sense, the reason for the seed's growing in the way it does is not external to it but consists in nothing more or less than the seed's own character as the seed of an oak tree, not of a birch. It is the specific function which the seed is capable of fulfilling, the form which it is capable of realizing — it is the *fully developed* character of being an oak which the seed *will* attain — that explains its growth. Aristotle calls this specific character the process of growth achieves its *final* cause or reason. The final cause of the seed's growth would be "oakhood" or "birch-hood." The final cause is so called because it explains the earlier stages of the process as means to the production of the final stage. To ask *what makes* the seed come to grow is to ask for the efficient cause; to ask *into what* kind of thing it is growing is to ask for the final cause. The efficient cause indicates the forces acting on *this particular* seed; the final cause indicates the *kind* of thing this seed will become.

**Materialist Exclusion of Final Causes.** Aristotle carefully distinguished what *makes* a change take place from the *results* of that change, an *efficient* cause from a *final* cause. But under the dominance of supernaturalism final causes were confused with efficient causes, and *ends* came to be regarded as themselves *forces*. Aristotle's distinction of two kinds of "causation" is quite compatible with naturalism, and has been accepted by most critical naturalists. The "final causation" which obliterates the distinction, and makes ends one kind of efficient cause, or force, cannot be accepted by any form of naturalism. And most materialists have disregarded final causes even in Aristotle's sense.

The mechanistic emphasis received great fortification from the revolutionary change in attitude that characterized the beginning of modern science. In the sixteenth and seventeenth centuries scientists began to place less emphasis upon final causes. They began to treat efficient causes, not qualitatively, as means to producing certain kinds of ends, but in terms of the exact quantitative measurement of their way of operating. This operation was formulated in the laws of mechanics, which treated efficient causes as the physical conditions of change of motion in time and space. The mechanist hence restricted the use of the broad term "cause" to the narrower notion of mechanical "force." Whereas on the Aristotelian conception natural change is understood in terms of the tendency of things to realize the "natures" or forms, the "purposes" or functions potential in them, on the mechanistic conception all events are understood as illustrations of mechanical law. Mechanical law implies that events occur solely because they are acted upon by mechanical causes, and that whenever these causes are the same, the effects are the same.

**Terminology: "Determinism," "Mechanism," "Teleology."** A few lines devoted to some traditional philosophic terms and their accurate meaning will enable us to avoid future confusion. A philosophy which asserts that each event in the universe is an instance of a definite causal pattern or law is called *deterministic*. A philosophy may be deterministic and yet not mechanistic (but not vice versa). The French astronomer of the late eighteenth and early nineteenth century, Pierre Laplace, concisely states the deterministic thesis when he says:

> We ought to regard the present state of the universe as the effect of its antecedent state and as the cause of the state that is to follow.

But he goes further, and expresses a mechanistic point of view in his next few words:

> An intelligence, who for a given instant should be acquainted with all the forces by which Nature is animated and with the several positions of the beings composing it, if further his intellect were vast enough to submit these data to analysis, would include in one and the same formula the movements of the largest bodies in the universe and those of the lightest atom. Nothing would be uncertain for him; the future as well as the past would be present to his eyes.*

For here he is assuming that the number of laws in the universe is forever a fixed and limited one, and consequently that it is theoretically possible, once we have understood what these laws are, and what the state of the universe at the time is, to predict or deduce completely every single event of the entire future. Determinism does not necessarily imply what mechanistic determinism does, namely, that it is possible for us to be in possession of a certain number of principles by which everything that will ever occur can be explained. In Chapter XVI we shall specify a form of naturalism which, though deterministic, is not mechanistic.

A deterministic philosophy may be teleological. Determinism asserts that each event is determined by antecedent causes. But it is possible for a philosophy to adopt this view and yet hold that the universe *as a whole* is teleological. Even super-

---

* *A Philosophical Essay on Probabilities* (translated by F. W. Truscott and F. L. Emory), Ch. 2.

naturalists have maintained a strict determinism while asserting that the universe as a whole illustrates design. The builder of a machine employs it as means to an end, yet it is in itself completely deterministic or governed by law. These remarks concerning the meaning of the foregoing terms are not meant to imply that the possible views are equally meritorious but merely to show what the possibilities have been in the actual history of philosophy.

We now turn to a second important piece of philosophizing for help in the understanding and intelligent criticism of materialism, this time once again by Hume.

**Hume's Analysis of Causation.**    Determinism means that, given a cause, a definite kind of effect will follow; given an effect, a definite kind of cause preceded it. With regard to the nature of this causal connection, an interesting question was asked by Hume. What does it mean to say, as most philosophers had said, that every effect *must* have a given cause, or that every cause *must* have a given effect? What does it mean to say that the effect is *determined* by the cause? Does it mean that an effect would be *inconceivable* without a cause? But this surely is false. When, as a cause, I drop a piece of paper into the fire, the effect is that it is burnt to an ash; and when, as a cause, I relax my hold on a book, the effect is that it falls to the ground. But it is *possible* that the paper should be unaffected by the flames, and that the book should rise instead of falling, under the very same conditions. In other words, to say that under these conditions the paper is unburnt and the book rises does not at all involve us in a logical contradiction. We all believe that these statements are false but we can prove that they are not self-contradictory. Chance is perfectly intelligible. This shows that the connection between cause and effect is not a "necessary" connection, in the logical sense; for this would be the case only if the opposite situation were self-contradictory. We can only say, then, Hume concludes, that a given cause always *has* been followed by a given effect, and that we always *expect* that it will be followed by the same effect (that is, that a purely chance situation will not arise) ; but we cannot say that a given cause *must* be followed by a given effect. His point is that causal connection is a matter of fact, and that our knowledge of it, like that of every matter of fact, is derived from experience or observation. And no empirical knowledge can ever be absolutely certain.

The deterministic viewpoint both before and after Hume has often been stated in ignorance of his distinction and in violation of his conclusion. This applies to both mechanists and others. A mechanistic viewpoint that ignores the distinction may be called a dogmatic or rationalistic mechanism.

**The "Reductive" Character of Materialism.** Let us now return to the general characterization of materialism. The assumption in broadest terms is that all realities can be "reduced" to material properties undergoing change of motion in space. This means (1) that all the sciences, biology, chemistry, psychology, physics, economics, sociology, and the others, treat at bottom of phenomena which, if analyzed in sufficient detail, prove to be only causally connected material phenomena; so that all sciences are in fact branches of the science of mechanics. (2) That what we call "mind" and its activities (thinking, understanding) are in fact complex movements in the brain, general nervous system, or other bodily organs. (3) That what we call "values," "ideals," "meanings," and "purposes" (human purposes, since no other are admitted) — "beauty," "happiness," "freedom," and the like — are nothing but names or subjective human tags for different physical situations or relations in which physical organisms find themselves. Thus all phenomena, including psychological phenomena (desires, hopes, motives, images, etc.) and social phenomena (tradition, civilization, nationalism, barbarity, etc.) are simply disguised forms of a basic physical reality and its causally changing relations.

**Advantages Claimed for the Materialist Hypothesis.** What is the justification of the materialist viewpoint? (1) It introduces, materialists have said, unity and continuity into our world-perspective. All things being conceived in material terms, we need not appeal to mysterious principles of explanation in order to account for a supposed relation between the material and the non-material. (2) It introduces simplicity and economy into our interpretation. If it is possible to employ one basic principle of explanation instead of two or more, the former is more desirable. The assumption that all things have a single characteristic, that of being material, and a single mode of activity, that of mechanism, is most intelligible. (3) It is most faithful to our experience. We know that all "mental" phenomena can be changed when physical conditions change. Ideas, emotions, meanings are impossible without bodily functioning; no mental event has ever existed except in a body. There can be a living brain without thought, but no thought without a brain. Similarly, "social" phenomena are known to be impossible without physical conditions. A tremble of the earth can revolutionize a society; a body of water can make the difference between war and peace. As the saying goes, had Cleopatra's nose been half an inch longer, the course of history would have been different. (4) It is most faithful to the conclusions of science. Physico-chemical changes are the most basic of all changes: they are possible without social, biological, and psychological changes, but the latter are not possible without them. As science takes no cognizance of final causes, so it ignores "values." Values are relative to man, different values to different men, while all men alike are at bottom complex physical organizations governed by the same causal sequences that govern the rest of nature. In the science of psychology, which had always been bothered by the so-called phenomena of mind, behaviorism has shown that only the physiological interpretation of human behavior has made a *science* of human behavior possible. Only mechanism explains why science can predict. On any other view we must abandon the scientific ideal of being able at some time to predict completely all future events. For this is possible only if, as in the

Laplacean assumption quoted above, we suppose a fixed and limited number of principles that always govern the universe.

We shall now digress again, in order to introduce further philosophic ideas that will prove useful to us in understanding and evaluating materialism. These ideas, however, have equal interest on their own account. They will concern us in the next four headings.

### Particular and General: the Nominalist-Realist Issue.

Since earliest times philosophers have differed over how the furniture of the universe, so to speak, should be interpreted. Some have felt that only *particular things* should be called "real." Others have felt that *kinds* of things are not less real than this or that thing. In the later Middle Ages, when this controversy was at its height, it took the form of a dispute as to whether "universals" are as real as particulars. By a "universal" is to be understood what is represented by terms like "white*ness*," "triangu*larity*," "father*hood*," "man*kind*"; by a "particular" we mean what is represented by terms like *"this* father (Jones)," *"that* white chair," *"the* triangle *just drawn on the board."* Those who denied the reality of universals were called *nominalists,* those who affirmed it *realists.* According to the realists, universals are qualities *common* to a group of particular things. The qualities which things have in common, they maintained, are no less qualities than the qualities which each of the things has individually. According to the nominalists, there are no universal qualities or kinds in this sense; there are only universal *names.* We apply these names to groups of things because it is to our *convenience* sometimes to refer to things collectively. But in actual fact only the individuals that go to make up a "group" are realities. Certainly a "group" does not *exist;* existence belongs only to individual things. And how, the nominalists conclude, can that which does not exist be called real? Historically, there have been many different formulations of each viewpoint, with various intermediate positions based on subtle distinctions.

The difference in intellectual attitude, method, and interpretative approach between the nominalistic and realistic viewpoint is very significant, and it can be stated as a much broader issue than the one we have just mentioned. Is nature to be described only in terms of particular things and of *facts,* or are *relations* and the *laws* to which facts conform to enter into our interpretation? Are relations and laws mere fictions, verbal conveniences? Are the similarities or common qualities which we ascribe to some classes of things and not to others purely arbitrary? Has the universe only a particular and not a general aspect; a specific and not a generic one? Applying the difference in approach to more special questions: Is society a reality not identical with a mere sum of individuals? Can we validly speak of "man" and "mankind," or only of this or that man?

**Plato on the Distinction between Sensation and Knowledge.** We are asking whether generality and law have as basic a status in the universe as particularity and fact. Let us ask, before venturing any conclusion, what the status of law and generality is in our process of *knowledge.* Here Plato (B. C. 427-347), the teacher of Aristotle, made a fundamental contribution. In human thinking, the general or universal takes the form of a *concept.* And what is the rôle of concepts in knowledge? Without concepts, Plato emphasizes, we should have not knowledge but only sensation. Sensation is merely the exercise of the senses on outward objects, it is merely animal contact with things. Knowledge, on the other hand, implies the grasping of *relationships;* it implies not merely feeling but understanding. Sensation is of particular things; knowledge is of the *character* of things. In sensing, we touch this or that table, taste this or that apple; in knowing, we think of tables as a *kind* of thing, a form of furniture, of apples as a *kind* of fruit. Or to put the matter in another way, knowledge takes place when we are able to communicate or use language, to be articulate or to think by using symbols. But if we reflect on what takes place when we describe or communicate,

we find that concepts, universal terms, are indispensable, even
in the most elementary kind of information. Thus suppose we
are describing a table. We can describe something only by
enumerating its properties. But to do this — to say that the
table's properties are brownness, smoothness, hardness, and so
on — is necessarily to assert general characteristics, to use universal terms.

**Merits and Limitations of Nominalism.**    If we accept
this Platonic conception of knowledge, we can formulate the
nominalist-realist issue this way: Do the concepts that we employ in the process of knowledge signify something objective,
or are they to be construed as human fictions and linguistic
artifices? The stock argument of nominalists is in the form
of a question: *Where are* relations and laws? Are they tangible? Can they be observed, measured? But in assuming that
the only realities are particular things in time and space, the
nominalist begs the question. Let us apply the nominalist position to two examples. We speak of "the state" in abstract
terms. There is, says the nominalist, no such reality as "the
state," nor even "a state," except in so far as this is a name
for a number of people living *in* a specific topographical re-
gion, *at* a definite period of time, and acting in this and that
way. Now the value of this nominalistic emphasis is in showing the danger of interpreting an abstract term like "the state"
as the name of a kind of substance or concrete object in itself
— the danger of "hypostatizing" concepts, to use the technical philosophic description of this process. There can be no
"state" without people and specific conditions. But to go to
the opposite extreme and *equate* the state with people and
topography is just as bad. The nominalist forgets that people
must stand in certain *relations* and act in certain *ways*. One
kind of relation and way of acting is what we call the "state."
To take our second example: The "law" of gravitation, according to nominalists, is only a name for the sum of all specific cases of mutual attraction by bodies. But here again,
while the sound element in this emphasis is that there can be

no law apart from specific cases of attraction, neither can there be action by bodies which is not a definite *kind* of action.

Nominalism interpreted as an emphasis against "hypostatizing" universals, or endowing them with a reality independent of particulars, is a healthy viewpoint. Certain philosophers have been inclined, consciously or not, to conceive of "laws of nature," for instance, as possessing a kind of independent power which compels facts to conform to them — a mythological or anthropomorphic conception reflected in our saying that laws "govern" facts. This *extreme* realism was characteristic of Plato's predecessors, the followers of Pythagoras; and Plato himself often gives the impression that he holds such a view. It held sway among Plato's followers in late ancient and early medieval times, and again in the later medieval period during the controversial era we mentioned. But so far as subsequent influence was concerned, nominalism emerged victorious in at least one sense, that nominalistic tendencies have been widespread in modern philosophy.

**Aristotle's Theory of Matter and Form.** In the philosophy of Aristotle, both nominalism and extreme realism are avoided. He distinguishes two aspects of every object in nature: *matter* and *form*. Thus in a statue, the matter may be clay, the form may be that of Zeus. The matter is what makes the statue an individual spatial and temporal thing; the form is what gives it its character. But while matter and form may be distinguished logically, they cannot exist separately. Clay cannot simply be clay with no form whatever; Zeus cannot be said to exist unless materially embodied. Hence the form (law, relation, quality) can *exist* only as the form *of* something or some things. But all things *do* have form, that is, character. Nature thus has two aspects according to Aristotle's view: specificity, individuality, here-and-nowness, concreteness, spatio-temporality, on the one hand; form, generality, character, on the other. The former aspect, which is what we can *sense,* signifies *that* a thing is; the latter, which is what we can *know,* signifies *what* a thing is.

Nominalistically inclined philosophers, in stressing that what is real must exist somewhere at some time, tacitly suppose that to assert this is to *exclude* the possibility that what is real can be non-spatial and non-temporal. But *both* may be true. For to say that facts, which are spatio-temporal, are real, is not to imply that laws, which are not, are unreal.

**General Remarks on Materialism.** The philosophy of materialism depends for much of its plausibility upon a process which only time has brought fully into the open — oversimplification. Half-truths are magnified into truths because of a failure to make one or two important distinctions. The emphasis on the physical as the basis of all phenomena does not warrant the conclusion that all phenomena are physical. The fact that some phases of scientific investigation favor the view does not mean that all phases do. The fact that some aspects of our common experience serve as evidence for it does not mean that this evidence can be interpreted in isolation from other evidence. And the fact that the view renders supernaturalistic explanation unnecessary does not mean that it is the only view which can do so.

**Materialistic Reduction Nominalistic but Not Consistently So.** It is obvious that in denying the "reality" of values, purposes, meanings, or what is the same, in reducing them to the exclusively physical, materialism involves a pronounced nominalistic tendency to interpret all phenomena in particularistic, spatio-temporal terms. The dictum of Hobbes that "all that exists is matter, all that occurs is motion" expresses this clearly. (Materialism is not at all the only nominalistic philosophy. In the next chapter we shall consider a completely antithetical philosophy, sensationalistic idealism, that is at least equally as nominalistic.) But now in the light of this, consider the materialist emphasis on mechanical law as the principle of all occurrence (motion). Is "law" another category, to be added to the two categories of matter and motion? Or is it a verbalism that we use because it is convenient to class a sum of events together which in fact are perfectly unique and have nothing in common? Now by "law" we mean something that could be described as *form* or *structure*. And to deny that the universe does in fact have a mechanical structure is to deny mechanism. Thus it would seem law is a category which materialism assumes covertly, this assumption being inconsistent with the Hobbesian maxim, that "that which is not body is no part of the universe."

**Reply to Alleged Advantages (1) and (2).** On pp. 202-4 above we attempted to state the case for materialism in four main points. To the first two we may reply as follows. It is not sufficient (as we showed in Part Two, p. 152) for a theory to be simple in order to be satisfactory. The more economical theory is preferable only when other factors are equal, and not merely because of its economy. Economy or simplicity is only a determining factor, and is secondary to adequacy. A theory may be too simple to explain all the facts. In such a case it is desirable to find another which has all the advantages of the given theory and which does more justice to the total evidence.

**Reply to (3) and (4).** First let us consider the claim that common experience favors materialism. Materialism is faithful to *part* of this experience when it is isolated from the whole. We do find that our mental states change when physical conditions change. But on the other hand we find, just as pervasively, that our thinking initiates changes in our physical actions. Now it may very well be that on the latter score our common uninterpreted experience is misleading and requires to be corrected. But materialism explains the difference in the two experienced phenomena only by denying the reality of "mind" and reducing it to physical states. The truth of the matter is that so far as common experience is concerned, the evidence is strongly against materialism. For this experience is overwhelmingly suffused with values, meanings, and purposes as well as with physical factors. We *rarely* experience a situation that is *purely* physical.

Turn now to the testimony of science. It is true that the modern development of science until the late nineteenth century favored the explanation of all branches of science in mechanical terms. In terms of its development in this century, however, even physical science has abandoned this ideal. The simple, pictorial explanations in mechanical or machinelike terms are no longer found to be adequate. This does not mean, as it is commonly supposed to mean, that the principle of causality or determinism has broken down. But it does mean that *mechanistic* determinism has shown itself to be inadequate and excessively simple as an interpretation. And in the development of psychology, although behaviorism is among the leading schools today, it is a far cry from the behaviorism of two decades ago, which, in the flush of a few experimental successes, rashly maintained that bodily processes were the only processes there are, that thinking is nothing but movements in the larynx or a form of speech, and that consciousness was an "illusion."

**Oversimplification in Materialist Reduction: the "Reductive Fallacy."** The error of materialism is that it confuses the *dependence* of biological, social, and psychological phenomena on physical phenomena with the *unreality* of such phenomena. To say that they cannot exist unless physical conditions exist and that yet the latter may exist independently, does not mean that they are "nothing but" physical. There cannot be thought without a brain, but from this truth the identity of the two does not follow. The physical may be a *basis* of all else, but it does not *exhaust* all. Values, ideals, purposes would not exist without a physical world, but this does not render them either physical or in themselves unreal. When materialists have said that non-physical phenomena are "illusory" they have in effect only reiterated that they are non-physical. As we have already pointed out in connection with the attempt to deny the reality of evil (p. 185), to call something that is definitely part of our experience "illusory" is merely to recognize that it is a different *kind* of reality from that which we happen to be emphasizing. To conclude, from the fact that A may occur without B but that B occurs only in connection with A, that B is "nothing but" A (or that B as such is "illusory") is to commit what has come to be known as the reductive fallacy: B is "reduced to" A.

**Empiricist and Rationalist Tendencies in Materialism.** In their opposition to supernaturalism and their emphasis on the exclusive reality of the physical world, materialistic philosophers would seem to be pursuing an empiricist attitude, revolting against assuming the reality of anything that cannot become an object of natural experience. But strong rationalistic tendencies crop up in a curious way. To hold that consciousness and purpose, the most pervasive factors of experience, are illusory, and that a deeper reality, matter, alone is real, is to sacrifice the universal testimony of experience to a dogma. Further, many mechanists have been inclined to emphasize the absolute truth of the causal principle, assuming in spite of Hume that the cause-effect relation is a necessary one; yet empiricism does not warrant belief in the certainty of any universal principle relating to fact. A good illustration of this tendency of rationalistic or dogmatic mechanism is to be found in the following statement by Büchner, whom we have already quoted as a very representative nineteenth century materialist:

> . . . We know with absolute certainty that all existence including sensation and consciousness, is one and self-dependent, ruled without exception by the law of cause and effect, and that no breaking through these boundaries set up by the necessity of Nature is possible at any point or at any time.*

Such an intrusion of *a priorism* is not in the original intentions of most materialists. But the manifestation of the rationalistic temper is something easily understandable in a doctrine that is reductive and that strives after clear-cut simplicity; for the achievement of such simplicity is hardly possible without some violence to the facts of experience.

---

* *Force and Matter*, Chapter on "Consciousness."

**Naturalism and Ethics.** What are the moral standards that go hand in hand with a naturalistic philosophy? There can be no definite answer, for the ethical views of naturalists have varied, and could vary to an even greater extent than they have. But the common features of naturalistic ethics as opposed to those of supernaturalistic ethics are not difficult to infer. The *validity* of moral standards will be established in a very different manner. If authority is regarded as the source of these standards, it will be the authority of society, of a legal code or of social tradition, and not the authority of something supernatural. If other sources than authority are recognized, these will be found in the desires, preferences, and abilities of human beings. For there are other possible standards of reference than divine will in terms of which "good" and "bad," "right" and "wrong" can be defined. Goodness will be a natural quality rather than a supernatural one. Since on a naturalistic point of view the soul is not an independent reality that can exist disembodied, the notion of personal immortality must be discarded, and our ethics cannot be an ethics of otherworldliness in the literal sense.

What about materialism in particular? It is a mistake to believe, as supernaturalists so often do, that materialism sanctions universal license and moral chaos. It is true that because of its nominalistic cast, materialism has usually resulted in an ethical philosophy far less imaginative and profound than one which a naturalistic philosophy is capable of achieving. But materialism does not necessarily entail the abolition of moral values. For in denying the "reality" of values, the materialist does not mean to deny that we do call certain types of situation value-situations. Standards that are held to be ultimately material realities do not cease to be standards. What we certainly can say, however, is that the materialistic hypothesis involves us in an artificial use of our language.

❖  ❖  ❖

# The Emphasis on Mind

We have called attention to the fact that the typical view of common sense distinguishes the "mind" or "soul" from the "body." The mind is vaguely regarded as something "intangible," the body as something "tangible" which changes and occupies space. Now this separation of mind and body has been, in one form or another, a fundamental principle in the world-view of various philosophers. It is too old to be dated in regard to its exact origin. But we find its importance already adumbrated by the Hebrew prophets, and it begins to find philosophic formulation in some of Plato's predecessors. In Plato, the soul, as contrasted with the body, is held to be immaterial and immortal; a view accentuated by the neo-Platonist Plotinus (205?-270), and by one of the most important of the early Christian Church fathers, St. Augustine (354-430), who was also deeply influenced by Plato. Under St. Augustine's influence combined with the vague but unmistakable assumption of it in the New Testament, the basic divorce of matter and mind, or body and soul, or flesh and spirit, dominated the whole of medieval philosophy, and was only partially modified in the thirteenth century by St. Thomas' introduction of more Aristotelian ideas. But it is in the view of Descartes in the first half of the seventeenth century that it receives its most deliberate and thoroughgoing expression.

**What Is a Dualism? Dualism of Matter and Soul.** Any philosophic theory which sets up, in its explanation or approach, two fundamental concepts, neither of which can be reduced to the other, is said to be *dualistic*. To apply the term "dualism" to a philosophy is usually misleading unless it is accompanied by a qualification. For there are many kinds of dualistic theory, and a philosophy dualistic in one respect is not so in another. The fundamental distinction and assumption of irreducibility between matter and mind is one kind of dualism (sometimes called "mind-body dualism"). Another kind is the dualism of faith and science (or "faith and reason") basic in various thinkers. Some philosophies contain a dualistic element not explicitly recognized as such by their exponents. We shall encounter one or two further types in this chapter.

**The Version of Descartes.** According to Descartes, the universe has two basic constituents, two kinds of "substance," body and mind. The defining characteristic of body, or matter — its essential characteristic, that without which it would not be what it is — is extension, or the possession of dimensions. The defining characteristic of mind (or mental substance) is thought, or the activity of thinking. Regardless of the *way* in which a body is extended (e.g., being round, hard, warm, etc.), it must be extended; regardless of the *way* in which a mind thinks (e.g., imagining, conceiving, abstracting), think it must if it is a mind. Now by "substance" Descartes, following historical usage, means that which "requires nothing but itself in order to exist." Only body and mind are substances, and everything in the universe is reducible to one or the other; but body and mind are not reducible one to the other — each is self-sustaining. Body has none of the properties of mind, mind none of the properties of body. The two realms are *absolutely* different. Strictly speaking, neither mind nor body is truly self-sustaining, for according to Descartes God (or the divine substance) is alone self-sustaining in the ultimate sense; the other two substances are substances by virtue of his power.

**Its Relation to Supernaturalism and to Mechanism.** The introduction of divine substance is significant, for it shows how a mind-body dualism inclines to supernaturalism as well. Supernaturalism on its side, as we saw, is most likely to assume a mind-body dualism, because this leaves room for immortality of the soul. But there can be no doubt that in Descartes the relation of God to the world is far more artificially introduced than in medieval philosophy, and the character of the relation is far less intimate than in the case of the medieval God. Medieval supernaturalism has a deeper ethical flavor; and its concomitant dualism is less an elaborate speculative approach to the nature of the universe than a principle required by it. The relation of body and soul on the Augustinian view is conceived along the lines of a warfare in which the soul is the seat of the forces of goodness. The dualism of Descartes, on the contrary, is saturated with the spirit of seventeenth century science, and the interpretation that he gives it is very different. Here we come upon an interesting drama of ideas. Cartesian dualism, because it affirms the substantial reality of the soul, cannot possibly be reconciled with any form of naturalism. On the other hand, it is deeply influenced by the mechanistic viewpoint that emerged from the procedure of the new science of its day. It attacks materialism, while it places mechanism on so solid a basis that the rise of the mechanistic world-view as a philosophy is today traced to the "Cartesian revolution"! What is the meaning of this? The answer is simple, namely, that for Descartes mechanism is not universal but applies only in the realm of matter. The material world is a perfect machine. The world of the mind is one in which the "will" is free to act without constraint. Descartes' dualism enables him on the one hand to cling to religious orthodoxy, and on the other to express his conviction of the philosophic implications of science. His total view cannot be called "mechanism" as we defined the term. But the mechanical theory that is part of his dualism, if it is less *sweeping* than the mechanism of the materialists, is just as *emphatic*. Later materialism leveled against Descartes its most powerful guns at the same time that it received from him its most powerful influence.

**Critical Remarks.** The fatal weakness of Cartesian dualism was revealed when Descartes came to describe the relation of mind and body in the human organism. The mind or soul, he suggested, might operate from a localized seat in the brain. It could communicate impulses to the bodily organs through nerves and blood vessels, and could be affected in the same way. But this conception was soon shown by Descartes' critics to be fraught with difficulties. The principal one was how the mind could have a "seat" in the brain. For this implies that it is located in space, or extended, and Descartes had emphasized that extension was the property of matter alone. Mind is defined solely by thought, and has none of the properties of body. Even if it can somehow function without being located, the manner of its interaction with the body necessarily remains mysterious. For how can two substances without *any* properties in common interact in *any* way at all? Descartes himself recognized the difficulty, and ultimately appealed to the convenient hypothesis of God to "explain" the interaction. In the light of such difficulties it becomes easier for us to understand the motivation of materialism, in which the problems of mind-body dualism are avoided. But materialism, in denying the reality of mind as a *substance*, fails to see that the concept of mind may connote a reality in *other* than a substantial sense. We shall presently encounter another attempt to avoid mind-body dualism, a denial that *body* has substantial reality. First we turn to the historical predecessor of this view, another type of dualism succeeding that of Descartes.

**Dualism of Knower and Known: Locke's Problem.** One of the important things Descartes assumed was (cf. p. 92 in Part Two) that critical inquiry reveals that the mind knows itself — its own existence and its own characteristics — with a greater certainty than it knows anything else. But Descartes maintained that by its intuitive powers the mind could go on also to assert with certainty the existence of body. Following the introspective method of Descartes (as it is sometimes called) John Locke set himself to examine in detail the powers of the mind and its claims to knowledge, and came to conclusions which directly or indirectly touched off some of the most controversial issues in modern philosophy.

**Representative Perception: "Ideas."** Locke was much impressed by the fact that when we perceive material things— whether through sight or sound, taste or touch, or any other sense — we perceive them only in part and from a certain *point of view.* Thus when we look at a house we see sometimes its facade, sometimes its rear, sometimes its corner, each constituting one aspect; when we hear a church bell, we hear a low sound if far away, a high sound if near; when we see something through a microscope, we observe a different texture from the one we observe with unaided vision; when we taste something, the taste will vary depending on how much or how little we eat, what we have or have not eaten previously; and so on. Locke felt that we could "know" material objects only in this way, through their sensed *appearances,* which could vary; in short, through what he called our *ideas* of them. Thus in order that perception should take place, three factors were necessary: the mind, the object, and the appearance of the object to the mind (the idea). The idea, according to Locke, is "in the mind," for how can there be an idea which is not in some mind? In perception the idea is in the mind only when the object as well as the mind is present. In imagination or in memory, we have ideas of absent objects. Locke's theory of perceptual knowledge is sometimes held to be a theory of *representative* (as opposed to direct) perception. The "idea" represents the object to the mind, it mediates between the mind and the material world. We directly experience only our own ideas; material objects we experience indirectly, via these ideas.

**"Primary" and "Secondary" Qualities of Objects.** There is a significant difference that is to be noted among the ideas we have of material things. Following the general lead of Democritus, and of Hobbes and Descartes as well as the scientists Galileo and Robert Boyle, Locke distinguished two kinds of qualities which objects have: "primary" and "secondary" qualities. The former are qualities like extension, shape, solidity, and motion. But the secondary qualities are not qualities in this sense at all. They are the powers which a material body has of exciting a certain kind of ideas in us—ideas of color, smell, taste, or sound. Now consider our ideas of shape, solidity, or motion on the one hand (our ideas of primary qualities), and our ideas of color, taste, or sound on the other (our ideas of secondary qualities). We find, according to Locke, an important difference. The former kind of ideas *resemble* their objective counterparts, an idea of a triangle resembles the physical triangular body, an idea of a body moving resembles the actual moving body. But the latter kind of ideas resemble nothing objective; for their objective counterparts exist only as powers or capacities. Thus shape, solidity, motion are objective and belong to the body we perceive even when we do not perceive it. But color, taste, sound are not objective; they belong to the body *only* when we perceive it. Or in other words, shape, solidity, motion exist as ideas and as objective qualities; color, taste, sound exist only as ideas (when the presence of the body excites them in us), and not as objective qualities. Thus the primary qualities are what Locke calls the "real" qualities, while the secondary qualities are merely powers which a body has of arousing ideas that we *suppose* have the same status as the ideas of primary qualities. Shape, solidity, motion are mechanical qualities, quantitatively measurable. Color, taste, sound are "sensible qualities," which exist (as ideas) only when objects are perceived by us. A body is square and occupies space whether we perceive it or not. But a body is red or sweet *only when* (though not "solely because") we sense it. Squareness is objective, redness is relative to the sense of sight. Our idea of squareness copies squareness; our idea of redness represents something (a power) but copies nothing.

**The Notion of Substance.** Locke found himself compelled to consider the question, How is it that we can perceive a material object as a unity — as a chair, a star, a man — and not merely as a jumble of qualities, hardness, brownness, smoothness in an undiscriminated mass? He reasoned that the qualities of an object are not all that goes to make it up. There must be something which, so to speak, holds the qualities together; something by which the qualities are borne or supported. This he called the *substance* of the object. This is the "substratum" of the qualities. For there cannot be merely squareness, hardness, and motion; there must be something which *has* the squareness, which *is* hard, which *does* the moving. There must be something *of* which the qualities are qualities. This substance cannot itself be merely a collection of qualities. For if that were so, these qualities would have to have a substratum to which they belong; if this in turn were nothing but qualities, a further substratum would be necessary. But this cannot go on indefinitely, and in general the confusion of substance with qualities, on Locke's view, reduces to absurdity. We can no more have qualities without a substratum than adjectives without a substantive. A substance, unlike a primary quality, cannot be directly perceived; and in fact we can say no more about it than that there must be such a thing. What it is we cannot say.

We must, in Locke's opinion, assume not only material but spiritual substance. The mental activities of perceiving, remembering, abstracting, or imagining, cannot take place by themselves: there must be something which does the imagining and perceiving, a self or soul. The concept of substance is one that appears in many philosophers from ancient times. The reader who goes on to study the works of thinkers like Descartes and Locke, for instance, will find that subtle differences in their treatment of this concept furnish a key to their respective views on many philosophic problems. And if he studies the history of philosophy as a whole, he will find that the evolution (or devolution, as the case may be) of this and many other concepts is a subject as fascinating as it is intellectually valuable.

**Implications of Lockean Dualism.** The dualism of Locke consists in a contrast between the knowing mind and the world that it attempts to know which results in an unbridgeable separation. The mind becomes insulated by a screen of ideas which alone are what it immediately experiences. Locke held that we do have knowledge of the physical world — the "external" world, as it has come to be known under unmistakable Lockean influence in our way of speaking, the world of things "without us." Real knowledge is defined by Locke as the agreement of our ideas with things. But the weakness of this view is seen as soon as we ask, How can we determine whether our ideas agree with their objects if these ideas are themselves the only way we have of knowing objects? A comparison would require that at least sometimes we could perceive objects directly and not representatively. This dualism leads inevitably to a barren form of scepticism. For if knowledge is something that refers to a reality behind appearance, this opens the way to the question, How can we be certain that we know the real world? Perhaps whatever opinions we have hold only of the world of appearance. Our discussion of knowledge in Part Two should have shown us that to the whole question of knowledge, the question whether it is or is not of something "real" is irrelevant. Whatever the answer to this, the actual knowledge we possess is unaffected. What our theories can predict remains predictable. Knowledge is a matter of verification, not of whether the evidence which serves to verify is or is not "real." Verification takes place within experience; whether this experience is the "real world" or whether it is a screen of ideas does not matter. Locke's dualism, resulting in a conception of knowledge that is based on an artificial approach, leads to an equally artificial scepticism.

**The Starting-Point of Berkeley.** Locke's eighteenth century successor, George Berkeley, realized the awkward implications of Locke's view. The scepticism which it justified could ask, not only, How do we know that our ideas correspond to the real world? but actually, How can we be sure that there *is* a world beyond the world of ideas? For we cannot get outside the screen of our ideas. Now one way to resolve these difficulties is to revise Locke's total theory by dispensing with ideas in the way he conceived them, as a kind of intermediate reality between the mind and the external world; to conceive of the world of experience (Locke's "ideas") and the world of nature (Locke's "external world") not as dualistically separated but as intimately interrelated. This we shall suggest in Chapter XVI. But this solution is not Berkeley's. Not ideas but the notion of a material reality behind ideas was what Berkeley felt to be superfluous. For ideas or appearances are unmistakably present to us. The proper question, he believes, is, Why suppose that ideas *represent* anything else at all, since we never are acquainted with anything but ideas?

Now Locke himself had anticipated such an objection, and had (in his own terms) dealt with it at some length. He admitted that we can never be certain that material objects exist. But what justifies us in this belief is (1) the very fact that we have ideas, for if we assume them not to represent anything we cannot explain how they are caused in our minds; and (2) the fact that we most often cannot avoid having ideas. We cannot at will abolish or create what appears to our minds, and this must mean that there is some external object which compels our sense-organs to function.

**Berkeley's Idealism.** To say, as does Berkeley, that only ideas in our minds exist, implies that whatever exists, exists only when it is perceived or thought of; for ideas, as Locke said, can exist only in a mind. Historically, those views which emphasize mind or what relates to mind (ideas) as the sole universal reality have been called *idealistic* (or spiritualistic, or mentalistic). Berkeleyan idealism is one among a number of different forms. Its author maintained that common sense does not, as is popularly supposed, support the view that perceived objects exist independently of consciousness. On the contrary, common sense gives us evidence that they exist only when we are conscious of them (i.e., when we have ideas) and gives us no evidence that they exist at any other time. Berkeley summed up his view in the maxim *Esse est percipi* ("to be is to be perceived") — the being of anything consists in its being perceived, that is, in its being an idea in a mind. In maintaining the Berkeleyan thesis, however, we need not identify the being of anything with the ideas of only one type of thought, perception, but (broadening his theory) may instead make use of the more general terms "consciousness," "thought," or "experience."

### Basic Presupposition of the Berkeleyan Theory.

Berkeleyan idealism rests on the view — we shall see its relevancy in a moment — that when we have an idea of anything (in perception or otherwise), it is a specific, or particular object that is present to our mind. It is not just a "house" that we perceive, it is a red, square, low house. And in imagining a house, it is a particular image of a house that we imagine, not "house" in the abstract. Indeed, we cannot think at all without thinking of something concrete and imaginal, something that we can represent to ourselves in sensible terms. And what we cannot think of we cannot speak of without indulging in mere verbalism. In Berkeley's own language, we cannot have "abstract ideas." Our ideas are, if not actual sensations, sensational in character. The reader will recognize here the view we have called sensationalism (cf. Chapter VII, Part Two). It identifies all experience, and therefore all knowledge, with sense-perception and sense-imagination. Any idea we have or form must be an image (visual, auditory, etc.), something representable in a sense medium. Berkeley's, like all sensationalism, implies nominalism; and we thus see how a view antithetical to materialism can be equally if not more emphatically nominalistic. (Nominalism, however, does not necessarily imply sensationalism.)

### First Argument: the Unexperienced as Inconceivable.

The simplest and broadest argument for Berkeleyan idealism

is that we *cannot possibly conceive* of anything existing independently of our consciousness, or thinking. For the very act of conceiving makes it an object of thought — an idea. So that it is impossible to conceive of anything but ideas, and ideas cannot exist apart from a mind. Or, stated differently: Everything must be an object that falls within experience, and cannot exist apart from it. For try to conceive it as existing apart. This very attempt must itself be part of conscious experience. We cannot, so to speak, get outside our experience. Thus to conceive of something unexperienced is a contradiction. It is to say that we conceive of something we do not conceive of. Now we can *say* that an object may exist independently of consciousness — that is, we can if we wish employ a verbalism. But we do not thereby conceive of that object. For to think of anything is to think of it in terms of specific sense qualities; and we cannot therefore really *think* of anything existing outside thought.

**Second Argument: Unintelligibility of Material Substance.** What, asks Berkeley, could Locke possibly have meant by the "substance" (or, as Berkeley calls it, the "matter") of an object as distinct from the sum of its qualities? The idea of substance has no defining characteristics. It is therefore unknowable, or, more accurately, not an idea at all. Whenever we wish to conceive of any object, we find that we can do so in terms of its qualities alone with perfect adequacy; so that the term "substance" is seen to be superfluous, an empty word.

**Third Argument: Inseparability of Primary and Secondary Qualities.** Locke admitted that the sensible qualities of an object, such as color, taste, or sound, do not exist apart from perception. Neither, says Berkeley, do the primary qualities so-called. Try to conceive of an object which occupies space and yet which has no color. This is impossible, yet it would be required on the view that the primary qualities exist independently while the sensible qualities (what Locke called "ideas of secondary qualities") do not. The only conclusion is that the primary qualities too are only ideas. For, since the sensible qualities do not exist independently of mind, and since the primary qualities cannot be conceived to exist apart from the sensible qualities, and since an "object" is constituted by nothing *more* than the primary and secondary qualities (cf. the preceding argument), the whole object must be mental, or an idea (or a collection of ideas). In virtue of this conclusion we ought no longer to use the terms "sensible" and "primary." *All* qualities are sensible qualities (ideas); *no* ideas resemble anything "external" to the mind.

**Fourth Argument: Discontinuity of Dualism.** To suppose a kind of being, matter, wholly unlike mind and its ideas, is to set up a discontinuity, and to make a complete scientific explanation of the world impossible. For how can mind "know" something absolutely unlike itself? The only plausible hypothesis is that ideas alone are the objects of knowledge. It is intelligible to speak of the mind as knowing an object that is also mental in character; it is unintelligible to regard it as knowing something with which it has nothing in common.

**Reply to Anticipated Objections.** Berkeley thought out his position with care and detail, and was aware of possible objections. (1) The first is that if there is no existence apart from consciousness, then the whole universe becomes nothing but the sum of the ideas which I, an individual, have. If I cannot conceive of anything as existing independently of my experience, then whatever does exist must exist as part of that experience. Only I (a mind or spirit) and my ideas exist, and when I cease to be conscious, nothing exists. This view is known as *solipsism,* or extreme subjectivism. According to it, not only "things" but other human beings exist only in so far as they are perceived or imagined by me, for I know them only as objects of perception, as ideas. In order to avoid solipsism, Berkeley holds that not one but many minds exist, each with its ideas; so that when I cease to perceive, other minds continue to do so. Above all, there is the mind of God. What we call "nature" or "the universe" is simply the totality of God's experience. Even if all human minds ceased to be conscious, nature would still exist objectively as the set of God's ideas. In terms of God's experience we can explain our own. For when we perceive, or have ideas, what this means is that we are participating in the experience of God.

(2) It is argued that if an object does not exist otherwise than as an idea, we should be able to will anything we wish as the object of perception, whereas the fact of the matter is that we perceive many things — actually the bulk of our environment — despite our will. In other words, if all things are mind-dependent, why is mind so helpless? why are its ideas cut out for it? The answer may be inferred from the preceding point. Nature or God's experience has a structure or order. We could not have ideas if we were not conscious, but when we do have them, what ideas we have are determined by the structure of the divine experience in which we participate.

(3) It might be argued that the Berkeleyan theory abolishes, or at least fails to do justice to, the real world as we know it. Berkeley insists, however, that it is the *materiality* and not the *reality* of the experienced world that he denies. His theory, on the contrary, is put forth as the only consistent theory of this reality. "The question . . . is not, whether things have a *real* existence out of the mind of this or that person, but, whether they have an *absolute* existence, distinct from being perceived by God, and exterior to *all* minds." *

**Critical Remarks.** *Confusion of Conceiving and Imaging.* Berkeley's point that it is impossible to conceive of an unexperienced object reflects, as we saw, the sensationalistic interpretation of thought. The error of his sensationalism is that it fails to distinguish between *calling up images* to the mind and *conceiving,* and uses the latter term with the former meaning. It is true that we cannot have an image of something un-

---

* From the third of the *Three Dialogues between Hylas and Philonous.*

experienced, in the sense that having the image is itself a form of experiencing. But this is far from the same as conceiving an object. We cannot have an image of a regular polygon with a billion sides; our powers of visualization are too feeble for this. Yet we certainly can *conceive* of it. For to conceive of something means to define its properties without contradiction. If there were no distinction between imaging and conceiving; if the latter meant no more than what the former usually means; human thought would be far more limited in extent than it actually is. Physics would be reduced to a shadow of itself, and mathematics would be all but impossible, for in both these sciences the amount of abstract thinking is very great. Once the distinction is drawn, we find that it makes no contradiction at all to suppose something existing unperceived. And we find too that Berkeley's argument that the primary qualities are inconceivable apart from the sensible qualities breaks down. We cannot indeed *visualize* an object in space without visualizing it in some color. But there is no contradiction at all in assuming that an object is extended and yet possesses no qualities which it would possess if it interacted with light and with an eye.

*Dilemma: Inconsistency or Solipsism.* Can Berkeley avoid solipsism and at the same time remain faithful to his basic assumptions? If nothing can exist apart from consciousness, how can other spirits and God exist apart from my consciousness? What grounds justify their being excepted from this idealistic rule? But worse, on Berkeley's view, what *reason* have I to suppose that there *are* other spirits and a divine spirit (as distinct from an idea of other bodies)? Have I an "idea" of another "spirit"? Berkeley admits that we cannot have an image of another spirit or of God, but says that we can have a "notion" of them. But not only is this term "notion" vague; its introduction is inconsistent with Berkeley's basic sensationalism, according to which there are no abstract ideas (or concepts) and all ideas are sense-images. Thus he is caught on the horns of this dilemma: If only "I," as a spirit, exist, I cannot get beyond solipsism — a view that is utterly fantastic; yet if, to avoid this, I assume the existence of other minds and the mind of God, the objection applies to them which applies to material things, that what is unperceived cannot be conceived to exist. Either solipsism or the sacrifice of the principle that *esse est percipi* is inevitable.

*Scientific Sterility of the Berkeleyan Hypothesis.* One of the valuable points emerging from Berkeley's analysis is that we can never be absolutely certain that objects continue to exist when we are not perceiving them. But to think that this verifies the Berkeleyan hypothesis is a mistake. *No* hypothesis about fact can be absolutely certain, as our brief sketch of scientific method indicated. Locke's scientific penetration shows itself to be greater than Berkeley's in realizing this. For as he says, the evidence of independently existing material objects "is as great as we can desire." * Although this hypothesis cannot be tested directly (for to observe directly is to perceive, and we want to know what the consequences are of an object's not being perceived), yet its predictions are always verified. Once we become acquainted with objects, we can specify when and under what conditions we will again observe them. Successful prediction is likewise possible on the Berkeleyan hypothesis — by introducing the concept of divine experience and communication with (or participation in) it. We can explain why our ideas are uniformly the same despite our will by assuming that God or a super-mind causes us to perceive uniformly, whereas on the opposing and usual hypothesis we account for this by supposing an objective order of things in relation. Pragmatically, the two views amount to the same, and differ only verbally. But if so, Berkeley's conception contributes nothing to our scientific understanding but an unfamiliar and (at least in some respects) unwieldy terminology.

*Its Reductive Oversimplification.* In abolishing the distinc-

---

* *Essay,* IV, 11, viii.

tion between "idea" and "thing," Berkeley is stretching the
term "idea" to cover both. This is a form of the reductive
fallacy (see pp. 210-11). To declare that things are "nothing
but" ideas, as Berkeley does, or that ideas are "nothing but"
things, as materialism does, is to oversimplify, albeit in respectively opposite ways. If in examining the difficulties of
dualism we felt better able to sympathize with the intention
of materialism (or perhaps of Berkeleyan idealism), now, in
observing the reductive artificialities of materialism and idealism, we may perhaps better understand the intention of a man
like Descartes, who by his dualism wished to ratify common
sense and avoid such reduction. Ironically enough, the responsibility for Berkeleyan reduction lies with Locke. For
had Locke not so elaborately established the usage of "idea"
as something representative, had he not been so inclined to
speak of the "idea" as a kind of distinct entity, Berkeley might
not have gone on to abolish the representation in the way that
he did. The criticisms made above of Berkeley are independent of the Lockean theoretical framework. The dualism of
knower and known, like any other dualism, commits us to
the difficulty of bridging some troublesome gap. Berkeley was
a child of Locke's indiscretion, repudiated before he was born
by a father fully responsible for his birth. His argument
against discontinuity is sound if it is interpreted as a protest
against dualism. But the elimination of the material world is
not the only way to correct this dualism.

*Value of Attack on Material "Substance."*	One of Berke-
ley's major services to philosophy is his critique of the idea of
substance in the Lockean sense. His analysis succeeds in showing that to ask *what* it is that "possesses" qualities is to be misled by a grammatical convention. The object *is* the sum of
its qualities organized in a certain way. Berkeley's objection
against the notion of substance is not merely a bias of his
nominalism; for while it does emanate from that strain in him,
it merely illustrates well how a nominalistic emphasis can be
sound. If we stripped his point of its sensationalistic termi-

nology, and reformulated it, it would amount to an experimental pragmatic criticism of the significance of a concept which refers to something that cannot possibly be identified in experience. This inauguration of the modern revolt against the concept of an unknowable reality undoubtedly influenced Peirce in his formulation of pragmatism. A naturalistic viewpoint like the one we shall indicate in the next chapter may profit from Berkeley's critique. In speaking of matter or the material world, it will now understand these conceptions in terms of ascertainable properties rather than as an intrinsically hidden substratum.

**Hume's Critique of Spiritual Substance.**  It took the critical penetration of Hume, Berkeley's successor in the vanguard of British philosophy, to see that the latter's arguments against material substance could be applied with at least equal force to spiritual substance, or the notion of a simple, permanent spirit. Berkeley had concurred in Locke's view that the operations of perceiving, imagining, etc., were the activities *of* something, the mind; and both had continued in adherence to the Cartesian principle that knowledge of our own mind or self is more direct and certain and basic than any other knowledge. Introspection they regarded as the starting-point of all deliberate inquiry. Hume, putting this introspective method to a critical test, found that it revealed no *entity* or *substantial subject*. His view is best stated in his own words.

> There are some philosophers who imagine we are every moment intimately conscious of what we call our *self;* that we feel its existence and its continuance in existence; and are certain, beyond the evidence of a demonstration, both of its perfect identity and simplicity. . . . For my part, when I enter most intimately into what I call *myself,* I always stumble upon some particular perception or other, of heat or cold, light or shade, love or hatred, pain or pleasure. I never can catch *myself* at any time without a perception, and never can observe anything but the perception. When my perceptions are removed for any time, as by sound sleep, so long am I insensible of *myself,* and may truly be said not to exist. . . . [The mind or self is] nothing but a bundle or collection of different perceptions, which succeed each other with an inconceivable rapidity, and are in a perpetual flux

> and movement. . . . The mind is a kind of theatre, where
> several perceptions successively make their appearance; pass,
> repass, glide away, and mingle in an infinite variety of pos-
> tures and situations. . . . The comparison of the theatre
> must not mislead us. They are the successive perceptions
> only, that constitute the mind. . . .*

Hume's analysis is directed toward the formulation of a more
consistent empiricism. As the idea of unknowable substance
has no empirical justification in the material sense, neither has
it in the spiritual.

> Philosophers begin to be reconciled to the principle, that
> we have no idea of external substance, distinct from the
> ideas of particular qualities. This must pave the way for
> a like principle with regard to the mind, that we have no
> notion of it, distinct from the particular perceptions.†

**The Idealistic Strain in Kant.**   In the philosophy of Kant
we find an instructive example of a viewpoint that within the
framework of an original approach seeks to profit from the
work of men like those we have mentioned. For Kant (on
the usual interpretation of him) there exists a real world absolutely independent of human minds. In this he rejects Ber-
keleyanism. But the real world cannot be known by us as it
is "in itself." All we can know is the world that is created
when the real world sets our machinery of structuring or
ordering in operation. The outcome of this structuring is what
we call "experience." The knower is supplied by the real world
with the *matter* for experience—something not himself serves
to arouse in him raw, unorganized sensations like feelings of
sight, touch, etc.—the knower supplies the *form* for experience, and without this form experience would not be experience. We cannot experience things-in-themselves. This follows
from the very meaning of "experience." We can experience
at all only by endowing the unorganized or formless stuff of
sense with the organizations or forms involved in ordering
or "judging." It is as if, Kant says, we were born with blue
spectacles attached to our eyes. We should have no right to

---

* *A Treatise of Human Nature,* Bk. I, Pt. 4, Sec. 6.
† *Ibid.,* Bk. I, Pt. 4, Appendix to Sec. 6.

say that things are really blue, blue in themselves; yet in order to see them (one form of experience) we should have to see them as blue. Blueness would be a necessary condition of seeing. On this analogy, the forms contributed by the knower — space, time, the cause-effect relation — are necessary conditions for experience and understanding. Substance in Kant becomes one of the forms with which judgment organizes its data. Whereas Locke had required supposition of an unknowable stuff to hold qualities together as a unity, Kant makes substance a form of order, one of the conditions of experiencing being that qualities co-exist in this or that order.

**"Phenomena" and "Noumena."** Thus we know only what we can experience, and what we can experience is determined by the conditions which the knowing process permits as limits and possibilities. The world of experienceable things Kant calls the world of *phenomena* or *appearances*. The real world, unknowable, is the world of *noumena* or things-in-themselves. Against the criticism of Hume, Kant tries to save the notion of substance by interpreting it as he does, and making it applicable to the phenomenal or knowable world, rather than as Locke did, to the real world. Thus Kant is an idealist only so far as the world of appearance is concerned; but he is not a sensationalist, since for him the knower does not receive knowledge passively but plays a rôle in endowing the known world with the order and structure that it has.

God, the soul, and human immortality belong to the real world, the world which is the object of faith and not of knowledge (see Chapter VIII). The real world, though unknowable, is a necessary assumption. We can say only that it is, not what it is. Here we have another kind of dualism, resembling most closely perhaps the dualism of Locke. As Locke's separation of idea and thing generated Berkeley, so Kant's corresponding but much sharper distinction between appearance and reality generated the criticisms of positivism and pragmatism. Yet as Berkeley was in part the child of Locke, so were positivism and pragmatism the children of Kant and the grandchildren of Kant's own partial ancestors, Locke, Berkeley, and Hume. Though it may seem peculiar that a view which springs from another should be its severest critic, a bit of reflection shows that it is only natural. For the later view in a sense is the older one attempting to repudiate its earlier difficulties and inconsistencies in the light of new possibilities and new influences.

**Objective Idealism.** Many philosophers, though convinced that mind is the dominant factor in the universal scheme of things, have tried to conceive it as having a larger, more objective rôle than it has in a philosophy like Berkeley's. They have sought to oppose materialism and mind-body dualism and at the same time to vindicate the objectivity of the world. Berkeley himself did not *intend* to conclude with solipsism or subjective idealism. He pictured the universe as consisting of God, finite minds, and ideas in these minds. But even in his intended idealism, Berkeley drew too sharp a distinction between a mind and its experience (or ideas). Nature was a sum of ideas, so that nature and experience came to mean the same thing. Yet nature remained distinct from the minds in which it had its being, these minds being conceived in the substantial sense criticized by Hume. Objective idealism tries to equate nature and mind.

**Its Motivation.** The attempt to identify mind and nature in some sense, though most prominent in modern philosophy, has its roots in ancient philosophy. The intellectual reasons for such a type of view are not difficult to state. Objective idealists believe that the mental or spiritual alone is identified with life and with reason. And they feel that it is only in terms of the latter concepts that nature can be understood. To conceive of nature as mechanical and dead, as devoid of purpose, is to make it inexplicable. For that which is completely alien to man is completely alien to his way of knowing. Inexplicable too, for idealistic and materialistic outlooks alike, as we saw, is the supposition of dualism in nature. Objective idealism (and indeed all idealism) is most often associated with a more or less religious outlook, which militates against the assignment of equal status to the material and the spiritual, and is conducive to a thoroughgoing spiritual interpretation. The interpretation of nature in terms of mind may avoid supernaturalism (though this is controversial), and yet may give values a place of objectivity and absoluteness. For values relate to life and to mind, and if life and mind belong not to man alone but to nature as a whole, so do values. In this way objective idealists are able to assign to moral law the status of other universal laws. Let us go on to sketch two historical types of objective idealism.

**Spiritual Atomism: Leibniz.** In the seventeenth century G. W. Leibniz (1646-1716), a contemporary of Locke and Newton, ventured a spiritual interpretation of the universe which would at the same time reflect the renascence of natural science. As the physical scientists at that time were impressed by the concept of motion and used it as the leading idea in all of science, so Leibniz was impressed by the concept of force and felt that it must be the ultimate principle of the universe. The universe being complex and many-sided, Leibniz reasoned that it must therefore ultimately be composed of *simple* elements, of parts which are themselves incapable of any further division or analysis. These ultimate units or atoms are not substances in Locke's sense of the term but spiritual substances in the sense of forces or units of energy. Leibniz called them *monads*. A monad, being no stuff, is really a set of activities, and for Leibniz these activities are "perception." Activities or perceptions are more than merely such: they are forces in the sense that they have a capacity—an unlimited capacity—to change, in other words, a potentiality. Leibniz's view is thus an atomism, an idealistic atomism as opposed to the materialistic atomism of the ancient materialists and Hobbes. In this atomism, however, no monad can interact with any other, since each is perfectly distinct from any other, and each is absolutely simple. Each is a distinct "viewpoint," a unique "perspective" on the world. Interaction would endow the things interacting with at least some degree of complexity,

and this would destroy their atomistic simplicity and uniqueness. Each monad can only "mirror" or reflect the activity of
every other monad. As forces or activities, the monads do not
occupy space. Though created by God, they are eternal. Leibniz
distinguishes perception from apperception, or self-consciousness. Though all monads are percipient, not all are self-
perceiving. And this distinction enables him to account for
what we distinguish when we speak of "the physical world"
and "the world of man." In the Leibnizian universe the monads
form a hierarchy, culminating in God, who is the highest
monad, distinct from all others. All monads are insulated
individualities, but the total interrelation and order of all
the monads (that is, the structure of the universe) results
from a "pre-established harmony" instituted by God.

**The Idea of the "Absolute": Hegel.**  Very different from
the spiritual atomism of Leibniz, and flourishing in an age of
romanticism unawed by science, are the early nineteenth century idealistic philosophies of Kant's German successors, especially Fichte (1762-1814), Hegel (1770-1831), and Schelling
(1775-1854). That of Hegel, most influential and most difficult, is very striking in its outlines. The whole of existence is
a web, a unity of which everything is an integral and indis-
soluble part. But this unity or whole — Hegel calls it the Absolute — is no fixed and static whole; it is an evolution or development, a process. Hegel interprets its nature by taking a
clue from the nature of man. Man's most significant characteristic is his mind or process of thinking, his striving to
acquire ideas, and to acquire always new ideas by modifying
older ones. Now this human process must be only an image or
reflection of the universal process. The Absolute is universal
Reason or Spirit, and the process of evolution or universal history is the process of Spirit thinking, becoming increasingly
conscious, realizing its potentialities. This development is a
necessary one, and a progressive one. All events represent
phases of Spirit's development. Human institutions, culminating in art, religion, and philosophy, are the highest manifestations of the absolute, universal mind. Now if the process of

world-history is the increasing consciousness of Spirit, and if Spirit is the whole of reality, this consciousness must be self-consciousness on its part. History, or the passage of events, and human experience, or thought about these events, are only two limited aspects of the one universal process, representing respectively the objective and the subjective aspects of this process. In Hegel, the Absolute or God is not distinct from the world, as in Leibniz, but is the very principle or process of its development. The teleological cast of this view is clear: everything comes to pass for a purpose, to realize the potentialities inherent in the Absolute spirit. Yet this view is also deterministic: the *way* in which things come to pass is through law. And the determinism is not merely one which maintains that things *actually* are governed by law but that they could *not possibly* have been otherwise, in direct contradiction of Hume's conclusion (see pp. 201-202 above).

**Critical Remarks; Empirico-pragmatic Difficulties.** We have refrained from criticism of the views of Kant, Leibniz, and Hegel. Such criticism is best left to the reader — after he has studied the views in question at first hand; for the major idealistic (or semi-idealistic) systems do not lend themselves easily to exposition, and criticism cannot assume a secure basis. But some general observations may be made. Even the foregoing sketches of the Leibnizian and Hegelian world-views are sufficient to indicate to the reader how thoroughly rationalistic in character they are — how *a priori* intuition, and, on the basis of this, reasoning which far transcends the world of observation, lie at the bottom of their speculation. Despite the important differences between the two systems — one an atomism, the other sometimes called a *monism* — both agree that mind is the sole "reality." They are thus both reductive, in the same sense that we found the materialistic and Berkeleyan views to be reductive, but in a different context and to a far greater degree. Unlike the material world, which in its ordinary sense is the directly observable world, the world of spirit of which the objective idealists speak is an *a priori* construction. Both the system of Leibniz, who preceded Kant, and that of Hegel, who followed him, depend in their essence on a distinction between appearance and reality. But the distinction is somewhat different from that of Kant. Whereas in Kant the real world is unknowable, for the other two our knowledge of the real world is of a deeper kind than our knowledge of the world of ordinary experience. If the reader will recall the distinction made above between two senses of *a priori* (p. 178), he will see that Kant's *a priorism,* obtaining solely in the world of experience or "phenomena," illustrates one of these senses, and that the *a priorism* extending to what transcends the world of experience, by which Leibniz and Hegel are dominated, illustrates the other.

The essential difficulty of these rationalistic systems is a pragmatic one. How are we to give empirical meaning to concepts like "monad," "Absolute," and so on? In what sense is the whole of reality reducible to the "activity of perception" or to the "self-consciousness of Spirit"? In what way are the data of the sciences and of common experience to be regarded as furnishing evidence for such conceptions? Leibniz has sometimes been defended on the ground that the conception of monads, which are atoms of force, is no more recondite and strange than the concepts of modern physics — those of "electron" and "photon," for instance. But this is based on a mistaken interpretation of modern science, which employs such terms for a complex network of experimental techniques and mathematical reasonings. Leibniz's speculations are not part of so solid a fund of scientific inquiry. In the latter, we are able to predict actual occurrences in nature; in the view of Leibniz we are not.

**The Poetic Interpretation of Speculative Systems.** If we look at the foregoing problem from another point of view, we may enter a very different plea for the world-views of men like Leibniz and Hegel. These perspectives, which seem so imaginative as to border sometimes on the fantastic, are not essentially different from poetic vision. They are the means of expression of men who are used to grappling with detailed problems of a moral, historical, and scientific character. Their validity consists not in any descriptive or explanatory value, for they are not empirically verifiable at least in the usual sense and all such schemes differ widely from one another, but in the imaginative possibilities and insights which they open to us. Interpreted in this way, they are not opposed to one another but are complementary, as the works of poets are. It is no doubt true that their authors intended no such interpretation, and that we should derive greater appreciation of their intended value if we studied them in detail. But the intent of a philosopher is not always the verdict of history.

An interpretation of this kind may be given, as we have seen in Part One, not only for philosophers like Leibniz and Hegel but for all speculative philosophy. The reader will do well to consider it carefully as he continues the study of philosophy. But there is another point that he will be well advised to remember; namely, that where speculative philosophy does possess poetic value, this does not imply that it may not *also* possess scientific value, as a broad interpretation of human experience in all its aspects. What is true is that not *every* theory of speculative philosophy can have *equal* cognitive (or interpretative) merit. But theories within a special science too may conflict. And as the development of scientific thought has revealed that conflicting viewpoints often had more in common than was at first supposed, so the development of philosophic thought reveals an unmistakable core running through even the most divergent perspectives.

❖ ❖ ❖

## CHAPTER SIXTEEN

# The Broader Conception
# of Nature

Especially within the last hundred years philosophers have been developing a perspective which seeks to benefit by criticising the major historical viewpoints and by extracting what is of value in them.

**Materialistic and Critical Naturalism.**  This framework of interpretation, which may be called *critical naturalism,* and which takes *many different* forms, is historically the offspring of both materialism and its idealistic critics. It avoids above all the hypothesis of a supernature, but its conception of nature is far broader and far more comprehensive than that of materialism: it finds a natural status for much of the subject-matter of idealistic philosophy. It regards the concepts of matter and motion as grossly inadequate for a speculative philosophy. It agrees with idealism in pointing to mind as an important fact; but it defines mind in terms of nature, not nature in terms of mind. Like materialism, it denies the existence of "final causes" taken as one kind of efficient cause or force; yet it finds room for the notion of ends and teleology, which it interprets as one among other kinds of relation in the natural world.

**Critical Naturalism and the Scientific Method.**  It might seem that the normal question arising at this point is, What is nature?  Critical naturalism, however, while refusing to identify "nature" with the world of space-time events alone, does not try to offer any compact alternative definition. "Nature," we found, is not capable of being defined in the way that a house or star is. It is not something that we can survey as a fixed, closed system of things, events, or laws. Indeed it is precisely in this attitude, which may seem destructive and negative but which amounts to the position that with respect to nature our knowledge is always partial and possesses vague boundaries, that critical naturalism is distinguished from the dogmatic tendencies of materialism. How, then, does it nevertheless exclude the hypothesis of any supernatural being or of any supernatural realm? Because it acquires its essential character not so much from a set of permanent principles as from the method which it employs. This method, whatever it may entail in the thought of individual philosophers, seeks to be harmonious with the scientific method. The supernaturalistic hypothesis is regarded as unsatisfactory because, resorting as it does to what is intrinsically incomprehensible and beyond possible experience, it explains nothing in a scientific sense but rather limits inquiry and the search for objective evidence. Critical naturalism is satisfied to claim less than other speculative theories but to possess a sound basis for what it does claim. In guiding itself by scientific standards, it commits no slavish worship of whatever scientific theories happen to be currently accepted, nor does it elevate scientific method to the status of a universal panacea. The reason is, first, that it accepts nonscientific experience as well as scientific—art and religion besides science—as contributing to a world-perspective; and, second, that the scientific method itself involves no such worship. It is important for us to remember that the scientific method by its objective techniques *approximates* to correct hypotheses; so that it is not any given conclusion on which our main reliance is to be placed, but the general method of establishing conclusions.

**The Ancestry of Critical Naturalism.** The foregoing really amounts to the assertion that modern naturalism is an empiricist philosophy in the broadest sense of the term. In this we must lay emphasis on the word "modern." For among the classical philosophers who may be regarded as closest in spirit to modern naturalism, an empiricist viewpoint (or a consistent empiricist viewpoint) is not always entertained. Two of these classical ancestors are Aristotle and Spinoza. Both conceive of nature in a diversified and broad sense, both avoid supernaturalism, and both — this is perhaps most significant — conceive of man as a part of nature. Yet there are sharp differences between the two, and between both alike and modern naturalism. Both believe that there are certain principles which are "self-evident" (though these play a much more significant rôle in Spinoza). For the most part, Aristotle's actual philosophic inquiry is definitely empiricistic, whereas that of Spinoza is rationalistic in the extreme. Aristotle emphasizes final causation and also believes in chance. Spinoza's philosophy excludes both in favor of a rigid determinism. But in spite of Aristotle's self-evident premises and in spite of Spinoza's rationalistic deduction of his entire philosophy from "first principles," neither of which is very relevant to the practice of modern scientific method, each of these philosophers represents to an unusual degree an attempt to embody in his philosophy the scientific method of his own day. Aristotle, indeed, not only practised both philosophic and scientific inquiry as we understand them today; he actually gave the latter its first systematic exposition as a method. For him, change was to be interpreted as the co-operation of means toward producing or realizing in an object some form or nature or essence. Natural events, as we previously said, were thus treated qualitatively in terms of the means needed to produce them as ends. Spinoza, on the other hand, wrote at the dawn of modern science, when the quantitative and measurable aspect of events was being exclusively emphasized and the appeal to final causes discarded. The science of his day moreover tended to conceive of nature as a great geometrical pattern, for it was intoxicated by its success in applying mathematics to the formulation of its theories and to the deduction of their consequences. It was natural, therefore, that a rationalistic, deductive method should find expression in Spinoza (and in his predecessor, Descartes) as the attempted philosophic counterpart of natural science. But the fundamental characteristic, to repeat, that makes Aristotle and Spinoza outstanding ancestors of modern naturalism is the way in which they conceive of nature and of man's place in it. In neither do we find the reductive fallacy, nor do we find an exaggerated emphasis on the traits of things human as typical of all reality.

**Spinoza's Conception of Nature.** Let us glance in the briefest way at the view of Spinoza. All that the contemporary naturalist includes in nature is for Spinoza embraced in "substance." Substance, or the order of nature, is both an order of extended things and a logical order of their "ideas" or intelligible aspects. Mind and matter are thus two "attributes" or ways in which the order of nature is illustrated. They are no longer as in Descartes themselves independent substances, the only substances in addition to the divine, but are exemplifications of the one all-embracing substance. Substance, which as the inclusive order of nature comprises the unity and interrelation of all that exists, also contains within itself all happenings. It is therefore "eternal" and "infinite" and "omnipotent," and for this reason Spinoza calls it "God" as well as "nature." Whatever happens, happens in accordance with fixed, necessary, unchangeable laws of substance (or God), and could not possibly occur in any other way. Spinoza is thus an extreme determinist. And here one or two comparisons are called for. (a) Spinoza's determinism asserts not merely that all events *are* caused, or governed by law, but that they *must* occur in the way that they do. It thus involves a conception of causality which, as we saw, Hume was later to criticize. (b) This necessary determinism resembles the necessary determinism later adopted by Hegel. But quite unlike the latter, it is not the instrument for the attainment of any goal or purpose. It is logical but not teleological. (c) But neither is this determinism a materialistic determinism or mechanism. For it does not like materialism reduce everything to matter and motion, nor are its causal laws exclusively mechanical.

For Spinoza there is no such thing as human "free will" in the sense that the "will" can cause things to happen without itself being subject to causes. A man, being one instance or embodiment of the attributes of nature or substance, a "mode" of both extension and thought (matter and mind), has the same status as all other "modes." His total activity is therefore one manifestation of universal determinism.

Bearing in mind this sketch of Spinoza's view, let us turn to some principles which seem to be characteristic of modern critical naturalism. We must try to see whether we can arrive at a conception of nature which, like that of Spinoza, interprets man and his institutions in natural terms, but which nevertheless avoids Spinoza's rationalistic method, and which modifies (in accordance with Hume's critique) the rationalistic formulation of determinism, all in harmony with an approach which better fits the contemporary testimony of experience and science.

**Naturalistic Rejection of "Appearance-Reality" Dualisms and of "Reduction."**  A view like that of Kant, which distinguishes a realm of appearance from a realm of reality, would not be called "reductive" in the usual sense. But conversely, there is a definite sense in which reductive views like materialism and rationalistic idealism (Leibniz, Hegel) may be called "appearance-reality" views. For in denying the reality of one or another kind of phenomena, they are tacitly making a distinction between what "is" real and what merely "appears" to be real.

When we say that critical naturalism adheres to a scientific attitude in defining what principles it will accept, we mean that these principles must be such as can be supported by the facts of experience common to all, and not such as disregard these facts or "transcend" them. From this it follows at once that it cannot accept any fundamental appearance-reality distinction. To imply that the facts which appear are not the "real" facts is to posit a realm about which *nothing* that we may say can be verified or refuted by evidence. But since the scientific attitude is our most reliable intellectual instrument, naturalism distrusts the notion of a reality necessarily hidden from us, for this very conclusion must have been arrived at by some other subjective, anti-experiential method. Now it is true that in ordinary common sense discourse we draw a distinction between appearance and reality — but of a very different kind. For instance, we say that the object we see before us "appears" to be a man but is "really" a dummy. Here, however, it is obvious that what we distinguish as the "reality" is *no less* a matter of observation subject to investigation than the "appearance" itself. It is the notion of an intrinsically non-empirical reality that naturalism regards as scientifically and pragmatically unwarranted.

In the same spirit, critical naturalism cannot accept the materialistic tendency to fit all things into the categories of physics and chemistry. For this too is equivalent to the denial that certain kinds of facts are "really" facts. To say that the phenomenon of a living organism is "nothing but" an arrangement of chemical compounds is to disregard relationships of which experience gives clear testimony. To say that values are no more than names given to purely physical situations is to dismiss one portion of experience *in favor* of another. Naturalism thus holds that values, meanings, purposes, ideals, life, mind, and society are not less "real" than the physically measurable world. With this important qualification, what it does say is that all these kinds of phenomena have their definite natural status *in* the natural world and that they cannot occur or act except in connection with its interactions. Critical naturalism says also that, since these realities have *arisen* in the world of nature, at one time nature may have been satisfactorily describable exclusively in physical terms. It is the task of such a view to explain how non-physical realities are found to be related to the physical. It must define them, or indicate the mode of their definition, in terms that avoid traditional difficulties and obscurities.

**The Reinterpretation of Causality.** "How can something not material be produced from something material?" has been a favorite question of materialists and anti-materialists alike. And further, how can new or unprecedented material events occur if the same causes always operate? These are the two main theses of materialism: that all realities are material, and that the functioning of the material universe is machinelike (mechanistic), devoid of genuine novelty. Now according to the critical naturalist these materialistic principles rest on a conception of the principle of causality — the classical conception — which is oversimplified and dogmatic. According to this classical conception, an effect cannot "contain more" than its cause; nor can it be "qualitatively different." In other words, a cause must be "equal" to its effect. But if we reflect a little on this principle, we find that it rests on no empirical evidence, and that where it is not vague in its meaning it is false. Water is certainly qualitatively different from the oxygen and hydrogen, the combination of which is its cause. As for the quantitative relation, by what means are we to determine whether there is "more" or "less" in the water than in its component elements? Is there or is there not "more" in an explosion than in a match flame and powder, in a landslide than in the rock disturbance that causes it, in the breaking of a window than in the moving stone which breaks it? More in *what sense?* If for an effect to contain more is for it to contain something *new,* something which is not found in the cause, this amounts to qualitative difference between the two; and we found that to deny this is false.

**Determinism and Novelty.**   There are two ways in which the critical naturalist may explain how non-material factors can arise in a universe that at one time presumably does not contain them. One is by appealing to chance, and supposing that new occurrences are spontaneous, accumulating to enrich the universe. The other alternative is to retain determinism, but to interpret it non-mechanistically. Mechanism implies that the laws of the universe are fixed and completed, and that therefore all "new" phenomena can really be fitted into a limited set of categories, or explained by a limited number of principles. Its dogmatism lies in the assumption that it is possible to frame principles of prediction applicable to all future qualities and occurrences in the universe down to the last particular.

On the reinterpretation suggested above the effect of a cause may involve conditions different in some respect from those which give rise to it. In this way, a new total set of conditions is generated, and the conditions under which the original cause will operate next time are not exactly the same. Thus new causal factors may continually arise, and at the same time influence the circumstances under which the old operate. When hydrogen and oxygen are combined in a certain proportion to form water, a new condition is added to the sum of the old conditions, thereby enlarging the possibilities of new kinds of change (new relationships), though the old conditions continue to obtain as causal factors. We may state the matter in other terms. Laws of nature are illustrated repeatedly, in certain patterns or kinds of relationship. But the *specific conditions* under which they are illustrated are never the same. That is, while the laws do not vary, the *facts* do; for each fact is an individual or unique occurrence. But now among the many new facts a new uniformity or pattern or repeated relationship may be exhibited, so that a new law is added to the old. Thus when the earth was first formed, this set of conditions involved geographic laws. We can suppose that physical laws, holding under ever differing conditions, each causally generated by previous conditions, at one time were exemplified under that set of conditions which we call "life," or "living matter." Along with the physical laws, repeatedly followed under the varying conditions, there were gradually manifested what we call "biological laws." As living organisms developed, that set of conditions constituting "mind" or "mental activity" arose. And thus together with the physical and biological laws exemplified under these conditions, psychological laws obtained. Then the development of human organisms resulted in the conditions of "society," and social laws obtained. Similarly were developed value-conditions, meaning-conditions, and the like. Thus without abandoning the assumption of determinism, which finds support in experience, the critical naturalist is able also to explain the existence of novelty and variety in the universe, which likewise is in accordance with the testimony of experience.

**Three Meanings of "Chance."**    Although determinism and chance are ordinarily opposed terms, on the foregoing statement of determinism it is possible to define "chance" in such a way that the two are compatible. We may use "chance" as the name for the specific conditions under which laws are illustrated. It is a "law" that fire burns paper, but it is chance that a particular piece of paper I burn now should happen to burn in the particular way and under the unique circumstances that it does. "Chance" in this sense is not opposed to causation, but denotes the particular way in which an effect occurs. When we say (in this sense) that a brick fell "by chance" from the roof of a building, we do not mean (a) that our subjective expectations were startled, which is one meaning of "chance," nor (b) that the falling of the brick violated a law or was not in accordance with any law, which is another meaning, the one incompatible with "cause," but (c) that a certain law has been exemplified in a unique way.

**The "Free Will" Problem.**    One of the controversial issues in the entire history of philosophy has been that of whether "the will is free." Does the principle of causality apply to the choices and decisions we make, to acts that we "will," as well as to everything else? If we consider ourselves as merely behaving organisms, we find that we call some of our acts "voluntary" acts, and others "involuntary." For the former alone do we regard ourselves as "responsible" in a moral sense. We find also that we have a "feeling" that some of our actions are performed "freely." Many supernaturalists and idealists have strenuously maintained that the will is "free," that the decisions to act voluntarily are not causally governed by prior conditions. Materialists, on the other hand, have maintained that the so-called acts of free will are only disguised forms of physical action, every act being in fact conditioned by antecedent causes. We do not, the materialists admit, *experience* any constraint when we decide to perform one of a number of alternative acts, but actually the choice we do make has a cause which in turn has had a cause and so on; and it is such a cause, not an "uncaused cause" called the "will," that is responsible for the act which results. The issue has sometimes been called that of "free will against determinism." It has been said that if determinism is universal, men cannot be held morally responsible for their actions. For if each act is determined by previous acts, and these by others previous to them, man is merely the product of the chain of causes and conditions that make him up. If this were the case, such things as punishment, praise, and blame would become meaningless.

**Some Clarifications.** One of the reasons for the interminable character of the free will debate is that disputants do not understand the same things by the terms they use. If we take the term "will," we find that it is often used to denote a kind of entity or independent agent that a man employs in order to make choices. This usage is now acknowledged to be naïve and untenable, a hold-over from an outworn system of psychology. We shall be on sounder ground if we regard the act of willing or making voluntary choices as a function of the entire human organism. The view of those who reject determinism in human volition is then that certain of our choices are not the effects of any cause. Now the settlement of this question cannot be achieved by simply observing a given man and noting his actions. For each camp will interpret these actions differently. We must try to decide the question by considering which answer (if either) is most harmonious both with our prior knowledge and with the evidence derived from relevant sources.

**"Freedom" as a Form of Determination.** The view that some of our choices are uncaused, far from giving meaning to the notion of moral responsibility, actually makes it meaningless. For what is uncaused is a matter of chance, and a matter of chance is nothing more nor less than an *accident*. And surely it is meaningless to say that we are "responsible" (subject to praise or blame) for what is an accident on our part. In fact it would be meaningless to speak of "choices" or "decisions" at all if they were purely spontaneous. And if determinism in human volition is held to be false, not only are our choices a matter of pure chance but also the execution of our choices, so that anything we may "voluntarily" do is subject not to our own determination but to accident. But are we then not in a dilemma, faced with an inability to explain what we mean by responsibility? For does not the other alternative, that human choices like everything else are causally determined, likewise shut the door? Not if we make one or two distinctions. Consider the case of a watch, mechanically ticking. If the watch's movements were not causally determined but were matters of chance, it would be nonsense to speak of it as telling time. Causally determined, the watch can tell time. But its movements must be determined by factors *within itself,* if we are to speak of the *watch* as the thing that tells time. If it is hindered by an external force, if it is interfered with, as we commonly say, then even though it be a mechanism we may say that it is no longer "free" to function. Consider now not a mechanism but an organism, and we can see that the same point applies. Spinoza pointed out that the freedom of a man consists not in his being undetermined but in his being determined by forces and conditions arising from his own nature and within himself, as contrasted with his being determined by something that coerces him. "'Freedom" of will and determinism are therefore not opposed. Human freedom is one kind of determination, what is roughly called "self-determination." In this sense alone can we be called "responsible" for our voluntary acts. But the organism must not be considered as a self-sufficient, artificially isolated unit. The determining factors are not only our state immediately preceding a choice but our bodily constitution, our past development, and our present relation to the environment. For this reason we cannot be regarded as *wholly* responsible for any given act. We are, for better or worse, to a great extent the products of factors beyond our control. This in itself is no mystery but a fact of nature. Life in society and the world in part *define* what an "organism" *is*. This general solution of the free will problem by identifying freedom with self-determination, though it originates with Spinoza, is the classical solution not of the naturalists but of the idealists. Kant and his successors took it over from Spinoza and made it prominent in modern philosophy.

**Self-Determination and Human Intelligence.** If the freedom of a man consists in determination of his choices by factors within himself, what factors are these? We often say that it is man's intelligence or reason (in the broader sense of the term) which governs his so-called purposive activity. We can give this a rather exact meaning. To say that man has intelligence means that he can modify his conduct to meet new situations. He can not only change, but grow. He can profit from past experience. If man could not learn from experience, punishment and reward, indeed the very idea of responsibility, would not be applicable. Thus so far as man is concerned, freedom and responsibility mean determination by intelligence. It is this concept which enables us to distinguish between the negative sense in which a watch is free to tell time and the positive sense in which man is free.

**The Status of the Non-material.** Critical naturalism in its modern version is at one with Spinoza and with Aristotle in holding that life, mind, and value are phases of nature, neither more nor less "natural" than its physical phases, and in suggesting, as opposed to the mechanistic view, that there may be an unlimited number of other phases potential in nature. It arrives at these conclusions, however, not in the rationalistic manner of Spinoza by deducing them from an *a priori* conception of what nature *must* involve, but by an attempt to form hypotheses empirically on the basis of the results of the sciences and the broadest implications of our total experience.

And it interprets the determinism of nature not in the Spino-zistic sense that events could not possibly occur otherwise than as they do, but in accordance with Hume's critique, as a guiding hypothesis the assumption of which is better justified than its contrary. In pointing to the fact that nature has biological, social, and psychological dimensions as well as physical, naturalism does not commit the error of isolating these from each other, or of endowing each of them with the same kind of physical efficacy. As factors in nature, their presence makes an unmistakable difference, but one that must be carefully defined and not confused with the operation of material forces. Thus mind is regarded as a factor influencing events, but not as a force independent of other natural processes.

**The Interpretation of Mind.** To define "mind" is a very large problem which, of course, cannot be adequately dealt with here. But we can indicate the approach of critical naturalism. There are two extremes which it attempts to avoid: the idealistic conception of mind as a substance, or self-sufficient entity, and the materialistic indentification of mind with the brain or nervous system. The difficulties in the former extreme have already been stated. The latter confuses the assertion that mental or conscious phenomena, feeling and thinking, could not exist *unless* nervous processes occurred in the body, with the assertion that such phenomena *are* nervous processes. But an image, for example, called up in memory, is clearly not identical with the physico-chemical process that makes its occurrence possible. "Mind" for the critical naturalist signifies a *set of functions* and not a simple entity or thing (whether brain or spiritual substance); it comprises a wide range of both capacities and activities on the part of the human organism. Mind is therefore an aspect of the organism's behavior. We perform not only so-called physical activities, like breathing, walking, digesting, grasping; but also "mental" activities, like remembering, inferring, abstracting. Mind is a phase of the human organism's living, as that living is a phase of natural processes. But for naturalism to point our conception of mind in this direction does not in itself give a detailed *account* of the mental functions of the organism. This belongs to psychology, which aims to explain them in accordance with scientific standards. That the achievement of such an aim is still far from complete may be readily admitted by naturalism, for it has no. desire to deny the significant differences between the mental and other functions and uncritically lump them together. Such a course was taken — unsuccessfully, it is now generally acknowledged — by the crude behaviorists in psychology. There are still many who feel that the mental functions are essentially different from the others, and that they can never be investigated by the same methods. Among the students of this camp are those who believe that not only the mental functions but all of living matter is the expression of a "vital force" in the world, and also those who hold these functions to represent something miraculous and incomprehensible. Naturalism places its trust (its "faith," in the third sense of this term we distinguished in Chapter V of Part Two) in the historically demonstrated capacity of science to attack and solve such problems. Rather than rush to explanations which are unverifiable and irrefutable, the products of reckless intuition, imagination, and vague tradition, it adopts the more difficult but saner course of admitting the limitations of our present knowledge and meanwhile using the best available method of overcoming them. Even apart from the positive justification of this position, it would still be preferable to the dogmas which now confidently claim the field.

**Knowledge as a Natural Event.** Naturalism opposes not only the assumptions of materialism, Cartesian dualism, and idealism, but also the subtler dualism of Locke with regard to knowledge. On Locke's view man is a knower, and nature is the object of his knowledge. Nature is not known to him directly but only representatively by the ideas that he has of it. It is something "outside." From this point of view, as we have seen, we are faced with a "problem of knowledge," giving rise to scepticism in a destructive form: If we know only our own ideas directly, how can we ever be certain that our "knowledge" is knowledge of the "real"? From the naturalistic point of view this problem does not arise. If our scientific theories are experimentally corroborated, if they enable us to predict future experience successfully, and can be applied technologically, it is. idle to ask whether this knowledge is "real" knowledge. To say that it is knowledge of "ideas" rather than "things" is only a verbal distinction. For the critical naturalist knowledge is itself a natural phenomenon. Man is a part of nature, not somehow an external spectator of it, and still less an external spectator with smoked spectacles that he cannot remove from his nose. The activity of knowing is as much an event as anything else. There is, of course, a sense in which all knowledge involves a knower and something known. But this distinction is not an absolute one which forever separates all things known from all knowers, man from nature. It is a distinction of two aspects of an activity that occurs *within* nature; and it simply means that now this, now that — different phenomena in nature — become objects in another natural phenomenon, a knowledge-situation. The reader — to end with an important warning — will understand that when we use terms like "within" nature we are speaking metaphorically, and are not naïvely interpreting nature as a kind of box. It is not in spatial but in logical terms that we are speaking. And the purpose of using one spatial metaphor to combat another is precisely to show that the formulation employed by the dualistic view lies at the bottom of its difficulties. Every theory must be judged not merely for what it says but for how it says it.

**The Interpretation of Value.** Here again, critical naturalism avoids two extremes, one, the denial of the "reality" of value, the other, the erection of value into a reality transcending all human relationships (or even nature as a whole) and possessing absolute or independent validity. For the naturalist, value is a natural phenomenon, and not something that can exist apart from natural — some would say, more specifically, human — situations. This is to deny the "absoluteness" of values. But though values are relative to the specific situations in which they obtain, and human values to human affairs, their reality is thereby not denied, as is supposed by the supernaturalistic argument stated above on p. 184; for when value is said to belong to a given situation, that is the same as saying that a certain kind of *property* belongs to it, and one property is no less "real" than another. This recognition of the natural status of values enables us to realize the complexity involved in their study, because it recognizes that no absolute formula will suffice to explain and legislate for all cases. Moreover, on the naturalistic view, the universe as a whole is neither a "good" nor a "bad" one. "Good" and "bad" (and other designations of value) are terms that apply in *specific* situations, though of course each specific situation will at the same time be a certain *kind* of situation. For supernaturalism, God is good, and nature, his product, may (always except in the views of certain deists) likewise be called good. But Spinoza, identifying God and nature, virtually stated the naturalistic interpretation of value when he held that God (substance, nature) cannot be called either good or bad. These are predicates relative to man, and to situations in which some element of human need or desire enters.

**The Interpretation of Purpose.** As the naturalist believes that there is no mind which is not *a* mind, and no value which is not one relating to some given area of experience, so he approaches the notion of purpose. To say that all nature displays a purpose is to assert something incapable of investigation. Nature contains not purpose but *purposes*. Purposes are ends or goals, properties of situations in which organisms strive to attain them. And once more the naturalist avoids two extremes, that of the materialist, which holds purposes to be illusory because all human actions are mechanistically determined, and that of idealists who hold that purposes represent a causal effect of the future upon the present. Our discussion of "freedom" of action should enable us to understand why purposes may influence actions which nevertheless are determined causally. For in envisioning goals, we strive to attain them by *determining our own* actions in that direction. The goal is not a "cause" in the narrow modern sense of that word but is rather a factor in the environment *the present awareness* of which causes us to act in a definite direction.

**The Naturalistic Philosophy of Experience.** What the critical naturalist finds in nature he finds in that aspect of nature called man's experience. Experience articulates nature. It is not a specific faculty of man, nor an entity somehow connected with man's body. It is not a screen through which nature appears, as the followers of Locke assume, nor is it the whole of nature, as idealists suppose. Man's experience consists in his *experiencing,* and his experiencing consists in his doing, feeling, and participating. Experience is a process. It is a dimension of nature, in which nature, so to speak, finds its expression. In experience the richness and unlimited possibilities that belong to nature are, to the finite extent of which man is capable, felt, thought about, and realized. From one point of view experience for the critical naturalist is a panorama revealing to us changes of different kinds, particular things and ever-repeating laws, variety and uniformity, many objects and many values. But it reveals and reflects only in the sense that all these phenomena are its warp and woof. Experience not only reveals, it is, growth and death. For the critical naturalist the warp and woof is an indefinitely complex one. In experience he finds many experiences, to none of which he denies significance. If, as we suggested previously, he finds no intrinsic mystery in the universe in the sense of some unknowable reality before which his understanding must surrender, he nevertheless acknowledges his wonder at the very fact of existence. Critical naturalism is imaginative naturalism. It is able to recognize not only the experience of the scientist but that of the mystic, if we use the latter term to mean one who can experience what, though it be in the natural course of events, defies simple description and arouses some of man's deepest responses.

❖   ❖   ❖

# Ethical and Aesthetic Values

We have had some occasion to see that an interpretation of human values is an integral part of a speculative philosophic outlook. Thus most supernaturalists attribute value or goodness both to the affairs of man and to nature as a whole, whereas naturalists find the latter predication meaningless.

**World-Views and Human Values.** The ascription of goodness to nature is usually associated with teleological views, even if, as in Hegel, they are not supernaturalistic (or explicitly supernaturalistic) in character. The philosophies of Leibniz and Hegel imply not only that goodness belongs to the universe but that everything occurring within it is in a fundamental sense right or good. Leibniz's reason is that God, having created the universe, must have created a universe better than any other that could possibly be created. The existence of evil must therefore be an element in the perfection of the whole, and could not possibly have been better adapted to the perfection of the whole. The reader is no doubt familiar with the literary reflection of this view in Pope's verse, "Whatever is, is right," and with the classical satire of it in Voltaire's *Candide;* and we ourselves have already considered (Chapter XIII of this Part) the ideas in terms of which it can be controverted philosophically. For Hegel the moral justification of whatever occurs lies in the fact that its occurrence is a necessary step toward the evolutionary advance that consists in the realization of Spirit or Reason. This unfolding of the whole constitutes universal progress, and the development of human institutions is instrumental to it. Ethical views like those of

Leibniz and Hegel are sometimes designated by the term *optimism* — in its philosophical meaning, the view that all things tend to achieve ultimately the character of "goodness." Optimism was aptly if ironically characterized by the British philosopher F. H. Bradley (1846-1924), himself an objective idealist, as asserting that "this is the best possible world, and everything in it is a necessary evil."

The general character of our philosophy influences our attitude in the interpretation of values, and the converse is equally true. For example, those who believe that we cannot make any moral distinctions unless it is true that the "soul" is "immortal," obviously cannot accept a naturalistic point of view. Or if they insist on so doing, they are committed on their own view to denying the validity of moral distinctions. For on the naturalistic position the soul or mind is no "substance" or independent being, and there is no immortality in the *literal* sense of life after death.

**Problematic Questions concerning Human Values.** Apart from its larger implications, the subject of human values forms a special branch of philosophical inquiry with special problems. It is the philosophical study of the relations of men and their institutions in society and in nature. Among the questions it asks are: Is there a standard of "right" conduct that applies to all members of the human race? On what basis would such a single standard, or differing standards, be determined? What does "goodness" or "badness" mean in human conduct? What is "duty"? Does right conduct imply curbing our natural desires, or seeking their fulfilment, or some other alternative? Such questions are questions about *moral* or *ethical* values. They belong to *ethics* or *morals,* concerned with human conduct in society. There is another kind of values, not unrelated, which emerges from the attempt of men in society to express their experience and to respond to the sensuous aspects of their environment in a very special way. These are *aesthetic* values, including among other things the values of art. We turn to moral values first.

**Moral Values: the Subject-Matter of Ethics.** If ethics is the philosophy of human conduct, how does it differ from the sciences of psychology, sociology, and anthropology? These sciences also are concerned with human conduct. But the sense in which they are is not the same. Their problem is to give us the facts and laws of society and of societies, of the behavior of man and of men. Their function is to tell us how men act and why they act as they do (i.e., what the laws are which govern these actions). Ethics, on the other hand, is concerned not with the description and explanation but with the *evaluation* of human conduct. In the former sciences, the concepts of "rightness" and "wrongness," "goodness" and "badness" do not occur, except as part of the actual judgments men are found passing, and they are not concerned with the conditions under which these concepts are *correctly* applied to conduct. We must not suppose, however, that ethics has no connection with psychology, anthropology, and sociology. On the contrary, the judgments and distinctions of ethics can be made more accurate, precise, and sound the more they are based on the factual knowledge that may be furnished by these and other sciences, and the more this knowledge grows. In one sense this is obvious. An understanding of moral values relating to man must surely be increased if we know as much about man as we are able. This by no means implies that the increase of special scientific knowledge bears a direct ratio to increase of moral understanding, but it does mean that moral evaluation is on a far firmer basis when it utilizes than when it ignores such knowledge. If ethics is itself to aim at a procedure as much in accordance with scientific method as possible, this must certainly be one of its policies.

**What Constitutes a "Moral" Situation?** What distinguishes mere physical behavior from conduct in which a so-called moral element enters? In other words, under what conditions is conduct subject to ethical evaluation, to the application of ethical judgment? This is no easy question to answer. There are some who draw a sharp distinction between moral

and other kinds of conduct, so that whatever we do is taken
to fall into a fixed category. Thus it is held that killing is a
moral act and eating a non-moral act. But if we insist on this
rigid distinction the question becomes doubly difficult, for we
must then give hard and fast characteristics that draw the line.
There is, however, another way of looking at the matter which
perhaps is more faithful to the facts of human conduct, namely,
that although doubtless not all actions are moral actions,
all actions *may* under given circumstances assume moral significance. Thus for example, eating, though ordinarily an act
with no moral consequences, may become one in the case where
we were to continue our normal eating habits when the amount
of food was insufficient for all the members of our family.

**Conditions of Moral Conduct.** Moral conduct (conduct
which it is meaningful to evaluate or judge morally) is conduct that (1) is voluntary, and (2) affects the basic direction
of our living. That a moral act must be voluntary or purposive
is not difficult to see. We cannot judge a man's action as
"wrong" if as a result of turning in sleep he causes his wife
to fall from the bed and be killed, or if he performs an act
under extreme coercion, or if he is insane. For responsibility
implies purposive activity. Purposive activity is the adoption
of a means to the attainment of some end or aim. But the second factor is also necessary. For an act may be voluntary and
consist in no more than deciding what to eat for dinner. Although, as we said, such an act is *potentially* moral, it cannot
be judged until it affects the fundamental pattern of our conduct. But just what is meant by "fundamental pattern of our
conduct"? We may define an individual's act as having moral
significance if it affects his intentions and actions (a) toward
the purposes of other individuals, or (b) toward the institutions of his society (religion, government), or (c) toward the
formation of his own character. It must not be imagined that
an act affects the basic pattern of our conduct (i.e., falls into
one or another of these classes) only if it is of great magni-
tude or importance. Consider the act of stealing a book. This

does not revolutionize our status in society, nor does it completely establish or transform our character. Yet it may be said to affect the basic direction of our living in the sense that it *contributes* either to the nature of our relations with others, or to the habit-formations which form our character, or to the type of relation we bear to religious ordinances and social (or legal) codes.

In ethics any claim to precision and completeness is dangerous, and the foregoing definitions are made as suggestions, not as finalities. In a full study even the points thus far mentioned could be expanded and qualified indefinitely. What appear to be simple distinctions, such as that between voluntary and involuntary actions, can be subjected to a good deal of analysis. For instance, we say that actions done under compulsion are involuntary. But as Aristotle pointed out, we must distinguish different kinds of compulsion, and it is not easy to say whether each is involuntary. To be carried from one's path by the wind is involuntary, but what about throwing goods overboard to save a ship in a storm at sea, or performing a shameful act under a dictator's command? The reader will profit by formulating his own analyses and comparing them with Aristotle's in Book III of the *Nicomachean Ethics*.

**Means and Ends.** We described voluntary conduct as the selection of a means to attain an end. It is important not to conceive moral conduct too narrowly. Sometimes there is a tendency to emphasize an action by itself, overlooking the choice of the end to which the action is only a means. Ethical evaluation is equally applicable to the *kind of ends* we select and to the *way* in which ends are achieved. And the term "conduct" is applicable even to a choice of ends *without* our acting specifically to achieve them, as in the preference for a certain kind of government as a human goal. Some moral philosophers have laid more emphasis on means, others more on ends, but they have not always formulated it in these terms, which were influentially employed by Aristotle. If we examine the usage of ethical terms both by philosophers and laymen, we find that the terms "right" and "wrong" relate to means or acts, while the terms "good" and "bad" usually relate to ends or goals. For example, to killing (as an act) we apply the judgments "right" and "wrong"; to wealth (as an end), the judgments "good" and "bad." But means and ends are nevertheless relative. Wealth may be an end relative to industrial activity as a means, but wealth (i.e., the multiplication of wealth) may itself be a means to (say) pleasure. And our application of ethical predicates will be appropriate to whether it is being considered in the capacity of means or end.

**Conventional and Critical Morality.**   We can distinguish different kinds of moral standards or criteria of evaluation. But before any such alternative approaches are considered, it is necessary to distinguish two different *attitudes* which underlie the very notion of moral criteria. Sometimes, when we speak of a morality (i.e., a set of ethical standards) we mean something to which we *conform,* a number of customs, traditions, or laws belonging to the society of which we are part. But morality may also be conceived as a set of distinctions which we *arrive at.* The former, which we may call *conventional morality,* implies a set of rules and prohibitions, to accept which is called "good" and to act in accordance with which is called "right." The latter, which we may call *critical morality,* implies a set of principles which are the results of ethical inquiry or analysis, of thought and reflection and the weighing of alternatives. The difference between conventional and critical morality is not an absolute one. There is no such thing as a conventional (group, social) morality based on no reason at all, purely arbitrary, and perfectly static. Some critical or reflective element lies at the bottom of the most rigid social code, and resides in the men who govern its functioning. Moreover, no adherent of conventional morality fails as an individual to do some thinking that falls outside his code. Similarly, there is no such thing as a purely critical morality, one totally divorced from social habits, influences, or institutions, and arising in an intellectual vacuum. No one who prizes stability and sanity can disregard conventional morality altogether. Nevertheless the ethical methods or attitudes involved in the two senses of morality are not to be confused. They embody the general differences between the methods of authority and science. Conventional morality might well be called authoritarian morality; and critical morality, scientific morality. In the former the emphasis is on conservatism, conformity, tradition, law; in the latter, it is on criticism, investigation, comparison, the absence of dogmatism or conclusiveness.

**The Hebraic-Christian Ethical Tradition.** *Authority as a Basis.* Conventional morality is not the less conventional because there happen to be different societies. Ethical standards may differ widely, yet may share the characteristics of conservatism and authority. The social morality of Western society rests on one ethical tradition in particular, the Hebrew-Christian. We saw that this tradition is based on the assumption of supernaturalism, and that this in turn finds all ethical distinctions set forth in God's Word. Moral standards of a fixed, permanent character are laid down, to observe which is morally correct, to transgress which is morally evil. These rules are authoritarian. We cannot ask, when confronted with a moral prohibition or command, Why? To conform is a duty not to be questioned or analyzed. The point of reference is not man but God. The extreme authoritarian position is sometimes formulated: Had God chosen to legislate the very opposites of his present commandments, the former would have been the morally correct ones.

*Moral Sanctions.* It might seem as if the "reason why" we should obey the divine word is that obedience carries with it rewards; disobedience, punishments. Now it is true that rewards and punishments are associated with conduct in the Hebrew-Christian tradition. But here an important distinction must be made. Reward does not function as an *end,* which justifies respect for God's Word. It does not justify the *rightness* of conformity. Conformity is not a means to an end without which it would have no ethical basis. It is intended as an *end in itself,* which requires no rational justification. It is good at the same time that it is right. What, then, is the ethical status of reward and punishment? The answer is that they function as devices by which obedience to an authority is guaranteed. A system of promises and threats which serve to enforce a definite kind of conduct (usually conformity) is known in ethics as a system of moral *sanctions.* Some of the forms of sanctions in modern society are the penal system of a legal code and the threat of ostracism which conventional morality tacitly exercises. Now reward may be the "reason why" an adherent of the Hebrew-Christian ethical outlook obeys, in the sense that it is the force which *causes* him to obey. But in another — the principal — sense, reward is not the "reason why" in the sense that it is the justification of his obeying; for obedience to God is assumed to be *its own* justification. There are certain significant differences in Old and New Testament regarding the nature of their sanctions. The leading one is that the former makes no explicit mention of a future life but places rewards and punishments in a given lifetime or in future generations; it offers an ultimate kingdom of God on earth. The latter offers a kingdom of God in heaven — the otherworldly idea of a final judgment culminating in salvation or perdition. Salvation would seem, on first thought, to be an ultimate ideal of man, a highest good. It is in so far as it consists in the achievement of perfect obedience to God's will. It is not in so far as it is something to which the latter is merely a means. That as something distinct it is actually a reward derived from a moral sanction and not itself the highest good, is shown by the fact that it is contingent upon a last judgment which determines *whether* a man *has* pursued the highest good — obedience to God. On the Christian view, which is essentially the Hebrew view in a different setting, it is not because we shall be saved that obedience is good; it is because obedience is good that we shall be saved.

*Mechanical Conformity versus Active Faith.* The Prophets of the Old Testament emphasize that it is not the letter but the spirit of the law observance of which makes for righteousness. In the Gospels of the New Testament Christ is represented as upholding the same view against the Pharisees. Is this a revolt against authoritarian morality? The answer is decidedly in the negative. It is against the mechanical, meaningless type of conformity that these moralists are protesting. Their view is that it is not the mere performance of an outward act that constitutes obedience to God but the conscious willingness to obey. Unless the individual convinces himself of the rightness of obedience, unless he possesses or achieves an unshakable faith, rightness does not truly belong to his actions. Thus the sinner who sincerely repents is more virtuous than the nominal conformist. This emphasis on faith is an emphasis on "the heart." ". . . What the Lord doth require of thee," we read in Micah, is "only to do justly, and to love mercy, and to walk humbly with thy God." And Christ says, in the Gospel of Matthew, "Blessed are the poor in spirit: for theirs is the kingdom of heaven. . . . Blessed are the pure in heart: for they shall see God."

**Some Forms of Ethical Intuitionism.** On the Hebraic-Christian view, moral standards are revealed to us by divine authority. Many philosophers have believed that, on the contrary, it is we who are the authority in moral values. What makes anything good is a sense or feeling on our part that it is so. To predicate goodness of anything means that we intuitively approve of it. And to know what is good we must appeal to intuition as arbiter. Thus intuition in ethics is both a *condition* of rightness and goodness and *knowledge* of rightness and goodness. But there is no single theory known as "ethical intuitionism," any more than there is a single school of "intuitionism." There are various forms, and the following are some of them.

(1) The view that we are, as human beings, equipped with a special psychological faculty of "moral sense." By means of

our "moral sentiments" we are able to judge some things as justifiable, others as not.

(2)    The view that the criterion of value in any moral situation is not a moral sense that is a special faculty common to every human being, but *some* feeling on the basis of which the value is determined. On the preceding interpretation of "intuition," intuition is a universal faculty and all men are at least in principle capable of the same evaluations. On the present interpretation, it is something that may vary with different individuals, who owing to their differing feeling-reactions cannot be regarded as subject to the same ethical standards.

(3)    The view that we have *a priori* ethical intuition. Whereas the two preceding views suppose intuitive ethical knowledge of a sensory character, applicable to particular ethical situations, the present view supposes intuitive knowledge of universal ethical principles.

(4)    The view of Kant, which, like any other view of his, is difficult to state apart from the complete outline of his system. Intuition here takes the form of "conscience," which expresses the "practical reason" of man, as his scientific capacities reflect his "speculative reason." The universe is governed by moral law as well as by physical law, and it is the former which man's practical reason in the form of his intuitive conscience apprehends. To do right and know what is good we must act in accordance with this moral law, and we do so act whenever we follow our conscience. The moral law is absolute, and to obey it is duty, the supreme obligation. The will to act in accordance with duty is what Kant calls the "good will."

**Fundamental Differences among Intuitionists.**    It is illuminating to note how wide the differences can be among those who employ essentially the same method in ethics. Within each of the foregoing types of view, moreover, differences could be pointed out that set off the exponents from one another.

It is obvious that the first two of the preceding views are empiricistic in emphasis while the last two are rationalistic.

Form (4) implies the objective nature of moral standards, in the sense that they are inherent in the constitution of the universe. Form (1) is objective in that the faculty of moral sense is held to belong to all men, but not in that values transcend *mankind*. Consequently, for a view like (1), moral value is inseparable from human desire or approval, whereas for (4) something may be good even though we may never desire it or approve of it. Form (4) is thus close in one respect to the authoritarian Hebraic-Christian morality, while (1) is quite remote from that. The empiricist theories (the first two) differ from one another in that the second allows for a *relativism* of values, supposing as it does that the feelings on which moral judgments are based may be any feelings at all and hence variable in different persons. Among empiricist intuitionists, who link value and desire, some have held (as a psychological assumption) that what men as a matter of fact desire (and hence intuitively stamp as good) is pleasure. Some have held further that men desire primarily their own pleasure, while others (chiefly in the "moral sense" school) have supposed that men have intuitive sentiments of sympathy and benevolence. But any of these special psychological assumptions, as well as the general position that value is nothing apart from *some* relation to human preference and desire, is fully as possible in ethical philosophies which are anti-intuitionistic.

**A Basic Assumption in the Authoritarian and Intuitionistic Approaches.**   The reader who remembers the discussion of authority and intuition in general, will have no difficulty applying the critical arguments to the sphere of ethics, though many new interesting points can be raised. There is, however, one which touches the heart of all ethical theory.

The basic supposition involved in the authoritarian and intuitionistic approaches is that moral acts and moral ends can be evaluated as *discrete, self-contained units* which possess definite characteristics like rightness and goodness. A given act or end is supposedly something that can be judged *intrinsically,* or *as such*. Thus, for example, on the authoritarian and Kantian positions an act of stealing or lying or marital adultery is regarded as wrong whatever the circumstances. And on the empirical intuitionist view, even if an act be regarded as now wrong, now right, the reason (though strictly, by definition there is no reason for a judgment that is intuitive) lies wholly in the character of the specific act itself. Whatever moral judgment be passed, on a *kind* of act unqualifiedly, as in the former, or on a *specific* act unqualifiedly, as in the latter, it is assumed that a given instance of moral conduct can be absolutely isolated and therefore judged absolutely.

**Consequences: the Continuity of Moral Conduct.** Now we may well ask whether an assumption of this kind can be made by a critical ethics. In the first place, to assume that any criterion of moral judgment is final and not subject to further examination is a form of dogmatism, antithetical to the scientific attitude. Secondly, the assumption that moral acts and aims are capable of absolute isolation is contrary to the testimony of common experience. To steal a weapon from a madman and to steal a book from a library are both acts of theft, but they cannot be evaluated purely as such. The act must be considered in relation to some purpose, that is, as a means to some end, and its status when so conceived is not always the same. A blanket rule cannot morally legislate for all time and all circumstances, and an intuitive evaluation of a specific act becomes a blind judgment in overlooking the possible network of relations in which the act is embedded. Similarly in the choice of an end. Authoritative and intuitive approval of certain kinds of ends and of certain specific ends neglects the fact (a) that an end may cease to prove desirable in the process of achieving it, (b) that an end we choose cannot be separated from other ends we have chosen and will have to choose, and (c) that our ends may become undesirable in the light of circumstances external to ourselves. For instance, the aim of contributing money to an indigent person, though at first judged as good, may become bad in view of his extreme sensitiveness, or in view of the consideration that it may do us more harm than him good, or in view of the fact that a more urgent cause requires our aid, or in view of the discovery that the apparent indigence conceals psychopathic miserliness. Thus for a critical morality the moral value of acts and goals can never be judged with finality in isolation but must always be examined in the light of possible *consequences*. Means and ends cannot be separated, specific circumstances governing them cannot be ignored, the interrelation of our ends cannot be immediately determined.

**The Nature of General Principles in Ethics.** The foregoing does not at all imply that it is impossible to formulate general principles of conduct, or that intuitive insight has no place in moral judgment. It denies only that general principles or intuitive approval are *alone* capable of justifying evaluation of specific instances of conduct. General principles are essential for our understanding of particular situations. Without having some general policy we cannot deal with a special case, just as without a hypothesis in natural science we cannot interpret a set of facts and predict facts not yet known. But principles of conduct are simply one kind of hypotheses. And just as all hypotheses stand ready to be discarded when the facts show them to be inadequate, so moral principles cannot pretend to be more than *guides* to conduct, tools for dealing with specific situations. Once they become eternal legislators for conduct, they become no less anti-scientific than hypotheses that are exalted as infallible truths. In the same way, "intuition" may legitimately function in conduct not as unquestioned arbiter but as fruitful insight guiding our action and as spontaneously reflecting the basic desires which can never be wholly ignored whatever choices we do make.

**The Pleasure-Criterion: Hedonism.** If it is true that what turns out to be morally "good" is something that we desire, it is nevertheless not true that whatever we desire is good. In Chapter XII we distinguished between what we desire and what is desirable. The morally desirable is what we would desire after examining the interrelation of all the ends which concern us and as many consequences as we can foresee. The task now confronts us of saying *what* it is that is desirable or good.

One famous answer, dating from ancient times, is that what makes anything good is the pleasure it yields (sooner or later), or the pleasure associated with it. This view is called *hedonism,* from the Greek term for "pleasure." Some intuitionists have been hedonists; but we may consider the view in its most favorable light, as prescribing the weighing of the consequences of actions to determine the pleasure associated with them, and the deliberate choice of actions in accordance with pleasurable ends. Hedonism is wider than the view that only sensuous or animal pleasures are the ultimate justification of conduct, a view known as *cyrenaicism.* It is a psychological as well as an ethical theory. It believes that the reason men *ought* to pursue pleasure as their ultimate end (i.e., the reason why it is good to do so) is that by nature they are pleasure-seeking animals. Leaving the reader to consider the merits of this widely-held but very dubious psychological assumption, we may note briefly the difficulties in ethical hedonism.

**Criticism of Hedonism.** (1) If the term "pleasure" be used in its usual meaning of pleasurable feeling or pleasurable reaction, then, as we suggested in Chapter XII, the facts of common experience and of history seem to prove that hedonism is narrow and arbitrary in its criterion of moral goodness. For many acts and choices universally regarded as desirable and approvable are actually inimical to pleasure in any precise sense — the captain going down with his ship, the martyr going to the stake.

(2) If pleasurable emotion were the criterion of goodness in conduct the consequences of our acting according to it would more than likely interfere with rather than promote our interests in the *long run,* our *total* interests. What is pleasurable to one individual is not necessarily so to another. If each

were to. act according to the criterion of ultimately attaining the pleasures that most satisfy him, conflict would result which would be detrimental to the general welfare of most concerned.

(3) That pleasure, considered in itself as much apart from consequences as possible, is *a* good, no one can deny. But it is another matter to regard it as the criterion of judging whether anything is good. Aristotle, in his analysis of pleasure, gives another reason why the pursuit of pleasure as a primary end is inimical to our general welfare. He points out that the greater the pleasure of an activity the more it interferes with any other activity. Pleasure absorbs our attention and distracts us from all else. It follows that if the multiplication of pleasure is our *primary* end, the wisest consideration of our *total* affairs is impossible. The wiser alternative is to select our ends *first* and *then* make them as pleasurable as possible.

(4) Pleasurable feelings and emotions, like all feelings and emotions, are variable and short-lived. They are unstable and dependent on accidental circumstances. To make them, therefore, the deciding factors in our conduct is to base that conduct on something unstable and impermanent. Here again we may say that pleasure should be added to permanently desirable conduct, not conduct fitted to the inevitably impermanent nature of pleasure. It is true, perhaps, that what is good must sooner or later involve pleasure, but not that whatever involves pleasure is good. The failure to make this distinction is a principal failing in hedonism.

**Pleasure and Happiness.** If the hedonist were forced to admit that there are instances of moral goodness which do not involve pleasure, he might state his theory in another form, namely, that pleasure is at least the greatest good. This really amounts to the same thing, and the foregoing objections remain. Hedonism was among the earliest of ancient Greek moral philosophies. Plato and Aristotle, when they came to criticize it, felt that it nevertheless contained a valuable emphasis, which they tried to preserve by making a distinction it had not made. This was the distinction between pleasure and happiness. Happiness or "well-being," not pleasure, is the highest good. Pleasure is fleeting and unstable; happiness is precisely the attainment of a basic stability. To define rightness and goodness in terms of what contributes to happiness is to avoid the foregoing objections. The confusion of happiness with pleasure has been a leading cause of much needless controversy in ethics, and theories we might otherwise be in sympathy with appear unsound because of a failure to make the distinction. A notable example is that of *utilitarianism,* whose best known exponents are the British philosophers Jeremy Bentham (1748-1832) and John Stuart Mill (1806-1873). This view takes its cue from hedonism in making pleasure the highest good. Not, however, my or your pleasure but the pleasure of society as a whole. The popular maxim representing utilitarianism is "The greatest happiness of the greatest number." But by the term "happiness" the utilitarians unfortunately *mean* no more than "pleasure," and they use the terms synonymously. It is not hard to see how a good deal of vagueness and difficulty in their emphasis would be eliminated if the necessary distinction were formulated.

**Happiness as Harmony, the Development of Man in Society.** Ethical theories which stress happiness as the highest good (or most desirable of ends) and the ultimate criterion for all other goods are called *eudaemonistic* theories (after the Greek *eudaimonia,* or "well-being"). Now many ethical philosophies, perhaps the larger number, have been eudaemonistic, yet have differed radically from one another. But this is understandable, for the important question is, What is *meant* by "happiness" or "well-being"? One of the profoundest and most influential interpretations is that of Plato and Aristotle (who, despite significant points of disagreement and differences in statement, share the same general theory), the gist of which is as follows.

**The View of Plato and Aristotle.** Men aspire to possess many kinds of goods, but the most fundamental of these

— the most lasting — is happiness. All other goods are for the sake of happiness, but happiness is aspired to for its own sake; it is not a means to anything else but is completely self-sufficient. What constitutes happiness? How do we determine it? How can we find an objective standard of evaluation? One thing we know, namely, that we shall recognize "happiness" when we find something self-sufficient or not a means to anything further. Let us consider the everyday world. What we mean when we say that such-and-such is "best" for any creature is the achievement of what that creature is most capable of achieving. The good of a musician is to pursue and succeed in music, that of a philosopher to pursue and learn from philosophy, that of a financier to loan and profit. The good of a deer is to graze in an open pasture, while the good of a monkey is to live in the jungle. Thus the good of a creature, or kind of creature, or indeed of anything at all, is determined by determining the *functions* which it is fitted to fulfill, or by determining what set of activities will best promote the *fullest and most harmonious development* of its life. The highest good of man, then, his happiness, will consist in the realization of his capacities or potentialities into a harmonious organization. This development will be a development in society, for on the Greek view man is essentially a social and political animal. The good of the individual and the good of the state are inseparable. Since the life of a man includes his relations to other men, the establishment of a harmony will involve the fulfillment of duties and obligations, the control as well as the exercise of his animal impulses, sacrifice and intellectual struggle as well as the pursuit of pleasure. Virtue, or the habit of right conduct, will be defined as the kind of conduct best adapted to the realization of harmonious development. Now the basic relationship that goes to make up such a harmony will be what a man's happiness consists in. But Aristotle points out that virtuous activity is impossible without the possession of material goods — friends, some degree of wealth, sound reputation, etc. — and that happiness is impossible without virtuous activity. Yet this is still not a complete picture. For though virtue is essential to happiness, it is not by itself sufficient. Plato and Aristotle believe that the happy man is the man who is capable of contemplation (whether it be the pursuit of art, science, philosophy, or any other reflective activity), the highest of human functions. The reason is that contemplative activity is the only kind that is *self-sufficient,* or pursued for its own sake as *an end in itself.* The contemplative man is, more than any other, not dependent on external circumstances as the source of his happiness. His happiness resides within him, while the man who pursues fame or wealth as his chief end pursues an end which by its very nature is prey to circumstances. The "happiness" achieved in the latter way is accidental and threatens always to be short-lived. A short-lived satisfaction is pleasure, not happiness. Happiness is not a state of mind or emotion at all; it is a fundamental relationship, embracing the whole of a man's interests.

There is a somewhat different way of expressing this moral ideal. The genuine happiness or well-being of a man consists not so much in his achieving what is *characteristic* or *typical* of his kind as in his embodying something of what is *perfect* of his kind. Thus contemplative or reflective activity, as the highest of human functions, represents the functioning of man in accordance with his *fullest* possible achievement, his most *complete* virtue or perfection or excellence. This version emphasizes, perhaps, a significant difference between the good of man and the good of other species of creature in the world. Whereas for other creatures the good of the species is thought of as attainable by any individual of that species, the good of man is attainable only by a relatively small number of men.

**The Epicurean Ideal.** An instructive alternative to the foregoing interpretation of happiness is that of the Greek philosopher Epicurus and his followers. Popularly *epicureanism* is interpreted as a crude form of hedonism, usually cyrenaicism, and is made synonymous with vulgar pleasure-hunting. But in fact it is the very antithesis of this. It counsels as the supreme good the diminution, not the multiplication of pleasures, on the ground that to multiply pleasures is to form new habits of desire, and that the man who has fewer desires to satisfy is happier than the man burdened by incessant craving. In achieving this good a man avoids dependence on external things for his satisfaction; he becomes emancipated. Here epicureanism shares the Platonic-Aristotelian conception of happiness as a self-sufficient harmony. Both point to the need of a reasonable amount of material goods, and to the intellectual pursuits as the most stable assurance of uninterrupted happiness. But the similarity goes no further. For whereas the Platonic-Aristotelian ideal is harmony in society, the epicurean ideal is harmony through withdrawal from society. The former is the harmony of the full life, the stability of "well-being." The latter is the harmony of the "simple life" that comes from avoiding obligation and responsibility. Epicureanism might be summarized as the view that the fewer a man's needs and desires, the fewer his duties and responsibilities, the smaller the chance of his contentment (achieved through the satisfaction of basic necessities and through contemplation) being broken. It is the philosophy of detachment and aristocratic aloofness.

Moral theories like the two preceding ones raise questions of fundamental importance. Is withdrawal from society in any sense less "right" than participation? Can happiness be achieved in either case? Aristotle warns us that whatever conclusions we come to in ethics must be regarded as approximate generalizations, with exceptions very likely; and we must guard against the possibility of legislating for all men and all societies. Can we call men "happy" who are incapable of the contemplative life? Does it make sense to speak of the contemplative man as in a state of well-being when catastrophic conditions prevail in society? Is happiness something that admits of degrees, so that we can speak of greater and lesser happiness? The reader to whom such problems come alive will inevitably discover a host of others that penetrate to the core of his living as well as his thinking.

**The Adaptability of Non-eudaemonistic Teachings.**
Ethical philosophies which define moral standards by some
other ultimate standard than human happiness may be termed
"non-eudaemonistic." Thus among non-eudaemonistic moral
philosophies would be numbered that of the Hebraic-Christian
tradition and that of Kant. In philosophy whichever view we
come to hold we are likely to find in alternative, even inimical
views, some valuable emphasis by which we can profit. Nowhere
is this truer than in ethics. If for example we accept an Aristotelian approach we need not reject *in toto* so different a view
as that of the Old or New Testament. We must distinguish
between the assertions about moral conduct made in the Old and
New Testament and the interpretation which these assertions
assume in their context. Now it is quite true that we cannot
abstract something from a context without losing some of the
meaning. But to a great extent the teachings of the Hebrew
prophets, the Sermon on the Mount, the Book of Job, St. Paul,
etc., are the result of an *independent* insight into human conduct, an insight not necessarily dependent on sectarian doctrine.
By wide consent, regardless of the particular cast of our
theory, we can subscribe to the admonition to pursue justice
and mercy and love; to the ideals of universal peace and universal charity. For Isaiah, Micah, and Jesus, peace is noble in
man because it conduces best to fulfilling the will of God; to
Plato and Aristotle, its value lies in its being a condition for
the fullest realization of man's capacities. Thus in different
contexts and for different reasons the moral value of the ideal
of peace is equally recognized. But in a critical theory (like
that of Plato and Aristotle) insight is accompanied by analysis. From one theory as from the other we may derive knowledge of certain pervasive human aims, but for the critical
theory it is not sufficient to know that justice, love, and charity
are values. The philosopher wishes to determine in what *sense*,
and *why* these are values; to examine their *possible* meanings;
and to know the conditions under which they do and do not
obtain.

**Human Values and the Conditions of Men.** At some point
or other the reader will probably reflect that the values which

are ascribed to man, and especially those which are held to be basic, depend greatly on the kind of "being" that man is thought to have. What kind of being is human being? Is there a "human nature" which, once discovered, provides a firm basis for the inquiry into human values? Further reflection suggests that we cannot pretend to answer such a question without difficulty. For the very concept of "man" cannot be investigated until we study the diverse customs, habits, cultures, and conditions of *men*. Thus, although it is true that the study of ethics and ethical values presupposes certain assumptions about man, the study of man presupposes certain assumptions about the values which help to recognize and define man in relation to other kinds of being.

We saw in Chapter Two that philosophies change as the social or historical experience of men changes. An age of confusion, of unpredictability, may increase the value assigned to tranquillity and peace. But such an age may equally well increase the importance or value assigned to violence and force. A philosophic response, after all, is an interpretation, not a passive mirror, of events and institutions. And a philosophic response, as we earlier pointed out, is itself part of the social and historical complex.

The general outlook and approach to the nature of man that has come to be known as "existentialism" is sometimes depicted as originating under historical conditions of a pervasive kind. Notable among these conditions is the deterioration of the churches, so far as their influence on personal religious experience is concerned. Equally notable is the spread of industrialism, with its harsh, impersonal impact on the affairs of men. Conditions of this sort were relevant to German existentialism of the mid-nineteenth century and afterward. French existentialism of the twentieth century arose in its fullest expression during and after the historical nightmare of Hitler and the Second World War. The ethical approach of leading existentialist writers focuses upon certain aspects of human life and experience which differ sharply from those considered as primary by the major ethical traditions. But it should be pointed out that there have been various manifestations of the so-called existentialist outlook throughout the history of Western thought.

**Kierkegaard: The Concept of the Supremely Intense Life.**
For the Danish theologian and philosopher Søren Kierkegaard
(1801-1855) the moral life of man is best understood in the
framework of religious experience. This, however, is to be
found not in what he calls Christendom, the life of propriety
and self-satisfaction, but in Christianity, the self's experience
of its relation to God. Kierkegaard's type of emphasis upon a
self—and particularly a self's relation to itself—is a con-
spicuous one in later existentialism; the emphasis upon God
is far less so, and some existentialists reject the idea of God
altogether. The notion of "existence" derives its significance
not from being a synonym of "what there is" but from the
crucial awareness by a self of what is ineluctably present to
it—of what it, in its condition, must deal with, concretely and
inescapably. Kierkegaard describes the self as "the conscious
synthesis of infinitude and finitude which relates itself to itself,
whose task is to become itself, a task which can be performed
only by means of a relationship to God."* Not to be willing to
be oneself is to be in a state of despair. It is, in the words of
the existentialist theologian Paul Tillich (1886-1965) to lack
"the courage to be as oneself." Despair, which for Kierkegaard
turns out to be the essential meaning of "sin," is the lot of a
man (or self) when he loses sight of the "eternal consciousness" within him. And the life of a man is a life of despair
when he fails to understand his finitude in the light of the
infinite and eternal, the being of God. Otherwise stated, the
self, in its perpetual process of becoming, fails to become
"concrete," fails to actualize its inherent possibilities, even as
the lowly acorn fails to actualize its inherent possibilities when
it does not become an oak. But the fulfillment of this state of
being, which requires understanding, also requires something
more than understanding, namely, "faith."

**Dread, Paradox, and the Absurd.**    The exemplar of the
man of faith, for Kierkegaard, is the patriarch Abraham of the
Old Testament. God, tempting Abraham, commands him to take

---

* *The Sickness Unto Death* (translated by Walter Lowrie), Part One, IIIA.

Isaac, his only son, to Mount Moriah and to sacrifice him as an offering. Abraham takes Isaac to the mountain, answering Isaac's questions gently but indirectly. He binds him and, taking his knife, is unhesitatingly ready to slay him when an angel of the Lord calls to him to desist, saying that he has proven his fidelity to God, and that he and his posterity will be blessed. Ethically speaking, we have here a bewildering state of affairs. Is not God commanding Abraham to do what is humanly and morally repugnant? Is not Abraham plunged into a contradictory, inscrutable situation in which his relation to God violates his relation to man? Is not moral conduct here rendered unintelligible? It is easy to draw the conclusion that only perfect faith—a kind of absolute belief in God as love—can explain the impeccable compliance of Abraham. But in his analysis (*Fear and Trembling*) of the meaning of the story Kierkegaard stresses the sorrow and aloneness of Abraham, and the torment of dread, in the course of his mission. In this portrayal, faith is not a pure state of simple acceptance. It is the consummation of a searing history of a self's feeling, in which the strength of the self emerges, its "eternal validity." The "knight of faith" believes what it is unreasonable to believe and accepts what it is preposterous to accept. His faith presupposes an achievement or "act" of "infinite resignation." Faith, says Kierkegaard, "is not an immediate instinct of the heart, but is the paradox of life and existence." Abraham acts, Kierkegaard says in a difficult phrase, "by virtue of the absurd." The absurdity of his situation actually constitutes and fortifies his faith. For him, an impossible, an unintelligible belief survives the valid testimony of the human understanding, in this case the testimony that readiness to slay another person cannot be justified. What is humanly (or finitely) impossible and contradictory is transcended by a conviction of what must be divinely possible.

Is Abraham, after all, a willing murderer? According to Kierkegaard, we cannot view Abraham (i.e., any truly heroic man) in terms of ethical considerations alone. Ethical principles, he points out, are universal, and the unique meaningfulness of Abraham's acts is a "particular," not reducible to any universal principle. This too, says Kierkegaard, is paradoxical and absurd; for how can there be meaning in human life apart from principles, that is, without standards of measurement? And yet we cannot shrink from acknowledging the unmeasurable. Dread and paradox are fundamental in all human striving. We have to accept the irreducible particularities, and the unclassifiable individuals, of human life, and the mysteries of eternal and infinite being, if we are not to remain in a state of triviality and frustration—a state of despair. After a point, analysis and thought break down, and only faith, a miracle, can take over. The ethical life, then, in its supreme form must be more than ethical.

There are many problems in Kierkegaard's moral outlook, but his perspective on man, in which this outlook is located, depends upon his perspective on the world in which man has his being. One might ask to what extent Kierkegaard conforms to and to what extent he departs from the classical Christian conception of man as inherently sinful. Is it necessary for him to distinguish between a hero and a saint? But the more theoretical philosophic problems are serious indeed. We have progressed far enough in our consideration of philosophic concepts and methods to leave it to the reader to explore for himself the difficulties and insights that the foregoing account involves.

**Emotion and Knowledge.**   An important trait that underlies the method of Kierkegaard, and perhaps of all thought which is called "existentialist," is the treatment of deep human emotion ("passion") as an avenue of knowledge. There had long been a preponderant tendency in philosophy to contrast the emotional attitude with the detached or dispassionate attitude. In the present century, a distinction between the "emotive" and the "cognitive" is regarded as basic by many philosophers. Emotion is considered to be the opposite of "reason" and to interfere with "objectivity." Knowing implies an impersonal stance. From Kierkegaard's viewpoint, on the contrary, it is only through strong passion and intense feeling that the most revealing knowledge can be reached. And in the same way, only depth of emotion can ensure true moral consciousness. Two contemporary existentialists, greatly influenced by Kierkegaard and yet as different from him as they are from each other, reflect his conviction that human feeling is the keynote of the most basic concepts. Thus Martin Heidegger (1889-     ) says: "Only in the clear night of dread's Nothingness is what-is as such revealed."* And according to Jean-Paul Sartre (1905-     ), the meaning and nature of human freedom "reveals itself to us in anguish."†

**Aesthetic Values in Human Experience.** Among human values, there is one kind which, though extremely difficult of definition, can be said to be closely associated with the creation and appreciation of art, and with our experience of those qualities in nature to which art is intimately related. They are the aesthetic values, and the branch of philosophy concerned with their study is *aesthetics*. Sometimes aesthetics is defined as the philosophy of art, and sometimes its principal concern is alleged to be the nature of beauty. There are many who consider these definitions as identical; but it seems clear nevertheless that they are not, for beauty can be found elsewhere in nature than in art, and the concept of beauty is only one among others in the philosophy of art. The reason why the value of beauty has been stressed is that in so doing we can conveniently (if not accurately) interpret the three disciplines of logic, ethics, and aesthetics (the so-called normative sciences) as respectively concerned with the three basic values that the ancients distinguished, truth, goodness, and beauty. But in any case, the interpretation of aesthetics as the philosophy of art is perhaps broad enough to cover questions concerning the nature of beauty, since it is necessarily concerned in part with the relation of art to other things. In aesthetics, as in ethics, many questions arise calling for close philosophic study, affecting and affected by our general philosophic outlook. Our purpose here can only be to indicate a few directions in which this study can proceed.

---

* "What is Metaphysics?" in *Existence and Being*.
† *Being and Nothingness*, Ch. I, Sec. V.

**Factors in Artistic Creation.** To say that art is a human institution, though it may sound like a commonplace, is significant. Human institutions are part of society, and society is part of nature. How, then, is the phenomenon of art, one of human life and conduct, different from other natural phenomena? In other words, under what kind of conditions does that type of activity we call art arise? We do not call a sunset, a cavern, a natural rock bridge, or a bird song works of art, and we do not cite these as instances of painting, sculpture, architecture, and music. The reason is that they are not products of deliberate or purposive activity. "Art" has traditionally been contrasted with "nature," works of art with works of nature. What is usually implied by this contrast is not that art is supernatural or miraculous but that its results are those of conscious activity. Works of art exist in a medium—words, notes, plastic materials, bodily movements — and what are these but natural materials? These are the vehicles or instruments by which artistic insight is expressed. Artistic creation involves, then, (a) a manipulation or arrangement of natural materials, which (b) is purposive. But this still is not sufficient. For we fulfill these requirements when we use a hammer to drive a nail into a door, yet this is not (at least by itself) artistic activity. What is further required is (c) that the product of our activity should be regarded as an end which justifies its own existence. The nail in the door does not justify its existence except as a means to something else. But the hammering and chiseling of a chair yield a product which can justify its existence as a chair, and it is therefore a work of art, though its relative aesthetic *value* (determined by a number of factors) may be great or small. Now arts like furniture and architecture, as distinct from, say, music, are "functional" arts; they have a practical character in a sense which music does not have. But the preceding example should make it clear that whereas some art may be functional, certainly not everything which is functional is art. In the case of arts like music, painting, poetry, the cinema, the drama, and the dance, it is much more obvious that artistic products fulfill the third requirement.

**The Nature of Art: Three Interpretations.** To suggest, as we have done, what factors are necessary for art to exist, does not suffice to characterize art as a major phase of human experience distinct from religion or science. We may note three influential and divergent approaches, among the many that philosophers have taken.

*Art as Penetration to a Reality behind Experience.* Many philosophers have seen in art a means by which we reach and bring to ourselves what science and ordinary experience cannot. To deny this function to art, they believe, is to give it the status of a kind of play, a manipulation of materials without purpose, and on the side of aesthetic appreciation to make it as frivolous as a game. But there is no more reason to conceive of it as a game than there is to conceive of science as such. Science is concerned with expressing the properties of the world of appearance. The world of reality cannot be expressed in terms of formulae, nor, indeed, in ordinary language at all. Just as the mystic cannot express himself by ordinary means, so art, by its employment of sensuous materials (and even literary art uses words not to inform but to suggest) tries to *exhibit* rather than to formulate the results of the artist's insight into reality. In this sense the artist is a kind of mystic, concerned as all mystics are with the nature of a reality otherwise inaccessible. By responding to works of art (the aesthetic response) we are able to penetrate to what is eternal and unchangeable, and thus to liberate ourselves from the transiency of mundane experience.

There are many forms which an interpretation of this kind takes, and some are very different from others. One is the view of Arthur Schopenhauer (1788-1860). Another is the view of Plato, that there is an absolute Form or Ideal of Beauty to which all things called beautiful must conform (or strive to conform) if they are truly to possess that property. Absolute Beauty is eternal and unchangeable, whereas all beautiful *things* in the natural world, in fact *all* things in the world of sense, are transient and corruptible. In terms of such a view artistic activity would be the search after an Absolute, and the products of this activity would be the avenue to it. The greatest works of art would be those which succeed in this to the greatest degree.

*Art as an Instrument of Pleasure.* If art is something that has human value, some philosophers argue, it must be interpreted as existing for human satisfaction. Now the value of science consists in its furnishing us with knowledge. Art, however, is not concerned with knowing nature and predicting its ways but with manipulating it for our pleasurable contemplation. Art lacks not only cognitive value but practical value, in the usual sense, and if it were not a means to pleasure it would have no value whatever. Although it is true — so the argument continues — that many things which give us pleasure are nevertheless of small significance in human affairs, while art is of great significance, this substantiates rather than refutes the present interpretation. For in the first place, the pleasure yielded by art to both artist and spectator is not any pleasure but a special kind of pleasure, sometimes called aesthetic pleasure. And in the second place, this kind of pleasure is more enduring than is ordinarily the case. Works of art, therefore, are not mere stimuli to gratification but permanent sources of enjoyment. Aesthetic pleasure, like all things valuable, is not easily bought, and its attainment is difficult.

The reader will recognize in this interpretation of art the emphasis of hedonism — aesthetic hedonism. Like the preceding interpretation, it is statable in many forms. One, somewhat crude philosophically, is that of the novelist Tolstoy. Tolstoy considers art to be a spreading or contagion of emotion by the artist. The wider the appeal of the emotion, and (here a strong ethical emphasis enters) the greater the number of moral sentiments it inculcates, the greater the art. Thus peasant airs, appealing to and emotionally affecting an innumerably wider group of people than Shakespeare does, are truer and better art, regardless of bourgeois prejudices on our part. In Tolstoy we have a curious intellectual combination—an ethical viewpoint stressing self-discipline and Christian humility, and an aesthetic viewpoint that is unmistakably hedonistic. Still more curiously in the light of this, the hedonism is one which seems to make immediate pleasure the fundamental purpose of art and artistic judgment, rather than acquired pleasure in the broader hedonistic sense mentioned at the end of the last paragraph.

*Art as the Intensified Expression of Experience.* Each of the foregoing interpretations assigns to art a special function, one severed from the course of ordinary experience. There is a third view which regards art as rooted in the warp and woof of all experience. On this view, art is experience that is consciously reshaped. The artist relates to his environment in a certain *kind* of way. The creation of art results from the artist contributing his personality, knowledge, memory, and imagination, and the environment contributing the materials that go to excite these into activity—sounds (in the case of music), animate and inanimate forms (in the case of sculpture, dance, furniture, architecture), living characters and events (in the case of the drama and the novel). The environment feeds the artist, the artist moulds the environment. Art is the deepening or intensifying of experience by imaginative transformation of it. Similarly, the enjoyment of art consists in a relation between the spectator's past life, knowledge, and imagination on the one hand, and the artistic object with all that it embodies and suggests on the other. The stuff of which art is made is the culture of a people and the personal life of its individual members. Art *reflects* experience and *adds* to it. In Plato we found a strain that nourished the first of the preceding interpretations, but we can find in him another that supports the present one. He and Aristotle, in characterizing art as an "imitation" of nature, did not mean a duplication of nature, an unimaginative copying of sights or a slavish parroting of sounds — this would be not art but a travesty of nature. The "imitation" signified that the subject-matter of art is that of all experience, and reflects human life with the inevitable interrelation of man and his surroundings that this implies. The tendency to look upon art as duplication is one extreme, the tendency to regard it as pure concoction of personal imagination is another. The one implies an indiscriminate identification of art with the rest of nature, the other an irreparable separation of a realm of art from a realm of nature.

**Critical Comparison of the Three Theories.**  The first of the three theories we have considered suffers from the objections that can be brought against any view resting on an uneliminable appearance-reality distinction, the second from those that can be brought against a view influenced by hedonism. If all art is an attempt to capture a fixed reality normally hidden from us, who is to determine when this has been accomplished more or less? All criticism becomes impossible, for no one can say about a hidden reality more than individual intuition prompts him to. Critical standards become equally impossible if the principal function of art is taken to be pleasure. No one can take another's pleasure as not enduring and legitimate, but only his own; so that if another than ourselves makes an aesthetic judgment contrary to ours, it must be accepted as equally valid so long as it is a sincere one. The first interpretation, emphasizing an objective reality, and the second, emphasizing subjective reaction, are both subjective as far as aesthetic standards are concerned. Both are removed from the body of social, public, human experience. Here the merit of the third interpretation is evident. It can interpret even the most individual manifestation of creation, or of enjoyment, as one that yet falls within the body of human experience. It also is able to embrace, perhaps in even more coherent form, the merits of the other two views. If we interpret the first liberally, as serving to emphasize that art is not a mere transcript of experience but reveals something in it not revealed in the ordinary course of experience, it is identical with the emphasis that art enriches experience and elicits from it new significance. The second theory is correct in implying that the justification of art is its contribution to human enjoyment, to experience that proves more desirable. The third view serves to show, however, that this element consists not in pleasure, even enduring pleasure, primarily and as such, but in the general enhancement of welfare and happiness, in which pleasure (as we showed in the ethical context) is a concomitant factor. The specific pleasures of aesthetic experience are not undervalued by this view; they are only subordinated to the rôle that art plays in the whole of life.

**The Aesthetic and the Moral.** What is the relation between aesthetic and moral activity, between aesthetic and moral values? We agreed above that the moral aspect of our lives is not something with fixed qualities sharply demarcated from the other aspects. All of our experience and conduct may assume a moral character under certain conditions. In this respect, each of our aesthetic experiences (whether as artist or spectator) *may* have moral significance, and certainly the sum of these experiences will have it, in the sense that it bears upon our total set of habits. Conversely, what we call our moral conduct or moral life *may* be endowed with an aesthetic value. Nevertheless despite this interpenetration and mutual influence, practically speaking, a distinction can be drawn, and if it could not there would be no meaning to "mutual" influence. A moral act or experience, we said, is moral in so far as it has a definite effect upon our relations to others, our own development, or our intellectual creed. An act of aesthetic appreciation or creation, on the other hand, is relatively self-contained and is centered in the object rather than in its effects or implications. Its significance for the basic pattern of our actions is irrelevant. Our attention is arrested and absorbed, and not, as in moral activity, pregnant with possible overtones or implications. Let us give an example where aesthetic and moral values can be distinguished in a single situation. A man who has borrowed a manuscript from a collection, defaces it in an idle, absent moment. He suddenly becomes conscious of the moral character of his act — its effect on others, on his own self-control, on his intellectual principles. But, just as suddenly, he is arrested by the pattern which his pen has been creating, and he is now in the midst of an aesthetic situation, exploring the qualities of a sensuous medium, and concerned solely with a value resident in the object he is contemplating. A man may go to church purely in the light of the moral significance involved, and another may go to church purely for the aesthetic significance of the services, each blind to the alternative possible significance or to their fusion. A man may, of course, bring his aesthetic experience to bear on his moral conduct, and perhaps also vice versa, but this is, strictly speaking, adventitious to the *character* of that experience. It may be, and probably is, also true that an aesthetic value is *greater* when it harmonizes with and promotes a moral value, when it takes on a moral value, and vice versa; but this too is an independent question that does not erase the distinction. Further, it is true that aesthetic experience may be enhanced when we come to aesthetic activity prepared for it, and cognizant of historical, technical, and psychological information relating to it (though this holds much more for appreciative than creative activity). But all this subserves acts of aesthetic contemplation, and is a means to increasing the intensity of any given one. In moral activity, each moral incident or choice primarily serves to accentuate the larger pattern or whole of conduct; in aesthetic activity, the larger pattern primarily serves to accentuate each aesthetic experience. Perhaps the ideal would be for each of our acts to enhance the totality of our conduct, and for the totality of our conduct to make each of our acts an end in itself. This would mean that each of our acts would at once have the maximum of aesthetic and moral value.

❖   ❖   ❖

# The Interpretation of Religion

No consideration of philosophic problems can fail to be influenced by that fundamental institution of man which we know as religion. We have already seen in detail that faith as a method, and supernaturalism as a world-view, are associated with at least *one kind* of religious outlook. We must now consider religion deliberately, and try to discover what philosophic implications this phase of human experience yields, just as we have considered science, art, and morality.

**Sociological and Philosophical Approaches to Religion.** Religion may be studied from at least two points of view. The first considers it as it actually functions in society, as a phenomenon which takes different forms among different groups and even among different individuals. This study is interested in knowing a set of facts and a set of social and psychological laws. It is, therefore, strictly speaking a branch of the social sciences — comprising conclusions drawn from history, sociology, anthropology, and psychology. The other approach to religion, which is the one that will most concern us here, may be called the philosophical as distinct from the sociological (the former) approach. The philosophy of religion is concerned with questions like the following: What are the essential or defining characteristics of "religion," which enables us to find what the various forms of religion have in common? Is there such a thing as religious knowledge, or religious insight, either distinct from or opposed to scientific knowledge? What, in general, is the relation between religion and science? But such questions are not independent of the sociological study of religion. In order to answer them, as in order to answer problems in ethics, we must constantly draw on the results of the empirical sciences, so that we may have a factual basis for our analysis.

**What Is Religion?**   Suppose that our empirical investigation of different peoples and different persons has revealed to us that there are numerous ways of human activity all actually called or calling themselves by the name "religion." For example, we commonly speak of a man's "religion" as involving certain beliefs on his part and membership in a church. We speak also of men as adhering to a given religion which does not involve church membership. We speak of certain kinds of beliefs as "religious" beliefs, exemplified by the Christian religion. But we also call other, very different kinds of beliefs, like those of Buddhism and Mohammedanism, religious beliefs. We speak of "primitive" religion, the religion of primitive cultures past and present. We speak of "pagan" religion, the religion of societies like the ancient Egyptian and Greek. Sometimes we speak of a man as adhering to a "religion of his own," something private. And so on. Now if we are to define "religion" we must take account of everything to which we apply the word, and, among the characteristics displayed by all of them, find those which are *common* to all. We cannot define "religion" in a given way and then, when told that our definition fails to include such-and-such within its range, dismiss that as not "really" being an instance of religion. To do this is to employ a *prior,* concealed definition — one not based on examination of the phenomena actually denoted by the term. For in seeking to determine what religion is, we are not arbitrarily defining a term, we are inquiring into a set of human activities and attitudes.

**Two Typical Definitions.**   *Religion Identified with Belief in the Supernatural.*   Popularly, religion means belief in God, that is, in a supernatural being. That this definition is inadequate is shown, first, by the fact that such great Oriental religions as Hinduism and Buddhism are not strictly theistic at all, and not supernaturalistic except possibly in the sense that the mythological accounts of the world that they embody involve the assumption of supernatural agencies. Second, there are many whose religion is explicitly non-supernaturalistic and who are nevertheless generally recognized as deeply religious; for example, Spinoza, and a number of non-supernaturalistic mystics. It is, however, equally objectionable to identify religion with some kind of belief and nothing more. It would then be indistinguishable from a philosophy, and the term "religion" would suggest no more than the sociological history of a given viewpoint.

*Religion Identified with Faith.* It is understandable that in the light of objections like these, what should be stressed as the core of all religion is not *what* we believe but *how* we believe it. In popular usage we imply something like this when we say that a person believes or does something "religiously." What is held here to constitute religion is unshakable conviction or "faith" in certain truths. But this needs to be made more precise. It cannot mean that religion is the set of beliefs in which we have *most* faith. The beliefs we are most convinced of are those of common sense and immediate experience. Religious faith, then, must refer to beliefs that go beyond what we have experienced in the past or experience in the present. This definition is designed to include within the scope of religion what we hear called "a religion of science" or a "religion of communism," the scientific method and the specific political ideal representing beliefs that dominate human life. But again we seem not to have touched the *principal* element in religion. For a man's dominant human ambition may be to demonstrate his superiority to all mankind as a pianist or as a boxer — a faith which goes beyond the immediate present and past but which surely does not constitute what would be justly called a religion. Thus while the present definition does touch an *important* factor in religion, it remains inadequate and imprecise.

**Worship and Ritual.** The essential element in religion is sometimes said to be "worship." But as soon as we reflect on the meaning of this notion, we find it to be far from simple. To "worship" sometimes means to adore, to revere intensely. Sometimes it involves the additional suggestion of awe. And sometimes it is used intransitively, not as directed toward an object but as signifying a kind of meditative state. In all these senses, what is emphasized is an attitude. But sometimes the term "worship" is used synonymously with acts of "ritual," and from this it seems desirable to distinguish it sharply. Worship strictly does not imply anything more than a kind of attitude, whereas ritual implies a definite kind of *performance.* Worship does not imply that the attitude be assumed regularly, whereas it is of the essence of ritual that it be scheduled or repeated on specified occasions. In all of the great organized religions, worship is closely *associated* with the performance of rites (or vice versa), but the distinction nevertheless can be clearly made. The term "ritual" may be understood broadly to cover acts purely private. If, however, an individual at a given moment were to fall on his knees in a sudden gesture of adoration, this would express worship but would not, despite the physical act involved, constitute a ritual; for it is spontaneous, and not scheduled. Perhaps the idea of prayer in the traditional sense of the word combines the elements of worship and ritual. Whether public or private, it seems to imply, in addition to a meditative attitude, a *habitual* setting aside of time for the purpose.

**Organized and Personal Religion.** We have tacitly assumed that religion may relate not to a group only but to an individual, that it may in some sense be private or personal. What is involved in organized religion? We may distinguish two major aspects, which may be called the dogmatic and the ritualistic aspect. Most organized religions possess a body of fixed principles regarded as unalterable truths, and these we call their dogmas. In addition they possess a ritual procedure. An organized religion could not consist in a body of beliefs alone. There would be no sense in calling it "organized"; it would more accurately be called a school of philosophic thought —though hardly that, either, if its methods were solely those of faith and authority. On the other hand, an organized religion could not consist in ritual alone: it would be organized, no doubt, but would amount either to a fraternal organization or to a school of art. Dogma and ritual, then, are complementary in organized religion. The performance of ritual is an outward manifestation of *belief* in the dogmas; belief in the dogmas gives *meaning* to the performance.

Ritual may, as in private prayer, be a part of personal religion; and like all ritual, it would imply some belief or outlook that rendered it significant. But we should not call this belief dogma, for it would probably be the outcome of a personal intuition rather than of authority. In any case, personal religion implies greater emphasis on attitude and psychological makeup than does organized religion. Organized religion has sometimes taken cognizance of the importance of a direct relation between religious conviction and the individual. Thus the tendency of Protestant Christianity has been to emphasize "faith" above "works" and to interpret this as the essential import of the New Testament Gospels.

**Religions and Religious Attitudes.** Organized religion has normally insisted on the inseparability of religion and ethics and the dependence of the latter on the former. On this view the source of our ideals of conduct is our religious faith. One might, however, as plausibly adopt the reverse position, and hold that the character of our religious faith depends on our ideals of conduct. Thus organized religion has often been faced with the problem that there are men with high moral ideals — and these ideals may coincide with those of organized religion — outside the Church. Of these, some do and some do not profess a "personal religion." A distinction insisted upon by Dewey is that between having a *religion* and being *religious*. Having a religion, in his view, means belonging to a group that professes fixed dogma and practises established ritual. Being religious, on the other hand, means consciously holding a fundamental kind of attitude, the nature of which we shall consider below under Dewey's philosophy of religion. The distinction in its broadest terms would seem to be in accordance with historical fact. Adopting it, we would say that it is possible to belong to a religion and yet not to be religious, and to be religious without having a religion. Dewey, in fact, for reasons to be stated later, considers a combination of the two detrimental to the religious attitude; for in his terminology "religion" is synonymous with "organized religion," and the term "personal religion" would be replaced by "personal religious consciousness."

The religious attitude has usually been identified with *piety*, and a distinction has been made between orthodox and *natural* piety, the latter signifying piety without supernaturalism. In these terms, we would say that merely to conform or subscribe to a religion and be a member of its body is possible with a total absence of piety or religious consciousness; while one may be said to be pious (to "worship," if we use more formal terminology) even without conforming.

### Humility, or Consciousness of Individual Subordination, as Basic in Religion.

If we glance at the types of religion that have manifested themselves historically, we find that we can divide them according to the world-view which each takes for granted. All religion would seem to involve some world-view. But for a religion to be a religion rather than a crude speculative philosophy, it must serve to bring home to the individual the *human significance* of this world-view. And here we come to those essential characteristics on the basis of which we might perhaps define religion. All religions or religious attitudes properly so called assume that there is a power, or force, or ideal to which human life must be adjusted in the appropriate way. This dominant force reminds the individual of his essential subordination in the universal scheme of things, and the religious resultant is humility. But in the general

framework of this definition, tremendous differences of interpretation are possible. *What* this dominant force *is*, *what* humility consists in, *how* the religious life functions, are the questions that distinguish one philosophy of religion from another.
We shall shortly go on to consider some of the approaches to
religion that have been prominent both traditionally and in modern times. The number of modern interpretations is great, and
in giving somewhat more attention to the naturalistic-humanistic interpretation, the purpose has been to acquaint the
reader most fully with one that at once is as distant as possible from the traditional, is eloquently defended, and is highly
plausible philosophically.

**Further on the Meaning of "Worship."** Recognition of
a higher power and subordination to it seem closely allied with
the idea of "worship." There appear to be three senses in
which this term is actually used: (a) Sometimes it assumes
the meaning of *mere belief* in a higher power to which we feel
subordinate. The assertion that a man "worships God" implies
that he "believes in" God. (b) Sometimes it is taken to mean,
not the belief itself, which is an intellectual conviction, but the
*consciousness of its significance,* that is to say, the *recurrent
recognition* of it. (c) Finally, it is taken to mean the ritualistic expression of the belief. We may, of course, use the term
in any of these senses so long as we specify which of the senses
we are employing when we do so.

**Animism and Supernaturalism.** The religion of primitive societies has often taken the form of what is called *animism.* On this view, magical agencies reside in natural objects,
which are therefore conceived of as alive. These agencies,
themselves non-material, exercise their power, both malignant
and benevolent, in an incomprehensible manner. They are usually conceived of hierarchically, as variously of greater and
lesser power. Beliefs of this kind, unrecorded in language, can
hardly be called dogmas in the usual sense of that term. But
the manner of their acceptance and their rigid status differ only

in degree if at all from beliefs properly so called. Rites in animism are the overt means of effecting adjustment to the magical powers, and in fact all ritual (where there is ritual) may be thus interpreted as overt expression of religious conviction. Animism may in one sense be regarded as a form of supernaturalism, though we have not previously so regarded it. In any case, it would be distinguished from theistic supernaturalism, which, whether more or less anthropomorphic, differs in conceiving of natural and supernatural as *distinct realms,* in substituting for *magic* the idea of *miracle,* and in the establishment of theology, that is, recorded dogma and polemic. As against animism, it *emphasizes* the subordination of man; subordination, in other words, is not merely a custom of psychological and social behavior but a principle elaborately developed.

**Mythological Pantheism.** As opposed to supernaturalism, *pantheism* conceives of "God" not as distinct from nature and as affecting it in non-natural manner, but as embodied in the universe or its processes. The supreme power is, to use traditional philosophic language, not a *transcendent* being (something that transcends the universe) but an *immanent* one (one that pervades the universe). Pantheistic world-views differ considerably among themselves, some being idealistic, some naturalistic, and all these, moreover, being either philosophically conceived or entertained in the wake of vague imaginative tradition. Organized Oriental religions like Hinduism and Buddhism are primarily pantheistic in the latter, or mythological sense. For example, the doctrine of Karma, or transmigration of souls, has the character less of a philosophic principle than of an imaginative bulwark for a moral outlook. The motivation of such doctrines appears to be not the explanation of the universe as it actually is and the formulation of a moral outlook on this basis, but the formulation of a moral attitude first and the subsequent creation of a cosmic system to lend it justification.

**The Pantheism of Spinoza.** Among philosophers, men as different as Hegel and Spinoza have been called pantheists.

Spinoza's philosophy is profoundly interesting because of the fact that a radically naturalistic outlook, which has ordinarily been associated with irreligion, becomes in his hands the basis of a deeply religious attitude. As we saw, Spinoza uses the term "God" for Substance, the unified total system of all facts and all possibilities. Conceived in this way, God has the attributes traditionally ascribed to the supreme being — omnipotence, infinity, etc. But that God in this sense is as far as possible from the idea of a personal deity follows from the character of Spinoza's determinism. No event could possibly have occurred otherwise than it does, which means, as Spinoza himself tells us, that God could not possibly have "chosen" to act otherwise than "he" does. A universal purpose or end being for Spinoza a myth, the immortality of the soul a fiction, where does the religious factor enter? In the recognition by man that he and all he possesses, being a part of God, are completely dependent on God — dependent not in the sense that he is subject to the whims of a deity but in the sense that he is an element of the whole. Man arises in God, and lives in God, and it is in this very concrete sense that he himself is divine. Such a view, as Spinoza reminds us, does not flatter man's emotions or his ego, and is hostile to what we should call the "will to believe." The truly religious attitude does not vainly make the universe to order for its own hopes but wisely reconciles itself to what must be. Thus our religious attitude should not be something which stands or falls with the hope that we shall somehow continue to be conscious after death. Religion need no longer be hostile to free intellectual inquiry. For as our inquiry grows, our understanding of nature grows — or, to translate this into Spinozistic terms, our awareness of our propinquity to God becomes greater. To *love* God means to *understand*. By understanding, the individual becomes humble, but he also becomes emancipated. The fact of death becomes something neither to be psychologically feared nor morally awaited; it becomes a fact of nature similar to the facts of life and growth. This humility and understanding, bringing with it natural piety and perspective, an achievement by Spinoza of what Santayana has called "the secret of peace," is surely as deeply religious as any attitude can be.

**The Relation between Organized Religion and Science.** Everyone has heard of the question so frequently discussed whether religion and science conflict or not. It is usually organized religion, religion in the historical or traditional sense, that is referred to in this question. Can the teachings and historical references of sacred texts and the dogmas of theology be regarded as truths when the results of scientific inquiry are? Now there is no doubt that some theories of science contradict sacred writings, whether of supernaturalistic religions or not. The systems of astronomy and geography, for instance, assumed by these writings are no longer acceptable, and the narration of miraculous events is at least inharmonious with the method of science. That such a conflict is inevitable was recognized comparatively early in the Middle Ages. Arabic, Hebrew, and Christian thinkers alike often debated the question whether much of the Bible was meant to be understood literally or allegorically. If allegorically, the conflict would be less direct; but conflict there still would be. For the question would still remain whether the *teachings* thus allegorically intended conflict with science. Belief in miracle might still be retained even though specific instances of miracle were intended allegorically. And in any case, the question would always arise whether the dogmas of theology, based on the teaching of the sacred texts, were compatible with science. It is sometimes alleged that they must be compatible since eminent theologians on the one hand and eminent scientists on the other have testified that they are. But (1) if we accepted this, we should have to explain why other eminent scientists and eminent theologians have held that they are not compatible. This goes to show (2) that neither those who say they are compatible, nor those who deny this, warrant our belief merely because they say what they do; it is the reason given for a view, not the eminence of those who advocate the view, that is important. Authority, as we have pointed out, is methodologically sound only when it is an equivalent substitute for independent scientific research, never when it is mere authority. Authority in science and theology is by no means necessarily entitled to the same respect when it purports to be authority in philosophy.

**Idealistic Philosophies of Religion.** Modern philosophies of religion feel called upon to reckon with the religion-science conflict. One type of attempt to lend a more adequate basis to religion than does the traditional conception is that of idealists or philosophers with strong idealist tendencies. These philosophers ascribe the conflict of science and religion to the fact that the latter lacks a correct, philosophical formulation of a world-view. The idealistic approach is offered to fill the need. So successful do idealists believe their philosophy to be in its application to religion that they regard this success as itself an argument for idealism.

Some recent idealists conceive of God, in Hegelian terms, as the Absolute, or infinite mind of which all things are reflections. Others, though they share the concept of an Absolute, try to formulate it in less impersonal terms and relate it more intimately to human experience. Thus for W. E. Hocking (1873-1966) God is not only the infinite absolute mind but stands to each of us as also an individual Other Mind. We know this other mind in knowing nature. The religious man is one for whom every experience is an experience of the Absolute Other Mind. Worship is precisely the attempt to gain a more and more profound consciousness of the absolute whole within which all things grow and develop. Such a consciousness is not of an abstract, speculative character, but is an immediate awareness or concrete experience in which all the traditional religious emotions are present on a higher, transformed plane.

**Panpsychism and Creative Evolution.** Another idealistic emphasis, similar in some respects and different in others, some proponents of which would not call themselves idealists, is that which conceives God both as a universal mind and as the creative force in the universe's evolution, the force which is responsible for both the emergence of the new and the increasing achievement of the good. In the opinion of W. P. Montague (1873-1953) this conception springs from the very nature of religion, which may be defined as "the faith that there is in nature an urge or power other than man himself that works for the kind of thing that man regards as good." The view of Montague differs from that of Hocking primarily in that, first, it is much less concerned with the traditional religious emotions and is more hostile to the structure of organized religion, and second, it is more concerned with a technical cosmology, or theory of the workings of the universe. It is inconceivable, according to Montague, that the universe can be an affair of merely mechanical causality and yet produce a *Hamlet*. The whole material world must rather be conceived of as intrinsically possessing consciousness. Only such a hypothesis can explain how mental phenomena arise and how the creation of new elements in the universe takes place. This form of idealism is known as *panpsychism*. It dates back in one form or another to ancient times, to the position which is known as *hylozoism,* and a number of notable modern philosophers subscribe to some version of it, though not necessarily with the present religious implications. God, for Montague, is the living universe, an all-inclusive Life, and in this respect is infinite. But the will of God is the creative force in this Life, the power making for good; and in this respect God is finite, for there is not one but many forces within him and in conflict with his will. Conceptions similar to that of Montague are expounded by E. S. Brightman (1884-1953) and E. W. Lyman (1872-1948). According to the latter, God may be conceived of as a Cosmic Creative Spirit. This spirit is not infinite in the traditional sense, nor is it eternal in the sense of being timeless; for the force of creative evolution is within time.

**The Idealistic Interpretation of Traditional Religious Concepts.** On views like those of Montague and Lyman the traditional problem of evil does not arise, for God is no longer infinite or omnipotent in the usual sense. It is perhaps equally interesting to note the points of contact between these systems of evolutionary panpsychism and traditional religion. Certain essential emphases in the latter are adopted but translated into more philosophical terms. God is a Creator, but obviously no longer in a naïve sense. God, moreover, is a "personal" God; not, however, in the sense that he is conscious of the destiny of each individual, but in the sense that he possesses the attributes of personality. In this respect religious panpsychism involves anthropomorphism. According to Montague, it is not an insult to God but the very reverse to ascribe to him an attribute (personality) which is also characteristic of human limitation. "If the universe has a mind, that mind would be more, rather than less personal than ours, for it would have more, rather than less of unity and organicity."

**The Naturalistic-Humanistic Philosophy of Religion.** There have been at least two noteworthy attempts in our century, by Santayana and Dewey, to interpret religion on the basis of a naturalistic philosophy. This type of interpretation assumes that when religion is looked at in a new light the historical value that belongs to it can be retained at the same time that it is made harmonious with science. Both Santayana and Dewey assume further that if the traditional interpretation is retained and the opposition between religion and science permitted to stand, there can be no reasonable alternative but to accept science at the expense of religion. How, then, is religion to be reinterpreted? We may begin with the older of the two naturalistic theories, Santayana's.

**Santayana's Interpretation of Religion.** According to Santayana, the only way to avoid the religion-science conflict and to understand the important place in human life which religion can have, is to realize that religion and science are not both enterprises which can attempt to discover *truth*. Or if they are, then it is truth in very different senses, and the scientific method alone can give us truth about matters of fact. Religion, then, can have nothing to tell us about the nature of the universe. In attempting to do so historically, it has amounted to pseudo-science or refined superstition. Santayana's interpretation is thus as much opposed to idealistic philosophies of religion as to traditional supernaturalism. But if this is what religion is not, what is it? Religion is essentially *poetry* — "in the sense in which poetry includes all imaginative moral life." It is poetry with a moral function, and it is this function that we must go on to define. The sacred writings of religion have the kind of value that mythology has, and the ritual of religion has the kind of value that drama has, a drama more exalted in its significance because we ourselves play a part. Religion, on this view, is no longer a matter in which there need be controversy or strife: there is no more reason for religions than for poems to conflict. One religion is not "true" and another "false"; one religion may be *better* than another in the sense that its symbolism and poetry are richer and morally more elevating. If religion possesses "truth" in some sense, it is the truth which all mythological poetry has, not *literal* or *factual* truth, but *symbolic* or *imaginative* or *moral* truth. Thus the Old and New Testaments are epics, dreams, in the same sense that the works of Homer and Dante are.

**The Concept of "God" Reinterpreted.** In Santayana's philosophy of religion, "God" is not the name of an actual being or reality. It is a name for the highest ideal of man. It is a symbol for perfect truth, beauty, and goodness, for the ideal of happiness. Thus, to ask the traditional question whether "God exists" is to ask an empty question. *That* God is, is a position which becomes dependent upon, and which derives its meaning from, an answer to the question *what* "God" is. (See in Chapter Thirteen the discussion of the classical arguments for the "existence of God.") If Santayana's interpretation is adopted, the old issue of "monotheism" versus "polytheism" vanishes. On his view Greek philosophers like Plato and Aristotle are not guilty of inconsistency when they speak sometimes of "God" and sometimes of "the gods." For when they refer to the gods, they mean to symbolize *special* ideals of man; thus Apollo is a symbol of beauty, Zeus of power, Athena of wisdom. When they speak of God, on the other hand, they mean to symbolize the *unified* or total ideal of man, happiness or perfection or harmony. The variation of expression serves a moral purpose.

Again, on an approach like Santayana's, the issue of whether "God is dead" (Nietzsche) needs to be given flexibility of meaning. If "God" is the name of the highest ideal of man, the issue can only be whether such an ideal has died or has become irrelevant to what we wish to call "religion."

**The Significance of Prayer.**    God being no longer interpreted as an actual being, prayer likewise must be reinterpreted. In its usual sense prayer is an address to a supernatural being serving either as petition or as thanks for certain desired effects. Santayana regards this as essentially similar to superstition and magic. It is a vain magnification of our individual sorrows as somehow the concern of a creator who will miraculously disturb the course of the universe for our benefit. Prayer, he feels, should be an instrument by which we seek to accomplish spiritual rather than material things. It is a symbolical attitude in which we remind ourselves of our ideals and clarify them; it articulates what we prize most. It reconciles us to the inevitability of natural forces and reminds us of our limitations in the face of them. It inculcates a spiritual discipline and a contemplative attitude, which as Santayana (following Aristotle) says, "are their own reward."

**Piety, Spirituality, and Charity.**    Along with the new light in which the concepts of God and prayer appear, the traditional religious attitudes take on a different significance. *Piety* is no longer directed toward a supernatural being but to the vast universe in which we are bred and in which we develop. Such a piety is justified by the fact that nature gives rise in us to those interests responsible for our aspiring to goals or ideals. Ideals always express natural impulses or interests.

They are not magical agencies beckoning our conduct from somewhere in the future; nor are they absolute standards superimposed on us to curb our natural impulses. An ideal is the ideal *of* something. Piety is the attitude that looks to the *source* of our existence and our ideals. Piety, however, is by itself not the highest expression of a religious attitude. Gratitude to the source of our existence can, taken alone, degenerate into ascetic humility, purposeless and completely resigned. What Santayana calls *spirituality* is the highest expression of the religious attitude. Spirituality looks not to the source of our being but to its fructification or *perfection*. "To be spiritual is to live in view of the ideal." Although all ideals have a basis in nature, to be conscious of a direction interrelating these ideals or goals is to be more than pious. Spirituality is not merely a striving to achieve this or that goal but an awareness of a total or unified perfection which each of these goals subserves. "Spirituality is nobler than piety, because what would fulfill our being and make it worth having is what alone lends value to that being's source." Finally, *charity,* as Santayana understands it, is justice, which a spiritual man, in spite of his spirituality, may forget. Justice is the realization that *other* creatures, other species, have *their* ideal ends, and that our own are not the only, nor the central, ideals in nature. Charity is *imaginative* justice, a perspective of tolerance and sympathy, without which our dominant ideal of happiness is narrow and incomplete. It is for this reason (its relation to happiness) that charity constitutes part of the fundamental religious attitude, and not because of a supernatural ordinance the ultimate rationale of which must forever remain mysterious to us.

**The Significance of the Historical Framework of Religion.** Despite the fact that he rejects the intellectual or philosophical *content* of traditional religion, Santayana insists that the framework or *structure* of traditional religion must be retained. We cannot merely have a "religion"; we must have a particular religion, a historical one, whether the one in which we are born or one which we adopt. We require a *vehicle* for our poetic (imaginative) vision of the human ideal, just as, in order to speak a language, we must speak a particular language. A man's religion is his moral language. Historical religion is the best vehicle, because of its richer accumulation of tradition and the deeper character of its epic. Santayana believes that if we examine a given historical religion we find that the values pointed out above have indeed always been present. He does not consider that his reinterpretation of religion is a *redefinition*, but rather that it has a historical basis. The values of religion have been obscured; they have been confused with philosophic or scientific values and have been associated, for the most part, with literal interpretations. It is in discarding the latter that the reinterpretation or new emphasis consists. The imaginative clarification of moral truth Santayana holds to be religion in its *primary* sense (as he calls it); literal belief is religion in its *secondary* sense. He believes that in the case of most great figures of historical religion the primary element *functioned* as most important, though they themselves may have professed literal belief or may have been unconscious of the implications of their own religious conduct. Once we come to realize that the *historical* association of the secondary with the primary elements is not *logically* justified, our religion will not only become purer but the tragic strife of religions will disappear.

**"Ultimate Religion."** Writing a quarter of a century later on what he calls ultimate religion, Santayana, it is interesting to note, no longer emphasizes the historical particularity of religion. Piety is now called respect for universal *power* (that of all nature), while spirituality and charity become fused and at the same time broadened in meaning, signifying love of universal *good*, the love or worship not only of our own ideals or goals of perfection but those of all living things. Emphasis on piety, or worship of universal power, corresponds historically, Santayana believes, to the religious emphasis of Spinoza; whereas spirituality or love of universal good represents the religion of Socrates. In making this con-

trast he perhaps fails to take into consideration the implications of Spinoza's philosophy. Though piety or humility do
emerge as most prominent in Spinoza's religious outlook, there
seems to be no doubt that love of universal goodness in Santayana's sense is an inevitable consequence of this attitude.

**The Approach of Dewey.**  Like Santayana, by whom he
is considerably influenced in his religious philosophy, Dewey
finds the reinterpretation of religion necessitated by the un-
questionable conflict between traditional religion and science.
Bearing in mind his distinction, stated above, between "religion" and "the religious," we shall in what follows agree to
understand by the former term "organized religion" (primarily supernaturalism) and by the latter an attitude that remains to be defined. As in Santayana, religious value turns
out to be moral value; though very unlike Santayana, Dewey
from the beginning discards the alleged interconnection between the pursuit of this value and the framework of historical religion.

**Two Senses of "Religious Experience."**  Dewey points
out that the term "religious experience" can mean two things.
The ordinary usage implies that religious experience is a special kind of experience, as scientific, political, moral, and aesthetic experience are; and as such it is supposedly to be
sharply distinguished from each of these, as each is from the
other. Religious experience allegedly gives us evidence for
"religious truths," as scientific experience gives us evidence
for scientific truths. In Dewey's own sense of the term, however, "religious experience" denotes an attitude, a quality in
human experience that may belong to *any* kind of experience,
whether scientific, aesthetic, or moral. It is not applicable to
any special kind of object or any special kind of belief. "It
denotes attitudes that may be taken toward every object and
every proposed end or ideal." There are, for example, scientific beliefs, but there are no "religious beliefs."

**The Meaning of "The Religious."**  According to Dewey
the religious quality or attitude enters our experience when we

perceive a fundamental *direction* in our living. We begin to harmonize the different ends we seek into an organized self, and into an attitude that persists despite changes in our environment. We achieve a fundamental perspective of this self in its relation to "that imaginative totality we call the universe." The religious attitude is the pursuit of *unified* ideals; in Santayana's language, its core is spirituality. "The religious attitude signifies something that is bound through imagination to a *general* attitude." ". . . We need to reverse the ordinary statement and say that whatever introduces genuine perspective is religious, not that religion is something that introduces it."

**The Conflict of Religion and Religious Values.** Historically religious values have, it is true, been associated with religion. Dewey feels, however, that this association not only is not necessary but has actually proved inimical to the best and fullest development of the religious attitude. Belief in fixed dogmas and fixed moral rules chains the mind to a perspective *imposed* upon it; such belief destroys the exercise of the human imagination in *gaining* a perspective. A genuine perspective requires freedom of insight, and liberation. The dogmas of religion, if they are not explicitly supernaturalistic, are likely to be at least anti-naturalistic. This means that the religious quality of experience is weighted down by them with something irrelevant. For the religious attitude is the pursuit of unified ideals. An ideal is a possibility that belongs to things natural, to ourselves as natural creatures. It is a possibility of growth, realization, and perfection. It follows, then, that

> A body of beliefs and practices that are apart from the common and natural relations of mankind must, in the degree in which it is influential, weaken and sap the force of the possibilities inherent in such relations. Here lies one aspect of the emancipation of the religious from religion.*

**Faith of Religion vs. Moral Faith, Free Intelligence, Natural Piety.** The gaining of a perspective and the pursuit of ends implies loyalty; without steadfast adherence, there

---

* *A Common Faith,* Ch. I.

would be no meaning to calling a quality of experience religious. Now loyalty in this sense is what we may call faith. But such faith is opposed to the usual sense of faith involved in adherence to organized religion. Since, as we have said, in a perspective attained by a truly religious attitude our pursuit of goals is freely arrived at, this faith is a faith *born* of free inquiry and not a faith in things closed to our examination. It is faith in the third of the senses we distinguished in Part Two (Chapter V). In this context Dewey calls it "moral faith." Conviction attained by free inquiry, *through* and not *at the expense of* understanding and knowledge, is the strongest and most uplifting kind of conviction. Intelligence and free inquiry are exemplified to the utmost in the scientific method.

> . . . Were we to admit that there is but one method for ascertaining fact and truth — that conveyed by the word "scientific" in its most general and generous sense — no discovery in any branch of knowledge and inquiry could then disturb the faith that is religious. I should describe this faith as the unification of the self through allegiance to inclusive ideal ends, which imagination presents to us and to which the human will responds as worthy of controlling our desires and choices.*

Intellectual liberation and faith in the sense described by no means imply the exclusion of piety and humility. On the contrary, they imply it directly. This piety springs from a realization that nature is the source from which all ideals spring and is the set of conditions without which no pursuit of ends can succeed. Dewey, however, emphasizes here too, that the humility is one we have naturally and willingly arrived at, not one superimposed upon us by fear or by the sanctions of religion. He believes that the name "God" might well be applied to the process which consists in uniting the *actual* in nature with the possible development of it that we call the *ideal*. It symbolizes, as in Santayana's version, the aspiration of man; the unity of piety and spirituality. Dewey emphasizes that the element of free intelligence in religious values does not mean that they become coldly intellectualistic and unemotional. In-

---

* *A Common Faith*, Ch. II.

telligence is not something rigidly distinct from or opposed to emotion. We can speak of passionate intelligence and ardor in pursuit of ideals. And the emotion aroused by the religious perspective growing out of intelligence is stable and "steady" emotion, the fruit of sanity, not a deviation from it.

**Common Faith: the Social Character of the Religious Attitude.** Religious faith (in the sense defined) is the fruit of the scientific attitude. And the perfection of the scientific attitude is itself one of the ideals in a religious attitude. The goal of unlimited success in human inquiry is a necessary part of an adequate perspective. Now as the scientific attitude of free inquiry is essentially co-operative and public, so must be the religious faith that is its consummation. The individual cannot have a genuinely religious outlook in isolation. His perspective must include as one of its ideals the welfare of the society of which he is an integral part. The multiplicity of organized churches as at present constituted are inevitably competitive in emphasis and they therefore militate against universality. But this need not always be. For men to retain the *ardor* of the historic religions and to direct this toward social welfare rather than toward the supernatural is the great desideratum. The ideal of universal brotherhood professed by religions like the Hebrew and Christian is inconsistent with the doctrine distinguishing between those who are damned and those who are saved, a consequence of the emanation of values from a supernatural instead of a natural source. The fundamental values and ideals of man can be achieved only by the community of men.

> The essentially unreligious attitude is that which attributes human achievement and purpose to man in isolation from the world of physical nature and his fellows. Our successes are dependent upon the co-operation of nature. The sense of the dignity of human nature is as religious as is the sense of awe and reverence when it rests upon a sense of human nature as a co-operating part of a larger whole. Natural piety is not of necessity either a fatalistic acquiescence in natural happenings or a romantic idealization of the world. It may rest upon a just sense of nature as the whole of which we are parts, while it also recognizes that we are parts that are marked by intelligence and purpose, having

the capacity to strive by their aid to bring conditions into greater consonance with what is humanly desirable. Such piety is an inherent constituent of a just perspective in life.

We who now live are parts of a humanity that extends into the remote past, a humanity that has interacted with nature. The things in civilization we most prize are not of ourselves. They exist by grace of the doings and sufferings of the continuous human community in which we are a link. Ours is the responsibility of conserving, transmitting, rectifying and expanding the heritage of values we have received that those who come after us may receive it more solid and secure, more widely accessible and more generously shared than we have received it. Here are all the elements for a religious faith that shall not be confined to sect, class, or race. Such a faith has always been implicitly the common faith of mankind. It remains to make it explicit and militant.*

**Conclusion.** Here, as well as anywhere, our survey of philosophical problems may be concluded. The intelligent reader will consider himself only on the threshold of philosophy. In discussing standards of valid thinking and method we have touched the field of *logic,* or *methodology.* We have discussed *epistemology,* or the study of knowledge, much of which overlaps with logic. We have delved into *axiology,* or the study of value. We have discussed aesthetic and moral values in treating of the philosophy of art *(aesthetics)* and the philosophy of conduct *(ethics).* We have dipped into the philosophy of science and the philosophy of religion. We have familiarized ourselves with *metaphysics,* or the formulation of the broadest and most fundamental characteristics of all experience. Certain types of problems we have not touched upon at all—e.g., those of social and political philosophy, the philosophy of history, and the philosophy of law. And many important philosophers we have not mentioned. We must remember that all of the "branches" of philosophy are closely interrelated. Their names are of use only for purposes of convenient reference and the question whether a given problem belongs to this or that field is of minor significance, for what is important is that the problem is there. From this point on the philosophically minded reader will study the history of philosophy and the philosophic literature of his own day, as a foundation

---

* *A Common Faith,* Ch. III.

for his own thinking. He will begin to find relative complexity in what he formerly held to be simple, and relative simplicity in what he formerly held to be complex. Above all, he will develop that disinterested passion for understanding which, as the basis of wisdom, becomes the most practical of all his pursuits.

# Selected Readings

∞∞∞∞∞∞∞∞∞∞∞∞∞∞∞∞∞∞∞∞∞∞∞∞∞∞∞∞∞∞∞∞∞∞∞∞∞∞∞∞∞∞∞∞∞∞∞∞

The following short list (one of many possible short lists) is designed for the reader who has finished this book and who wishes to begin further reading. For the most part, the selections here chosen are of the kind which not only investigate their subject but suggest broader implications. Many of the books listed are obtainable in paperbound editions. The readings are grouped under the chapter headings to which they are relevant.

## CHAPTERS I-IV
### (The Role of Philosophical Thinking in Human Life)

Plato, *Republic,* Book VI, 484-501.

Dewey, John, "The Meanings of Philosophy," in *Intelligence in the Modern World: John Dewey's Philosophy,* ed. J. Ratner.

Dilthey, Wilhelm, *The Essence of Philosophy,* trans. S. A. and W. T. Emery.

Whitehead, A. N., *Process and Reality,* Part I, Ch. I.

Waismann, Friedrich, "How I See Philosophy," in *Logical Positivism,* ed. A. J. Ayer.

Russell, Bertrand, "The Value of Philosophy," in *The Problems of Philosophy.*

## CHAPTER V
### (The Basic Methods of Inquiry)

Bacon, Francis, "The Four Idols," in *Novum Organum,* Aphorisms xxxvii-lxviii.

Peirce, C. S., "The Fixation of Belief," in *The Philosophy of Peirce: Selected Writings* (also titled *Philosophical Writings of Peirce*), ed. J. Buchler.

James, William, "The Will to Believe," in *The Will to Believe.*

Bradley, F. H., *Essays on Truth and Reality,* Ch. II.

Marcel, Gabriel, "Some Thoughts on Faith," in *Being and Having.*

## CHAPTER VI
(The Scientific Method)

Campbell, Norman, *What Is Science?*

Duhem, Pierre, *The Aim and Structure of Physical Theory,* trans. P. P. Wiener.

Nagel, Ernest, *The Structure of Science,* Chs. 1, 2.

Whitehead, A. N., *Science and the Modern World,* Chs. 1, 2.

Hanson, N. R., *Patterns of Discovery,* Ch. 1.

## CHAPTER VII
(The Roles of Reason and Experience in Human Knowledge)

Descartes, René, *Rules for the Direction of the Mind,* Rules I-XIV.

Spinoza, Baruch, *On the Improvement of the Understanding.*

Locke, John, *An Essay concerning Human Understanding,* Book II, Chs. 1, 2.

Hume, David, *A Treatise of Human Nature,* Book I, Part I.

Kant, Immanuel, *Prolegomena to Any Future Metaphysics,* Secs. 1-13.

Dewey, John, *Reconstruction in Philosophy,* Ch. IV.

## CHAPTER VIII
(Problems concerning the Scope and Extent of Knowledge)

Sextus Empiricus, *Outlines of Pyrrhonism,* Books I, II.

Descartes, René, *Meditations on First Philosophy.*

Hume, David, *An Inquiry concerning Human Understanding,* Secs. iv, v, xii.

Husserl, Edmund, *Cartesian Meditations,* Introduction, First Meditation.

Moore, G. E., *Some Main Problems of Philosophy,* Ch. IV.

Ayer, A. J., *The Problem of Knowledge,* Ch. 2.

## CHAPTER IX
(Immediacy, Communication, and Language)

Bergson, Henri, *An Introduction to Metaphysics* (also published as Ch. VI of *The Creative Mind*).

Croce, Benedetto, *Aesthetic,* Chs. I-III.

Stace, W. T., *Mysticism and Philosophy.*

Austin, J. L., *How to Do Things with Words.*

Buber, Martin, "Dialogue," in *Between Man and Man.*

## CHAPTER X
### (The Problem of Meaning)

Plato, *Cratylus,* 1-391.

Locke, John, *An Essay concerning Human Understanding,* Book III, Chs. I, II, IX, X, XI.

Peirce, C. S., "How to Make Our Ideas Clear," in *The Philosophy of Peirce; Selected Writings* (also titled *Philosophical Writings of Peirce*), ed. J. Buchler.

Royce, Josiah, *The Problem of Christianity,* Vol. II, Lectures XI-XIV.

Cassirer, Ernst, *Language and Myth,* trans. S. K. Langer.

Wittgenstein, Ludwig, *Philosophical Investigations,* Secs. 1-133.

Quine, W. V., *Word and Object,* Chs. 1, 2.

## CHAPTER XI
### (What Is Truth?)

Nagel, E., and Brandt, R. (eds.), *Meaning and Knowledge,* pp. 124-160, 166-176.

Aquinas, Thomas, "On Truth," in *Selections from Medieval Philosophers,* Vol. II, ed. R. McKeon.

Royce, Josiah, "The Possibility of Error," in *The Religious Aspect of Philosophy.*

Jaspers, Karl, *Reason and Existenz,* Lecture 3.

Brentano, Franz, *The True and the Evident,* Part One, Ch. I; Part Four. Ed. O. Kraus, trans. R. M. Chisholm, I. Politzer, K. R. Fischer.

## CHAPTER XII
### (The Concept of Value)

Moore, G. E., *Principia Ethica,* Ch. 1.

Dewey, John, *Theory of Valuation.*

Perry, R. B., *General Theory of Value,* Ch. 5.

Shirk, E., *The Ethical Dimension,* Ch. 1.

Hare, R. M., *The Language of Morals.*

Nowell-Smith, P., "The Meaning of 'Good,'" in *Readings in Ethical Theory,* ed. W. Sellars and J. Hospers, pp. 302-317.

## CHAPTER XIII
### (The Supernaturalistic World-Perspective)

Aquinas, Thomas, *Summa Contra Gentiles,* Book I, Chs. 1-9.

Hume, David, (1) *Dialogues concerning Natural Religion;* (2) "Of Miracles," in *An Inquiry concerning Human Understanding.*

Bradley, F. H., "On God and the Absolute," in *Essays on Truth and Reality.*

Taylor, A. E., *Does God Exist?*

Hartshorne, C., and Reese, W. L., *Philosophers Speak of God.*

Tillich, Paul, *Systematic Theology,* Vol. I, Part II.

## CHAPTER XIV
### (Materialism and Its Implications)

Lucretius, *On the Nature of Things,* Book II.

La Mettrie, J. O. de, *Man a Machine.*

D'Holbach, Baron P. H. T., *Common Sense.*

Büchner, Ludwig, *Force and Matter.*

Spencer, Herbert, *First Principles,* Part II.

Elliot, Hugh, *Modern Science and Materialism,* Chs. 5, 6.

Bertalanffy, L. von, *Modern Theories of Development,* Ch. II.

## CHAPTER XV
### (The Emphasis on Mind)

Leibnitz, G. W. (1) *Discourse on Metaphysics;* (2) *Monadology.*

Berkeley, George, *Three Dialogues between Hylas and Philonous.*

Fichte, J. G., *The Science of Knowledge,* trans P. Heath and J. Lachs.

Royce, Josiah, (1) *Lectures on Modern Idealism;* (2) *The Spirit of Modern Philosophy,* Lecture XI.

Lenin, V. I., *Materialism and Empirio-Criticism,* Introduction, Ch. 1.

Ryle, Gilbert, *The Concept of Mind.*

## CHAPTER XVI
### (The Broader Conception of Nature)

Aristotle, *On the Soul (De Anima).*

Spinoza, Baruch, *Ethics.*

Dewey, John, *Experience and Nature.*

Alexander, Samuel, *Philosophical and Literary Pieces,* Chs. IX, XI.

Santayana, George, *The Realm of Spirit.*

Woodbridge, F. J. E., "The Nature of Man," "Naturalism and Humanism," and "The Preface to Morals," in *Nature and Mind.*

## CHAPTER XVII
### (Ethical and Aesthetic Values)

*Ethical Values*

Plato, (1) *Republic,* Books I, II; (2) *Protagoras;* (3) *Gorgias;* (4) *Crito.*

Aristotle, *Nicomachean Ethics.*

Kant, Immanuel, *Fundamental Principles of the Metaphysics of Morals.*

Kiergegaard, Søren, (1) *Fear and Trembling;* (2) *The Sickness unto Death.*

Mill, J. S., *Utilitarianism.*

Sartre, J.-P., in *The Philosophy of Jean-Paul Sartre,* ed. R. Cumming, pp. 243-352.

Hobhouse, L. T., *Morals in Evolution.*

Sidgwick, Henry, *Outlines of the History of Ethics,* 3rd ed.

*Aesthetic Values*

Plato, (1) *Symposium;* (2) *Ion;* (3) *Hippias Major.*

Aristotle, *Poetics.*

Hegel, G. W. F., Selections from *The Philosophy of Fine Art,* in *Philosophies of Art and Beauty,* ed. A Hofstadter and R. Kuhns.

Tolstoy, Leo, *What Is Art?*

Dewey, John, *Art as Experience,* Chs. 1-5.

Croce, Benedetto, *Guide to Aesthetics,* trans. P. Romanell.

## CHAPTER XVIII
### (The Interpretation of Religion)

Nietzsche, Friedrich, "The Religious Mood," in *A Modern Reader in the Philosophy of Religion,* ed. W. Arnett.

James, William, *The Varieties of Religious Experience.*

Otto, Rudolf, *The Idea of the Holy.*

Santayana, George, *Reason in Religion.*

Niebuhr, Reinhold, *Reflections on the End of an Era.*

Russell, Bertrand, "A Free Man's Worship," in *Myticism and Logic* or in *Philosophical Essays.*

Tillich, Paul, "Religion," in *A Modern Reader in the Philosophy of Religion,* ed. W. Arnett.

Ayer, A. J., *Language, Truth, and Logic,* 2nd ed., Ch. VI.

Smart, Ninian, *Reasons and Faiths.*

# Index of Names

Anselm, St. (1033–1109), 176
Aquinas, St. Thomas (1225?–1274), 33, 40, 171, 213
Archimedes (B.C. c. 287–212), 59
Aristotle (B.C. 384–322), 5, 17, 21, 44, 103, 125, 196, 198 f., 205, 207, 213, 239–41, 249, 259, 269 ff., 283, 300 f.
Augustine, St. (354–430), 213, 215
Austin, J. L. (1911–1960), 142

Bentham, Jeremy (1748–1832), 270
Bergson, Henri (1859–1941), 110–117, 120
Berkeley, George (1685–1753), 101, 103, 124, 220–32, 235
Boyle, Robert (1627–1691), 217
Bradley, F. H. (1846–1924), 256
Brightman, E. S. (1884–1953), 298
Büchner, Ludwig (1824–1899), 197, 211
Byron, Lord (1788–1824), 119

Cassirer, Ernst (1874–1945), 140–2
Comte, August (1798–1857), 101
Copernicus, Nicholas (1473–1543), 72, 148
Croce, Benedetto (1866–1952), 122

Dante Alighieri (1265–1321), 300
Darwin, Charles (1809–1882), 44, 57, 145
Democritus (B.C. 460?–362?), 195 f., 217
Descartes, René (1596–1650), 6, 78 f., 81, 91–3, 96 f., 100 f., 104, 213 ff., 219, 228, 240 f.
Dewey, John (1859–1952), 126, 137–9, 140, 153 ff., 291 f., 299, 304–8

Einstein, Albert (1879–1955), 59, 72
Epicurus (B.C. 341–270), 22, 196, 272 f.

Faraday, Michael (1791–1867), 59
Fichte, J. G. (1762–1814), 234
Frege, Gottlob (1848–1925), 124

Galileo Galilei (1564–1642), 52, 57, 72, 82, 113, 217
Gauss, K. F. (1777–1855), 57

Harvey, William (1578–1657), 57, 82
Hegel, G. W. F. (1770–1831), 7, 17, 40, 234–7, 241 f., 255 f., 292
Heidegger, Martin (1889–   ), 279
Heraclitus (B.C. c. 540–475), 5
Hobbes, Thomas (1588–1679), 124, 196, 208 f., 217, 233
Hocking, W. E. (1873–1966), 297 f.
Homer, 300
Hume, David (1711–1776), 39, 96 f., 101, 103, 124, 181, 201 f., 211, 229 ff., 241 f., 250
Husserl, Edmund (1859–1938), 104–9

# Index of Subjects